In Their Own Words

In Their Own Words

✦

Hoosier Ancestor and Family Journeys

Philip M. Coons

iUniverse, Inc.

New York   Bloomington

In Their Own Words
Hoosier Ancestor and Family Journeys

The views expressed in this work are solely those of the author and do not necessarily reflect the views of the publisher, and the publisher hereby disclaims any responsibility for them.

iUniverse books may be ordered through booksellers or by contacting:

iUniverse
1663 Liberty Drive
Bloomington, IN 47403
www.iuniverse.com
1-800-Authors (1-800-288-4677)

Because of the dynamic nature of the Internet, any Web addresses or links contained in this book may have changed since publication and may no longer be valid.

ISBN: 978-1-4401-9766-6 (sc)
ISBN: 978-1-4401-9768-0 (dj)
ISBN: 978-1-4401-9767-3 (ebk)

Printed in the United States of America

iUniverse rev. date: 1/13/2010

"In all of us there is a hunger, marrow deep, to know our heritage - to know who we are and where we came from. Without this enriching knowledge, there is a hollow yearning. No matter what our attainments in life, there is still a vacuum, an emptiness, and the most disquieting loneliness."

(Alex Haley, Roots)

Contents

Preface

Genealogy is, of course, the study of a family history, but Philip Coons and his wife, Elizabeth Bowman, have gone above and beyond this simple explanation and created an impressive endeavor of ties to their ancestors. Getting to know Philip and Elizabeth through the descriptions of their own adventures as well as the images brought forth about their relatives is a delightful treat.

Perusing *In Their Own Words*, the reader will discover Philip and Elizabeth's love for those who have gone before them. This work is a unique way of looking at family history by using letters to and from their family members. Philip's personal thoughts on each writer, as well as an overview of each contributor's life, enhances the knowledge one obtains from each piece of literature. Truly, each contribution included is a grand piece of writing in its own right and elicits an inimitable way of looking at ones family history.

This book presents family lore, enhanced by the beauty of many parts of our country, enveloping the reader in the dangers and atrocities of war, as well as offering much more. Humor, desire, anger, and many other emotions can be found within the contributions presented here. *In Their Own Words* takes the reader on an adventure into early Americana, through several wars, bicycling pathways, and is definitely a romantic and entertaining read!

Karen Zach, 2009
Former Montgomery County Historian

Acknowledgments

In the early 1950s when my brother Steve was in the eighth grade he was assigned to write about our family's genealogy. This precipitated a love affair with genealogy for my parents, Harold and Margaret Coons, and maternal grandparents, Frank and Edith Richman. My paternal grandmother, Clara Coons, and her brother, William Edgar Van Cleave, had already been hard at work on their Van Cleave family genealogy since the early 1940s. I am ever thankful to my various family members in instilling a love for and fascination with genealogy and local history.

Of course, in deep gratitude, I thank my wife, Elizabeth Bowman, for her infinite patience with my genealogy addiction and forbearance in allowing me to take genealogy expeditions by myself in order to discover my roots. Dr. Bowman has even authored some segments of this book and has graciously typed several manuscripts. I've found that you can always tell who is a spouse in a genealogy and local history room at a local library; he or she is the bored or sleeping one sitting beside the other who is meticulously scanning census records, cemetery listings, or local history books. I'm grateful my wife is not like that!

Librarians who have helped me with research are far too numerous to name individually, but I wish to mention a few libraries, archives and historical societies where I have conducted the bulk of my research. These include the Indiana State Library, the Indiana Historical Society, and the Indiana State Archives in Indianapolis, Indiana, the Crawfordsville District Public Library, Montgomery County Historical Society, and Wabash College Lilly Library in Crawfordsville, Indiana, the Bartholomew County Public Library and the Bartholomew County Historical Society in Columbus, Indiana, and the Allen County Public Library in Fort Wayne, Indiana.

I want to single out several immensely helpful people in county clerk's offices in Indiana. Tina Jeffries works in the Bartholomew County Archives in Columbus, Indiana. This archival collection of Bartholomew County documents is magnificent and even has an index online.[1] Her colleague, Mary Ellen Sweet Grossman, is a trained genealogist who works in the Bartholomew County Clerk's Office. What a treat to have a trained genealogist on the staff of a county clerk's office. Finally there is Brenda Miller in the micrographics section of the Clerk's Office in Montgomery County, Indiana. All of these individuals have helped me immensely.

Finally I want to single out several individuals who have been of great help in Montgomery County, Indiana, Dian Moore and Dellie Craig in the Genealogy and Local History Department of the Crawfordsville District Public Library. They have been invaluable resources to me and always ready to help. Last, but not least, is Karen Zach, former Montgomery County Historian. Karen has written a number of articles about my family for Montgomery County newspapers. Together we have tracked down and typed Coons and Van Cleave family obituaries. We also have a friendly competition about who can get the most people in our Family Tree Maker computer programs; she's winning by a long shot!

About the Authors

William Allen:

It appears that Mr. Allen was from Johnson County. The 1850 federal census identifies a William Allen who may be the same as the author of this letter. Born in Kentucky, he was age 25, teaching school, and was living in Johnson County's Ninevah Township with the Dunhand family. Mr. Allen wrote a friend of our family about his experiences on the Oregon Trail and in the goldfields of California and Nevada.

Thomas Nelson Baker (1831-1865):

My great-great-grandfather, Thomas Nelson Baker, was born in Davie County, North Carolina and at age six months moved with his parents to a farm near Azalia, Indiana. He was a member of Company F, 39th Regular Indiana Volunteers and subsequently the 8th Indiana Cavalry. He died of dysentery in Indianapolis on August 14, 1865 while on his way home from the Civil War. Prior to his military service, he was a schoolteacher and married to Love Aurilla Shumway. While teaching Mr. Baker wrote a series of love letters to his fiancé, Love Aurilla. He also wrote a series of letters to her during the Civil War.

James Wilson Bean (1882-1964):

James Bean was a nephew of Alice Wilson Rogers, my great grandmother. His father was a physician. James was a Presbyterian pastor who was born in Fairfield, Iowa and ministered to congregations in Nebraska, Iowa, Canton, Ohio, and St. Paul, Minnesota. He wrote my great grandmother about his trip with his wife Harriet when he went to Clarion County, Pennsylvania in search of his Wilson roots.

Love Aurilla Shumway Baker Bland (1831-1918):

Love Aurilla Shumway Baker was my great-great-grandmother. Originally she was from Livingston County, New York. She came to Bartholomew County, Indiana with her parents, Charles Shumway and Jane Bevins, when she was a child. After the death of her husband, Thomas Nelson Baker, she married Marion E. Bland, a Bartholomew County physician.

Elizabeth S. Bowman:

Elizabeth Bowman is a psychiatrist and currently Adjunct Professor of Neurology who works part time in the Epilepsy Clinic at Indiana University School of Medicine. She has a part-time private practice in Indianapolis, Indiana. She formerly was a Professor of Psychiatry at Indiana University School of Medicine. Her academic interests include psychological seizures, the dissociative disorders, and the religious and spiritual aspects of mental health. As a psychiatric physician she enjoys teaching and writing. Her leisure interests include travel, photography, flower gardening, quilting and embroidery. Dr. Bowman keeps a travel diary on many of her travels.

Elizabeth Lapp Bowman (1879-1965):

Elizabeth Lapp Bowman, the grandmother of Elizabeth S. Bowman, was born in Story County, Iowa. She moved with her parents, Jacob Lapp and Amy Alward, from Iowa to Oregon in the early 1890s and then on to Orange County, California in 1898. "Lizzie," as she was called, wrote about her family's move from Oregon to California when she was in her late teens. She married Alva Edward Bowman, an Indiana native, in 1908 in Los Angeles, California.

Caroline Coons:

Caroline Coons, my niece, and daughter of my brother Steve, grew up in Indianapolis, Indiana. She is a graduate of the University of Colorado at Boulder with a degree in anthropology. She has worked and studied at the California Vipassana Center, in North Fork, California. Caroline did a two-year training program at the San Francisco Iyengar Yoga Institute and has a level one certification as an Iyengar teacher. She is quite a linguist and has some fluency in the French, Italian, and Greek languages. She is now learning Spanish. Caroline recently wrote a blog about her experiences hiking St. James' Way in northern Spain.

Clara Van Cleave Coons (1889-1967):

My grandmother, Clara Van Cleave Coons, was born in Montgomery County, Indiana. She married my grandfather, Merle Coons, in 1910. After my grandfather, an Indiana state legislator, died in 1940, she served five terms as Montgomery County representative in the Indiana House of Representatives. She also traveled throughout Indiana as a representative for the Webster Publishing Company, publisher of schoolbooks. She was intensely interested in Van Cleave genealogy and carried on a correspondence about this with her brother, William Edgar Van Cleave.

Harold Coons (1911-1999):

Harold Coons, my father, was born in 1911 in New Market, Indiana. He was the son of Merle Fuson Coons and Clara Leona Van Cleave. He obtained his AB degree Wabash College in Crawfordsville, Indiana in 1932 and LLB from Indiana University School of Law in 1936. He was a member of Beta Theta Pi fraternity. He married my mother, Margaret Louise Richman in 1938 in Columbus, Indiana. He served in the Army during World War II and retired as a major in the United States Army Reserves. For most of his working career he was an insurance adjustor, first in Indianapolis and later in New Albany, Indiana. During the latter part of his career he was a practicing attorney and was a Floyd County Superior Court judge in 1978. He was the chairman of the Floyd County Republican Central Committee from 1968-1976. When he was in the Army, he carried on an almost daily correspondence with my mother from February 1944 until his return to the United States in February 1946.

Margaret Richman Coons (1913-1998):

My mother, Margaret Richman Coons, was born in Columbus, Indiana in 1913. She was the daughter of Frank Nelson Richman and Edith Rogers. She married my father, Harold Coons, in 1938 in Columbus, Indiana. She graduated from Indiana University in Bloomington, Indiana in 1935 with a BA degree in Latin. She was a member of Kappa Kappa Gamma sorority.

Philip M. Coons:

Philip Coons is an Emeritus Professor of Psychiatry at Indiana University School of Medicine in Indianapolis, Indiana. He works part-time in private practice as a forensic psychiatrist. He has written extensively on the dissociative disorders. His leisure time interests include travel, photography, history, and genealogy. In the summer after his junior year in high school, he attended the Indiana University Geologic Field Station near Cardwell, Montana and wrote a series of letters to his parents about his experiences.

Edith Rogers Richman (1885-1968):

My grandmother, Edith Elizabeth Rogers Richman was born in 1885 in Ottumwa, Iowa. She was the daughter of Lannes Edgar Rogers and Nancy Alice Wilson. In 1908 she married Frank Nelson Richman in Studley, Kansas. She lived nearly all of her married life in Columbus, Indiana and then in Indianapolis. She accompanied my grandfather when he went to Germany in 1947 to be a judge at the Nuremberg trials. Her diary written that year describes her experiences.

Frank Nelson Richman (1881-1956):

My grandfather, Frank Nelson Richman was born in 1881 in Columbus, Indiana. He was the son of Silas Tevis Richman and Elma Jane Baker. In 1908 he married Edith Elizabeth Rogers. He obtained his JD degree from the University of Chicago Law School in 1909. He began the practice of law with his uncle, Charles Baker, in 1908 in Columbus, Indiana. He was a judge on the Indiana Supreme Court between 1940 and 1947. He was also a judge on the Nuremberg Trials American Tribunal IV in Nuremberg, Germany in 1947. Judge Richman wrote *Log of the Big Dipper*, an account of his boat trip in 1944 from Madison, Indiana to New Orleans with Clessie Cummins. He also wrote about his experiences as a Nuremberg Trial judge.

Silas Tevis Richman (1852-1938):

Silas Tevis Richman was my great grandfather. He was highly educated and attended Hartsville College in Hartsville, Indiana, and graduated from Asbury College (now DePauw University) in 1877. After a stint of teaching school, he went to medical school at Butler University in Indianapolis and received his MD degree in 1884. After practicing briefly in Columbus, Indiana he relocated to Princeton, Kansas in 1884. In 1882 he went to Chicago and entered Northwestern University Medical School from which he obtained another MD degree. He practiced medicine on the south side of Chicago until his retirement in 1929.

Thomas Nelson Richman (1942-2003):

My first cousin, Thomas Nelson Richman, was born in 1942 in Boonville, Indiana. He was the grandson of Frank Nelson. For many years Tom worked and wrote for *Inc. Magazine* in Boston, Massachusetts. He was a graduate of the United States Naval Academy at Annapolis and served two tours of duty in Vietnam. He wrote *The Ride to Fargo: A Journey of Imagination"* and a number of other travel articles.

Nancy Alice Wilson Rogers (1849-1936):

My great grandmother, Nancy Alice Wilson, was born in 1849 in Callensburg, Clarion County, Pennsylvania and died in 1936 in Columbus, Indiana. Her parents were Allen Wilson and Jane Gibson. She married Lannes Edgar Rogers in 1876 in Ottumwa, Iowa. She wrote *Memories* about her move at age 10 with her parents and nine other siblings from Pennsylvania to Ottumwa, Iowa. She lived her last 19 years in Columbus, Indiana.

Margaret Catherine Baker Seward (1834-1875):

Margaret Catherine Baker was born in 1834 in Azalia, Indiana and died in 1875 in Lucas County, Iowa. Her parents were Samuel Baker and Jincy Ellis, my third great grandparents, and sister of Thomas Nelson Baker. In 1855 she married Jacob Seward in Bartholomew County, Indiana. They moved to Iowa shortly after they were married. She wrote her brother, Thomas Nelson Baker, about Morgan's raiders being in Indiana in 1863.

William Edgar Van Cleave (1877-1946):

William Edgar Van Cleave was born in 1877 in Montgomery County, Indiana and died in 1946 in McAlester, Oklahoma. He was the son of Daniel Brewer Van Cleave and Anna Elizabeth Reynolds, my great grandparents. In 1906 he married Catherine Gunkle in Crawfordsville, Indiana. He graduated from the Kentucky University Medical Department in Louisville, Kentucky in 1905. For most of his career he served as a physician in the Indian Health Service. From 1916 to 1943 he was Medical Director and then Superintendent of the Talahina Indian Hospital in Talahina, Oklahoma. He wrote an article about his experiences in the Indian Health Service.

Wayne Arthur Van Cleave (1903-1984):

Wayne Arthur Van Cleave was born in New Market, Indiana in 1903 and died in Crawfordsville, Indiana in 1984. He graduated from Wabash College in 1924. In 1925 he married Autumn Alleen Hester. Wayne was a man of many talents and went on to have a distinguished career as teacher, band and choir director, bank president, and farmer. He won many local, state, and national awards for various types of grain. In 1958 he was the Indiana State Fair Corn King.

Introduction

Our ancestors and contemporary kin travel for all sorts of reasons; Emigration is one. In fact, the United States is largely a nation of emigrants. Our ancestors on the eastern seaboard began to migrate westward soon after the West was opened for exploration. Other reasons for travel include attending school, being sent off to war, moving to find a job, going on vacation, recreation, and tracking down ancestors.

I am fortunate in having been raised in a family that was interested in genealogy. My maternal grandparents, Frank and Edith Richman, spent part of their retirement traveling East in quest of their ancestors. Both of them wrote about their experiences as did a number of other members in my family.

When I started my hobby of genealogy, I wanted to extend what my family had already accomplished and find a few more ancestors another generation back or two. I wanted to trace these folks back to when they first came to the United States and I have been remarkably successful. My other aim in doing genealogy, which was just as important, was to find out all I could about these people. My quest to do so has taken me to many libraries, both in Indiana and seventeen other states. In my compulsive quest to find out more about my ancestors, I have amassed an astounding amount of material.

This book consists of but a small portion of the genealogical material that I have collected. However, in my estimation, what I have placed in these pages is the most important, because it consists of the firsthand experiences of my ancestors and contemporary relatives. It is written in their own words and consists of letters, diaries, and other such accounts. Where no such firsthand accounts exist, I have attempted to recreate their travels and migration paths in my own words.

History comes alive in these accounts and seems to jump out at the reader. Some of our nation's most important events are recorded in the following pages.

Editing has been held to a minimum. Some letters and diaries, for instance, are entirely unedited and contain the spelling errors or antiquated language of the authors. Other letters were edited to remove less interesting extraneous material.

Chapter One concerns the crossing of the Appalachian Mountains by my ancestors who lived in the eastern United States and is written entirely in my own words. For some the migration paths are known, for others unknown.

Chapter Two consists of several accounts of ancestors who left Indiana and moved further west. There is one letter from William Allen, a traveler on the Oregon Trail. Another account is by my great grandmother, Alice Wilson Rogers, who moved west from Pennsylvania to Iowa and then spent the remaining years of her life in Indiana following the death of her husband. A final account is by my great grandmother, Elizabeth Busenbark Coons, who, together with her family, moved back to Indiana from Missouri at the beginning of the Civil War.

Chapters Three through Five consist entirely of letters written during the Civil War and World War II. The Civil War letters are written by Union soldier Thomas Nelson Baker and the World War II letters were written by my father, Harold Coons. These letters include those written from the front to both wives and children. Both the wife and sister of Thomas Nelson Baker wrote letters during the Civil War from the home front.

Chapter Six is composed of two accounts of travel by train. One was written at the end of the nineteenth century my wife's grandmother, Elizabeth Lapp Bowman, and the other letters were written by my father as he was moved about the United States by troop train before being shipped to the European theater during World War II.

Chapter Seven is composed entirely of "love" letters that my great-great-grandfather, Thomas Nelson Baker, wrote to his wife, Love Aurilla, while he was teaching school in Madison County, Indiana and she was residing with her parents in Bartholomew County, Indiana.

Chapter Eight consists of diaries and accounts written about work. My grandfather, Frank Nelson Richman, was selected to be a judge at the Nuremberg Trials in Germany shortly after World War II ended. He wrote an account of his experience, and his wife, Edith, kept a diary during her entire year abroad. My great uncle, William Edgar Van Cleave, a physician and native of New Market, Indiana, was in the Indian Health Service and located in Oklahoma for most of his career. He describes his career in several documents. My father's first cousin, Wayne Van Cleave, wrote letters from Florida to his parents back in Indiana. These letters describe his experiences playing for a dinner club in Hialeah during the early 1930s.

Chapter Nine consists of accounts about school experiences. My great grandfather, Silas Richman, was a physician who moved about frequently to gain an education. Margaret Coons, my mother, writes a humorous anecdote about my not returning from school one afternoon. My submission consists of letters that I wrote at age 17 to my parents from the Indiana Geologic Field Station near Cardwell, Montana and letters to my parents from Wabash College in Crawfordsville, Indiana.

Chapters Ten, Eleven, Twelve and Fifteen consist of diary accounts of various trips that my grandfather, Frank Richman, my cousin Thomas Richman, and my wife and I have taken.

Chapter Thirteen consists of a letter that my great uncle, Joseph Bean, wrote about a genealogy expedition that he and his wife took to discover their Wilson roots in Pennsylvania.

Chapter Fourteen contains snippets of letters that my grandmother, Clara Van Cleave Coons, and her brother, William Edgar Van Cleave, wrote to each other about the possible paternity of their grandfather, Jesse Van Cleave, who was born out of wedlock.

Finally Chapter Fifteen contains a blog that my niece, Caroline Coons, wrote about her experience trekking St. James' Way in northern Spain.

All of these diaries, letters, and accounts have Hoosier connections.

Philip M. Coons, 2009

Chapter 1

Crossing the Appalachians

o o o o o o o o o o o o o o o o o o o o o o o o o o o o o o o o o o o o o o

"Two roads diverged in a wood and I took the one less travelled by,
And that has made all the difference."

Robert Frost [The Road Not Taken, 1920]

No first hand accounts exist of my Hoosier ancestors' crossings of the Appalachian Mountains. The only accounts that do exist are a few brief references to their journeys in county and local histories, obituaries, and a few oral accounts that have been passed down from generation to generation. It is time to collect these accounts and put them in writing before they are lost. What follows are brief vignettes from a number of my Hoosier ancestors.

Thomas Nelson Baker

The parents of Thomas Nelson Baker were Samuel Baker (1804-1849) and Jincy Ellis (1810-1873). Both were born in Rowan County, North Carolina. Their son Thomas was born March 1, 1831 near Lexington in Davie County, North Carolina. In September of that year the Bakers and their first-born child crossed the Appalachian Mountains on horseback and settled in Sandcreek Township, Bartholomew County, Indiana. Their new farm was located near Azalia, a Quaker settlement.[1-3] They traveled on horseback; Samuel walked while his wife Jincy rode and cradled six-month-old Thomas in her arms.[4] According to Arbuckle, settlers from North Carolina to Bartholomew County took the Wilderness Road across the mountains through the Cumberland Gap. They then followed an Indian trail through Indiana starting from the Ohio River.[5] It must have been a rather long arduous journey and it would have been necessary to arrive in Indiana before the winter snows came which would have made travel treacherous to impossible.

Daniel Brewer and Nancy Smith

Daniel was born in Conewago, York County, Pennsylvania on March 30, 1784 and died in Putnam County, Indiana about 1861. On October 5, 1805 he married Nancy Smith who was born in Kentucky. Their first and only child, Charity Brewer, my great-great-grandmother, was born January 28, 1815.

Daniel's father John was born in 1761 in Bergen County, New Jersey and died in 1822 in Shelby County, Kentucky. He married Janetje Van Arsdalen on April 3, 1781 in Conewago. An unsourced web document on Roots Web mentions that Daniel's brother Garrett moved to Mercer County, Kentucky about 1791.[6] Thus it appears that Daniel must have traveled from Pennsylvania to Kentucky with his parents when he was a seven-year-old child.

Daniel's fourth great grandfather, Adam Brouwer (1620-1692), had emigrated from Holland on the Ship *Stetyn* in September 1642. He settled in New Amsterdam and his son Pieter (1646-1700) settled in Bergen County, New Jersey. It was Pieter's grandson Daniel who moved from Pennsylvania to Kentucky.

Daniel's ancestors were part of the Low Dutch Company. They were from Holland originally and of Dutch and French Huguenot background. They migrated together across the American frontier and maintained their ethnic identity for nearly two hundred years. In the 1760s they moved from New Jersey to their newly formed settlement, Conewago, in Adams County, Pennsylvania. A number of groups of families moved on to Kentucky. Their favored route took them on the Pennsylvania Road over the Appalachian Mountains to Fort Pitt (now Pittsburgh) and then down the Ohio River to the Falls of the Ohio, near present day Louisville. They then traveled overland to Henry and Shelby Counties, Kentucky where the group had purchased a large tract of land from Squire Boone. Because of Indian attacks many in the group relocated to a second settlement in Mercer County, Kentucky. From there, beginning in the mid-1820s, groups of families began a migration to Johnson County, Indiana.[7-11]

James Busenbark and Elizabeth Good

My Busenbark line began with Johannes Busenberger (1686-1781) who came from the Village of Sehelen, County of Braunfels, Germany to America in 1710 and settled in Amwell Township, Hunterdon County, New

Jersey. His great grandson, James Busenbark, my third great grandfather, was born in Amwell Township on March 28, 1796 and died in Montgomery County, Indiana on February 10, 1784. James married Elizabeth Good in on December 3, 1818 in Butler County, Ohio. James' father John (1767-1837) joined his family in Butler County after serving in the Revolutionary War. We also know from census data that James was in Montgomery County, Indiana as early as 1830. James' third child Mary was born in December 1824 in Ohio and his fourth child, Henry, was born in 1827 in Indiana so James would have moved to Indiana between Mary and Henry's births in the mid to late 1820s. The only account of the Busenbark family's migration from New Jersey to Ohio reports that "Late in the seventeenth century, they having heard so much of the advantages in the far west, decided to brave the frontier. They started out with their children and baggage in a one horse wagon."[12] Their exact route is unknown, but they might have followed the same route as the aforementioned Brewer family but stopping near present-day Cincinnati and then traveling a short distance overland to Butler County, Ohio. The probable route that the James Busenbark family took from Ohio to Indiana would have taken them overland to Brookville, Indiana and from there on the Wetzel and Berry Traces to Putnam and Montgomery counties.[13]

The Coons Family

From me, the Coons family extends back seven generations to Michael and Rebecca Coons. Michael was born in Frederick County, Virginia between 1730 and 1740 and died about 1813 in Jefferson County Tennessee. Michael and Rebecca had ten children. Their ninth child Abigail was born in Shenandoah County, Virginia so it's likely that they followed the Great Valley Road which extends from southern Pennsylvania to North Carolina. It passes through the Shenandoah Valley in Virginia between the Blue Ridge Mountains to the east and the Allegheny Mountains to the west. Michael's son John (1767-1834) and his wife Catherine Carlock (1770-1849) were both born in Virginia but died in Montgomery County, Indiana. They had thirteen children, the first six being born in Jefferson County, Tennessee and the last five in Overton County, Tennessee. John's son, George Washington Coons (1797-1864), and his grandson, James Madison Coons (1826-1916), my great-great-grandfather all moved from Overton County Tennessee to Montgomery County, Indiana sometime between 1821 and 1829. Census data put them in Overton County in 1820 and Montgomery County in 1830. It is not known exactly when John arrived in Montgomery County, but James Madison Coons and his parents, George Washington Coons and Julia Ferree

(1804-1893) arrived in 1830 before the 1830 census was enumerated· Census data confirms that their fourth child, Robert, was born in 1829 in Tennessee and their fifth child, William, was born in Montgomery County in 1833. The exact route of the Coons from Tennessee to Indiana is unknown. They may have taken the Wilderness Trail which bisects with the Great Valley Road or they could have taken the Cumberland Trace to near present day Paducah, Kentucky and then gone up the Ohio River to the Wabash River and thence up Sugar Creek.[13] Another route could have taken them from Terre Haute up the Terre Haute Road, built in 1824, to Montgomery County.[13-15]

Adeline Elvira Gillette

Adeline Elvira Gillette, my great-great-grandmother, was born on January 29, 1814 in New York and died on February 10, 1880 in Hope, Bartholomew County, Indiana. She was the daughter of Asahel Gillett (1784-1835) and Lydia Hickok (1785-1887). She married Enoch Richman on March 20, 1834 in Darrtown in Butler County, Ohio. Although she and her family moved from New York (probably Ontario County) to Butler County, Ohio in 1820 nothing is known about the route of their move. It is clear that they did not take the Erie Canal because it was not opened until 1825. It's likely that at least part of their trip was on the Ohio River as that is the route that most emigrants from the east took to southwestern Ohio. Adeline's mother, Lydia Hickok, who was born in Massachusetts remarried after her first husband's death and eventually died at her daughter Calista Keever's home in Scircleville in Clinton County, Indiana.

Samuel Gilliland and Mary Trousdell

Samuel Gilliland, my third great grandfather, was born in Huntingdon County, Pennsylvania on May 2, 1807 and died in Montgomery County, Indiana on May 19, 1889. At age 16 he left home and traveled to Butler County, Ohio. Although we have no account of his route traveled it is reasonable to assume that he took the Pennsylvania Road to Pittsburgh and then traveled down the Ohio to Cincinnati. He lived in Ohio six years and married his first wife Mary (Polly) Trousdell on December 20, 1832. In October 1834 he moved to Montgomery County by using a wagon and two-horse team. [16-18] He probably followed the same route as the James Busenbark family.[13]

William Reynolds and Mary Miller

William Reynolds was born on December 7, 1796 in Henry County, Kentucky and died in Montgomery County, Indiana on September 19, 1834. He married Mary Polly Miller (1801-1872) in about 1822 near Frankfort, Kentucky and they had seven children. They moved to Indiana in 1830 after their fifth child was born. According to Armstrong, [They] "came on with a covered wagon with all the household goods and Mother Reynolds with two-year-old Napoleon in her lap; some on foot, some on horseback."[19] Their route is unknown.

Enoch Richman and Adeline Elvira Gillette

Enoch Richman was born in Camden County, New Jersey on February 14, 1800 and died on October 31, 1882 in Hope, Bartholomew County, Indiana. He married Adeline Gillette on March 20, 1834 in Darrtown, Butler County, Ohio. It is not clear how Enoch Richman got from New Jersey to Ohio, but it is certain that older brother Samuel and younger brother Eli "walked ...and carried their packs on their back from Philadelphia to Cincinnati, before there was a railroad." [20] Enoch may have accompanied them. Enoch and Adeline Richman moved to Decatur County, Indiana between the births of their third child, Samuel in 1846 and their fourth child, John, in 1848.

Michael Rogers

Michael Rogers, my third great grandfather, was born in October 1796 in Newbury, Essex County, Massachusetts and died December 10, 1882 in Bloomfield, Davis County, Iowa. His parents were Samuel Rogers (1761-1823) and Mary Davis (1762-). He married Rachael Sherwood (1769-) on December 19, 1843 in Guernsey County, Ohio. He lived in Licking County, Ohio from about 1840 to at least 1860. He was both a farmer and "boat captain." According to family lore, he would flatboat his farm produce down Ohio and Mississippi Rivers to New Orleans and then he would return via the Natchez Trace. He would, of course, have skirted southern Indiana as he made his way down the Ohio River.

Charles Shumway and Jane Bevins

Charles Shumway, my third great grandfather, was born on August 12, 1798 in Oxford, Worcester County Massachusetts and died on December 29, 1871 in Bartholomew County, Indiana. In 1819 he married Jane Bevins

(1801-1860) in Conesus, Livingston County, New York.[21] They moved to Bartholomew County, Indiana some time between the birth of their sixth child, James, in 1841 and the tax collection in 1842.[22] Charles and Jane Shumway moved with their five children as recorded in their daughter, Love Aurilla Shumway Bland's obituary: "Mrs. Bland, who was eighty-four years old, was a native of New York state, but came to Indiana with her parents, Charles and Jane Shumway, when a small child. The family traversed the Erie Canal part of the distance, and arrived at Cincinnati, Ohio, from where they moved to a place near Jonesville. Later they moved to Azalia, where on March 25, 1855 Miss Shumway, was married to Thomas N. Baker, my great-great-grandfather."[23]

The Van Cleave Family

Nearly all of my Van cleave relatives followed Daniel Boone from North Carolina over the Wilderness Trail through the Cumberland Gap into Kentucky. Many settled in Shelby County, Kentucky and later most removed to Montgomery County, Indiana. In fact, Squire Boone, Jr., (1744-1815), bother to the famous Daniel Boone, married Jane Van Cleave (1749-1829) in Rowan County, North Carolina on August 8, 1765. Squire and Jane moved from North Carolina to Kentucky in the mid 1780s.

My fourth great grandfather Ralph Van Cleave, sister of Jane Van Cleave above, was born on May 10, 1747 in New Brunswick, Monmouth County, New Jersey and died on September 15, 1798 in Shelby County, Kentucky. He and Lydia Combs (1746-1823) were married in 1768 in Rowan County, North Carolina. Ralph and Lydia moved to Kentucky in about 1785.[24] They likely would have traversed the Wilderness Road through the Cumberland Gap into Kentucky. Ralph's tenth child Thomas G. Van Cleave (1792-1856) and his wife Mary Van Cleave (1793-1870) moved to Montgomery County, Indiana sometime between the birth of their fifth child, Mary Jane, in 1826 and their sixth child, Matilda, in 1828.

Samuel Bowman and Mary Cain

Of my wife's family, a number of families including the Bowmans, Metzgers, and Ulrichs have Indiana Connections.[25] My wife's third great grandfather, Samuel Bowman, was born in 1825 in Pennsylvania and died on January 29, 1895 in Kosciusko County, Indiana. He married Mary Cain (1828-1880) in 1846 in Montgomery County, Ohio. They moved from Ohio to Indiana between their marriage in 1846 and the birth of their first child, Barbara Ellen, in 1848. The Bowmans were members of the German Baptist

Brethren Church. This group immigrated from Germany to Pennsylvania and Maryland during the early to mid-eighteenth century. During the late Eighteenth to early Nineteenth centuries they moved to Montgomery County, Ohio. This tight-knit group consisted of such family names as Bowman, Butterbaugh, Cripe, Metzger, Miller, Peterbaugh, Rench, Replogle, Shively, Ullery, and Ulrich. Replogle speculates that when these families left Pennsylvania that they took the Pennsylvania Road to Pittsburgh and then traveled by boat down the Ohio River to southwestern Ohio.[26]

Jacob Metzger and Esther Ulrich

My wife's third great grandfather, Jacob Metzger, Jr., was born on January 24, 1808 in Bedford County, Pennsylvania and died on January 18, 1884. On March 3, 1831 he married Esther Ulrich (1813-1896) in Montgomery County, Ohio. Jacob's father, Jacob, Sr., (1781-1862) moved with his wife Mary Peterbaugh (1783-1852) and five children, including Jacob, Jr., from Bedford County, Pennsylvania to Montgomery, Ohio in 1813. Jacob, Jr., and his wife Esther, moved from Ohio to Kosciusko County, Indiana sometime between the birth of their child, Isaac, in 1832 and their second child, Jacob, in 1834.

Interested readers may want to consult books or maps on American migration routes, of which there are many.[28-28]

Chapter 2

Moving West

○ ○

"Go West, young man, go west."

John Babsone Lane Soule in the *Terre Haute Express,* 1851

Alexander Wilson

Although Alexander Wilson never lived in Indiana, his granddaughter Nancy Alice Wilson died in Indiana while living her last nineteen years of her life with her daughter Edith Rogers Richman, my grandmother. He may have taken the same route to Iowa that his son Allen had taken when his family went down the Ohio River and up the Mississippi when they moved to Iowa in 1860.[1]

The following inscription appears on Alexander Wilson's tombstone in the Callensburg Cemetery in Clarion County, Pennsylvania:

"Father Wilson was born in Westmoreland County; came to this county in 1801 and settled on Licking Creek Curllsville; lived three months among the Indians without seeing a white man; was friendly with Turkey John the giant Indian, great hunter of that day. Removed to Clarion River, built the first gristmill near Callensburg. He blazed a road from Callensburg through the woods to Curllsville and conveyed Rob't McYarrah back to Concord Church, who preached the first sermon there. In 1857 he moved to the West; remained 6 or 7 years; returned to Clarion County where he died in 1876."

So, even before he moved further west, Alexander Wilson had proven his mettle by blazing a road into the Pennsylvania wilderness.

Alexander Wilson was born on June 24, 1779 in Harrisburg, Westmoreland County, Pennsylvania and died on October 9, 1878 in Callensburg, Clarion County, Pennsylvania. He outlived three wives: Jane McCombs (1781-1833) who bore him ten children, Jane Gwin (1771-1844), and Mary Ann Graham 1778-1864). He moved west to Delaware County, Iowa in the mid 1850s and was back in Clarion County, Pennsylvania by 1864. In Pennsylvania he was a farmer and saw mill operator. In Iowa he was a farmer. According to the 1860 Agricultural Census of Milo Township in Delaware County Iowa, he owned 120 acres, of which 80 were improved. He owned two horses and 12 cows and his farm was valued at $1200. The 1870 Agricultural census in Licking Township in Clarion County, Pennsylvania showed that he owned 185 acres, of which 20 were unimproved. By that time his farm was worth $9840 and he owned 8 horses, 21 cows, 40 sheep, and 8 pigs.

Exactly what prompted Alexander Wilson to travel further west to Iowa is unclear, although, in the 1860 Federal Census, he is living next to another Alexander Wilson who was born in 1808. This could not have been his son Alexander, Jr., who was born in 1821 and remained in Clarion County. His eldest child, Allen Wilson (1806-1879), was living in Wapello County, Iowa, but this was a little more than 100 miles distant and Allen did not move there until a few years after his father had moved to Iowa.

Nancy Alice Wilson Rogers

My great grandmother, Nancy Alice Wilson Rogers, was born on June 26, 1849 in Callensburg, Clarion County, Pennsylvania and died on September 13, 1936 in Columbus, Indiana. Her parents were Allen Wilson (1806-1879) and Jane Gibson (1811-1863). On December 25, 1876 she married Lannes Edgar Rogers (1851-1941) in Ottumwa, Iowa. She wrote *Memories* [1] about her move at age 10 with her parents and nine other siblings from Clarion County, Pennsylvania to Ottumwa, Iowa. She lived her last 19 years in Columbus, Indiana.

Memories is a wonderful document. It contains an excellent description of life in Pennsylvania and Iowa in the middle half of the nineteenth century. From housing to furnishings to transportation to the temperance movement, it's all contained therein. There are even descriptions of illegal behavior on the part of a business associate and a cross-dressed thief. Alice's submission is written as is; it is entirely unedited.

Alice Wilson Rogers

Memories

To the descendants of Allen and Jane Wilson, this twenty-fifth day of November, nineteen hundred thirty four with my prayer that your lives may be rich with the Christmas spirit, I send these memories of many years ago

Alice Wilson Rogers

Related by Alice W. Rogers in her 86th year to her daughter, Edith Rogers Richman, at Columbus, Indiana, in November 1934.

Last spring there came to Columbus a letter from my nephew James Bean containing the following paragraph:

"It occurred to me the other day that. I had never asked Mother about her father and mother and her recollections and impressions of them. And now it is too late. Your mother is the only tie we have left of that generation. I wonder if you would ask Aunt Alice about them and as she chats with you from time to time could I ask you to write it. Down. Anything that comes to her I would like to have about their appearances, their personalities. Just anything."

In response to that request the following notes have come.

In 1874 or 75, my sister Elizabeth and I spent the summer in Pennsylvania, dividing our time between our mother's people in Butler County and our fathers in Clarion County. While there, we stayed with an Uncle John Martin, married to our mother's youngest sister Margaret There were fifteen flowing oil wells on this farm on the Allegheny River Their daughter accompanied us on our visits to the other relatives.

One of the most interesting places was the home of George Gibson, mother's youngest brother, whose two sons had been had been confined in Andersonville Prison during the Civil War. One of them died in prison; the other was released. In looking through an album of photographs, my sister Elizabeth exclaimed, "Where did you get our brother Morrison's picture?" It turned out to be the picture of one of these cousins who had been prisoner, but the resemblance was very striking.

On Sunday we went to the Concord Church, which my mother had attended until her marriage, and heard a sermon preached by a cousin Reddick Coulter, a man who was paralyzed from the waist down. His mother's name was Elizabeth and she was the aunt for whom my sister was named.

After a few weeks spent with my mother's people we went to the home of my uncle, John Murray in Clarion County, a mile out of Callensburg.

My grandfather Wilson lived in this home in which my father's oldest sister, Hannah, was the wife and mother. My grandfather, as I remember him, was a man six feet tall, with an abundance of snow-white hair.

For the benefit of the young people who think we did not have nice things in those days, I shall describe the house. It was a large white house beautifully situated on a hill with big shade trees in the front yard, and with an orchard in the rear which continued up the hill. There was running water piped up the hill into the kitchen and the laundry. The house was well furnished throughout. Our meals were served on a porch screened with mosquito bar. After breakfast and prayers, grandfather would sit with his Bible on his knee, telling us stories of the past which our Aunt Hannah assured us were accurate.

Promptly at ten he would go to his room to exchange his warm wrapper for a lighter coat, always refusing to allow any one to wait upon him. Sometime during the day, the carriage would be brought to the door to take us, including our grandfather, to the home of some of our other relatives. In each of the home in which we visited several of the younger children of the family were living; in the home of our Uncle John and Aunt Hannah there remained two young men of approximately the same ages as Elizabeth and myself and who devoted themselves to seeing that we made the rounds of our relatives safely, comfortably and pleasantly. One of them,

Robert Murray located in Ohio.

One of the houses we visited was a large, two-story, stone house, one mile from Callensburg, built by and lived in by my grandfather in his young manhood. It was at that time occupied by a cousin. Both front and back of the house had double porches running full length. Grandfather insisted that Elizabeth and I go down to the basement to see a large trough, which he had himself hewn out of solid rock, in which milk and butter were set to be cooled by the spring water which was piped into the basement.

[Mother has always told me that great grandfather passed his ninety-ninth birthday, which they celebrated as his hundredth to humor him, and I see by the record that he was born June 24, 1779, and died August 4, 1878. So that tallies. He would have been ninety-five or ninety-six at the time of which she tells.-E. R.]

Our grandfather's tall clock stood in that house.

In Uncle Alec Wilson's home we found the solid mahogany sofa, upholstered in hair cloth which had stood in the parlor of our own home in Callensburg. We found dressers and mahogany chairs with inlaid backs, which had belonged to our parents, in the homes of our uncles and older cousins. My brother Alec tried to buy one of the dressers from Uncle John Elliot years afterward but he would not sell it.

Allen Wilson
Born Dec 17, 1806, died Dec. 12, 1879

His boyhood was spent on his father's farm. I remember hearing him tell of walking six miles to school and six miles home every day. Then he attended school at his Uncle David's. After that short period of schooling, he left home, buying his time of his father.

[It was customary for a son to work for his father until the age of twenty-one. When he did not do so, he paid a stipulated sum for each year, which arrangement was called "buying his time." E.R.]

In the home of his father there were several sons younger than Allen, so his services were not needed and he was able to leave home before the age of twenty-one. He bought land at the mouth of the Piney, eight miles above his father's mills on the Clarion River; he hired men to cut down trees, build a saw mill, a house for himself and shacks for the workmen, flat boats to carry lumber down to Pittsburgh where it was exchanged for dry goods, groceries, etc., for the operation of a general store which supplied the needs of the community growing up around this saw mill. All this was accomplished by the time father was twenty-one years old, at which time he had a hundred men working for him. He was married on Feb. 12, 1829, at the age of twenty-three to Jane Gibson. Their first child, Hannah, was born a year later.

In those days it was customary to celebrate any special event with the use of alcoholic drink. Allen received a congratulatory letter from one of his Gibson brother-in-laws in which he notified him of the shipment of a keg of brandy in honor of his niece's birth. Allen told no one except Jane of the fact but he definitely made up his mind that he was not going to bring the liquor into the midst of his working men, so he took his sled and horses at night alone to the station where he accepted the keg, started home with it, but when he reached the woods near his home, he drew out the bung and let the brandy drain out. It was a long time before he told his brother-in-law what had become of his gift, but by the time he did so, his brother-in-law also was devoted to the cause of temperance.

Along this same line is another story, illustrating a radical departure from custom. The original mill was replaced with a larger one. All the men in the community were expected to be present at the "raising" of the mill, at which plenty of food and liquor was always served. My father made up his mind that he would not follow custom in the serving of drink. He confided his plan to several friends, each of whom assured him that it was impossible to carry out. But he was not dissuaded, and assisted by mother with an unlimited quantity of hot coffee and good food, his mill was "raised." From that time on, he became known as an ardent worker for temperance.

In after years when the history of Clarion County was written, he was credited with being an outstanding leader in church, temperance and good works in the community. My cousin, Oren Elliot wrote to us about this history and told us of the prominent part our father had in it as a Christian leader. All his life he was a great reader and encouraged it with an abundance of books, so that when he moved to Callensburg, no one in town had so many books except the minister.

Before father's fifth child was born, he had become prosperous enough to take a partner who handled the selling end of the business at Pittsburgh and also the buying and shipment of supplies back to the mill and store. His name was John Morrison, and when a baby son was born near this time, he was named in his honor, John Morrison, and called by the latter name.

During one of his trips to Pittsburgh (a little earlier than the time of the partnership) father was asked to take a fugitive slave home with him. He took this fourteen year old colored boy home, taught him to care for the horses and he became coach man and house boy until the family moved to Callensburg. He used to drive the family carriage to church every Sunday with a great deal of pride.

This church was called "Rehoboth." Elizabeth and I were there at the time of our visit and heard cousin Oren Elliott preach. (This cousin later moved to California where he died. His three sons are all ministers there).

My father wanted an education himself, but failing to get more schooling, he transferred his ambition to his children for whom he planned good educations. However, his habit of reading developed his mind to such an extent that the following comment was made by Mr. Carson Reed, a son-in-law, to his wife, Mary, during the last years of my father's life. "Do you know that your father is a well educated man? He can speak intelligently on almost any subject." She replied: "Indeed I do. He has been a student all his life."

My father's business failure came through the dishonesty of his Pittsburgh partner, Morrison. He sold lumber, but instead of paying for the supplies, he charged them and kept the money himself. This state of affairs went on for a long time undetected, partly because of the inherent honesty and lack of suspicion in the character of father, who trusted Morrison implicitly. I remember hearing a story about something which occurred after father found out so many suspicious circumstances that he had gone to Pittsburgh to investigate. He was in Morrison's home in the library before an open fire with all his papers which he had brought from the mill spread out, going over figures with Morrison, when they were called to dinner. They went in, leaving things just as they were. When they returned, everyone of those valuable papers, evidence against Morrison, was gone. The excuse they made, was that a colored maid had come in to put the room in order and thought the papers were "trash" so she had burned them in the grate.

My father might have availed himself of the law of bankruptcy, but instead he ruined himself to satisfy his creditors and went to Callensburg to begin over again. He operated a saw mill for a man by the name of Moore. He had spent twenty-one years in his own mill work. After he cleared his entire indebtedness by surrendering everything except his household furniture, he bought a plain house in Callensburg where the family lived for ten years and where the three youngest children were born. He became an elder in the Presbyterian Church at Callensburg. During this time brother Alec was completing his college course at Jefferson College, Hannah and Annie were teaching in Western Iowa where grandfather had gone earlier; Morrison was in Elder's Ridge Academy, and Mary in Blairsville Seminary. Because of the needs of this large family, my father's earnings in the saw mill were no more than was necessary to meet expenses.

During his last year in Jefferson College, Alec contracted a serious throat ailment. A doctor in Pittsburgh advised him to go to a milder climate and introduced him to a planter from Natchez, Mississippi, who engaged him as tutor for his sons. Through the influence of the Presbyterian minister in Natchez, "The Natchez Institute" was organized and Alec was elected principal of it. He sent for sister Hannah to join him and become a teacher in the school.

When Alec was en route home to Callensburg for the summer vacation of 1859, he came by way of Iowa in order to visit his old teacher at Elder's Ridge Academy, Dr. J. N. McElroy. He was at this time pastor of the Presbyterian Church of Ottumwa. Dr. McElroy persuaded him to buy a farm, six miles north of Ottumwa, which he did, jointly with sister Hannah. After reaching home, he persuaded his parents to move west which they did the following April.

One of the reasons which influenced this decision was a failure in father's health. He was a man, six feet tall, very finely proportioned and of naturally rugged constitution. But the years of exposure and heavy lifting incident to saw mill operation, had developed chronic kidney trouble from which he never recovered and which made him more or less an invalid the rest of his life.

So we went to Iowa. We spent the last night at Uncle John Murray's home and left at dawn for Waterson's Landing where we got on a boat which went as far as Kitanning. There we took a train for Pittsburgh. These were wonderful experiences for the three younger children who for the first time, rode on a train, a steam boat and the cars which ran from the river up to the railroad tracks. We spent the night in the hotel at Pittsburgh and were joined in the morning by sister Mary who had just graduated from Blairsville Seminary. The next day we boarded "The Argonaut," a large steamer on the Ohio river, bound for Cincinnati. We spent Sunday there and on Monday got on a still larger and finer boat called "The Canada," which completed the trip down the Ohio river and continued up the Mississippi to Burlington, Iowa. The boat took about two weeks for the trip which was a great delight to all the family, especially the children. We spent the night in Burlington after disembarking and left in the morning for Ottumwa. The Burlington road had just been completed as far as Ottumwa. Dr. McElroy met us at the train and took us to his home.

Father and the older brothers and sisters spent the afternoon buying a team of horses, wagon and the essentials of furnishing and equipment to begin housekeeping in the new country home. The household furniture had not been brought from Pennsylvania. At daybreak the next morning father and these older children went out to prepare the house which had been built according to Alec's directions for the family. In a few days Morrison came in and took mother and the three younger children home. Father had bought cows, pigs and chickens.

We had reached Ottumwa on the sixteenth of April so that by the time we were settled, the season was getting pretty well advanced for corn planting. A few days after the family was settled, Dr. McElroy drove up to the door to tell mother "to wash the mush pot higher" for sixteen men would be there the next morning with horses and ploughs to prepare for corn planting. After that Morrison took a harrow and started into the field. He stopped for a drink, leaving his horses hitched to the harrow. When he looked toward them, he saw to his astonishment, that they were being driven along the furrow by his five-year-old brother, Robert, who, thus early showed two characteristics, energy and helpfulness, which distinguished him throughout his life and made him the successful and beloved man he became.

This new country home received the name of Plum Grove Farm because of a grove of plum trees, in front of which stood the house. The house was built forty rods back from the road with a pretty green meadow in front. A large elm tree and a big cottonwood grew by the side of the road which connected the farm buildings with the main road. The house was so much larger than any surrounding homes that it was frequently mistaken for a country tavern by travelers who stopped for accommodations. My father was so hospitable that he would never turn anyone from his door. This habit resulted in an incident which was a favorite story with my children when they were young.

One Saturday evening a girl came to the door and asked for lodging overnight. She was taken in and ate supper with the family. During the evening, father handed Elizabeth a considerable sum of money ($150.00 is my recollection of it) and told her to take it up to a small room at the head of the stairs and put it in a certain place which he designated. All this was discussed in the presence of this stranger.

The next morning after breakfast the entire family made ready, according to custom, for the six-mile drive to Ottumwa to attend church. The traveler went on her way.

As the wagon load of Plum Grove Wilsons reached the main road, they were joined by the family of Uncle John Wilson. Uncle John asked, "Didn't you keep a girl at your house last night? Well, she is hiding in the hedge back yonder." Sixteen-year-old Newton volunteered to go back home to investigate. He circled the field and came in at the back door where he stopped to pull off his shoes. As he entered the house he saw the dining room window was open. He slipped quietly upstairs and surprised the girl in the small bed room. He tried to catch her, but she evaded him, leaped from the second floor over the banister to the first floor and fled across the field. Newton lost time by stopping for his shoes and in his haste pulled on a pair belonging to some one else which did not fit him, so that he ran with difficulty, and the girl had gone a mile and a half before he caught her, just as she was climbing a fence. He seized her by the arms and marched her back to the house. Just as his prisoner stepped up on the porch above him, Newton saw the flash of a dagger which passed harmlessly between his body and his arm. In the struggle which followed Newton discovered his adversary was a man in men's clothing, with the girl's dress as a disguise. When he found no money on his person he let him go, but that episode marked the close of such wholesale hospitality.

One of my father's first acts was to canvass the community to secure the promise of the people to attend a Sunday School in the neighborhood school house. This was the first religious service ever held in the neighborhood. He acted as superintendent with his older children as teachers, and in a little while, he had Dr. McElroy come out to preach one Sunday of each month.

During the first summer, 1860, Morrison and Newton raised a large crop of corn, which they sold for five cents a bushel.

Alec and Hannah spent their summer vacation with us on the farm, returning to Natchez in the fall.

After the farm work was done, Morrison secured a country school, which he taught for three winters, turning all his earnings in to improvements on the farm. During this time he was tutoring with Dr. McElroy, taking the work of the freshman year of Jefferson College, which he hoped to enter as a sophomore in the fall of '63.

On Sundays Morrison would have me take the Bible and listen to him as he translated from the Greek testament.

During this time, of course, the Civil War was in progress, and the siege of Vicksburg had closed the lines so that Northerners were shut in the South. For two years my father and mother received only two letters from Alec and Hannah. One of the saddest pictures of my childhood is seeing Morrison with his arms around mother, pleading to be allowed to go to war. Mother would answer, "Just as soon as we hear from Alec and I know that he is not in the Southern Army. I could not have one of my boys fighting against another."

After the fall of Vicksburg, Alec was recognized by Dr. Orr of Ottumwa, was taken to General Sheridan's headquarters where he and Hannah secured passes through the lines and they returned home in the late summer of 1863. Typhoid fever brought up from the South brought tragedy into the home. Hannah was smitten first, then Mary, and when they were convalescent, Morrison was stricken and died, October 3, 1863. Mother came home from his funeral ill and died Oct. 21, 1863.

As I think of those terrible days, I am engulfed by such a wave of desolation that it is impossible to speak of them in detail. The whole course of our lives were changed. The happy carefree home life we younger children had known was gone forever. From that time our lives were adjusted to the stern necessity of circumstances.

My memory of my mother is of her remarkable gentleness of disposition. She was quiet in all her ways and so efficient in a sick room that she was called on frequently to minister to the needs of the sick and suffering in the homes of her neighbors in Callensburg. She was treated with the greatest consideration by my father and brothers. She was much smaller than my father and used to reach up to pat his shoulder when he was speaking excitedly and say, "Be calm, Allen, be calm." She was much loved by all her friends and neighbors.

Dr. McElroy opened a Seminary in Ottumwa and employed Mary as a teacher in it. Emily taught in a country school near there. Alec entered McCormick Theological Seminary. Hannah and Alec decided to sell Plum Grove farm and bought a smaller one of fifty acres on the south side of the Des Moines River just a mile from Ottumwa. We moved into a log cabin which was on the farm until a more comfortable home could be built. Newton was very successful at farming and in the summer of 1869 was building a concrete house.

Before this time I had taught country school intermittently from the time I was fifteen years old and Elizabeth had her first school the winter of '68 while Emily was home keeping house for father and Newton. Newton bought a reaper, a new implement for that day, and when he could spare the time from his own farming, he went from farm to farm with this reaper, helping with the work of other farmers. In later years, a woman of the neighborhood testified as to the unusual influence for good he exerted, and the respect of all the men of the community for this youth of twenty-two.

At one time he sold a load of hay to a lawyer somewhat unfavorably known for shiftiness. The lawyer disputed the weight and refused payment. The case came to trial. The lawyer summoned Dr. McElroy as one of his witnesses. Dr. McElroy's surprising testimony was as follows: "If Newton Wilson said that bay weighed 80 much, it did." Needles to say he won the case.

In the fall of 1869, my sister Mary and I went to Onarga, Illinois, she to teach and I to attend the seminary in that place. Brother Alec was pastor of the church there. He had been married for five years at this time.

As I have said before, Newton was building the permanent home for the family during the summer and early fall in the midst of his farming activities. Father became ill and the doctor in attendance asked for a consultation. The judgment of the consulting doctors was that our father had not long to live. I still have in my possession a letter written by Newton after he had heard the doctor's verdict, saying that he had decided to dismiss the men who were working on the house and give all his time to caring for father during the days remaining to him. The following morning after receiving that letter brother Alec received a telegram saying that Newton had died at midnight. He had spent the previous day in town on matters of business, had come home and had been stricken with a violent illness in the night. A doctor was called but did not reach the house until Newton's life had passed out, after terrible suffering of less than two hours' duration. We have since believed that he died from an attack of appendicitis. Alec, Mary and I left immediately for home, reached Keokuk at midnight on Saturday and could not leave there until Monday as no trains ran on Sundays.

Contrary to what the doctors had said of the likelihood of father's death, he began to improve and lived for ten years. It is quite remarkable to me that ten years to the day from the time I received Newton's letter describing father's condition, I received a telegram from Malvern, Iowa, which told of father's serious illness which resulted in his death.

That winter the family at home consisted of father, Elizabeth, Robert and myself. Robert clerked in town in a grocery store and walked back and forth day and night. In the spring, Harper, McIntyre & Co. hardware store wanted a clerk and accepted Robert for the position on the very high recommendation of the grocer who had employed him. He afterward became a partner in the hardware company.

The home had to be reconstructed along different line because, after Newton's death, there was no longer anyone to farm the land. Alec and Hannah sold the farm. Emily was married in the summer of 1870 and Mary in the following fall.

I was sent over to Streator that fall to help with the work in Alec's home. Hannah was teaching in Moulton where she met Dr. Barnes to whom she was married the following summer.

Father, Elizabeth and Robert moved into a small house in town located at the top of a very steep hill, where Elizabeth combined the duties of teacher in the Ottumwa schools and housekeeper. The work and the difficult walk over the two hills to Adams school was hard on her and they sent for me to come home to keep house. However, the president of the school board heard that I was coming and asked Elizabeth if I would be willing to teach, so before I came I had a place in the school for the following year. During the summer the chance to buy the Presbyterian parsonage for $1500.00 came to us and Robert, Elizabeth and I each put $500.00 into the purchase of this home on Jefferson Street, and furnished it as well. After several more or less unhappy experiences with help, we were fortunate in finding a good Swedish housekeeper who looked after our comfort most satisfactorily and we four had a very happy home together for five years. This was the happiest home life for us since our mother's death.

On Christmas Day, 1876, I was married but continued to live at home for a year thereafter, when we built our own home. The home on Jefferson street was sold as Robert went on the road as traveling salesman and Elizabeth went to teach at Ferry Hall. Father went East to visit his relatives in Pennsylvania, spent some time in Illinois with Alec and Emily, and was visiting Hannah at Malvern. A few weeks before Thanksgiving he wrote me that he would be in Ottumwa by Thanksgiving Day to spend the winter in our home. Before that time, he became ill and died.

Before he died, he asked Elizabeth not to allow his death to change her plans for her marriage in January, so she was married in the home of her sister Mary in January, 1878. So ended the home established by our parents, but the seeds of Christian joy and service planted in our lives by their teaching and example grew in the homes of the second generation and have borne fruit in the lives of their descendants, It is in the hope of arousing a pride in the richness of the family heritage that I have undertaken to recall and describe the foregoing incidents which reflect their courage and steadfast faith in God's care.

I know of no better way to close these memories of mine than to quote two verses of my father's favorite hymn.

Faith of our fathers! living still
In spite of dungeon, fire and sword;
Oh how our hearts beat high with joy
Whenever we hear the glorious word!
Faith of our fathers! holy faith!
We will be true to thee till death!
Faith of our fathers! we will love
Both friend and foe in all our strife;
And preach thee, too, as love knows how,

By kindly words and virtuous life:
Faith of our fathers! holy faith!
We will be true to thee till death!

Elizabeth Jane Busenbark Coons

My great grandmother, Elizabeth Jane Busenbark was born October 17, 1859 in Hannibal, Missouri and died April 15, 1922 in Montgomery County, Indiana. She married George Washington Coons (1850-1940) on November 30, 1879 in Montgomery County. Elizabeth's parents were Emmons Busenbark (1829-1910) and Anna Laura Gilliland (1838-1910).

Elizabeth Busenbark Coons and George Washington Coons

Emmons' mother was Elizabeth Good (1798-1842) and his father, James Busenbark, (1796-1874) was a wealthy Montgomery County farmer who "While the sons were working on the farm or farms, he made several trips to Missouri and Iowa, buying up land as money came in at home, and he later settled his three sons, William, John and Henry in Linn County, Iowa, and two, Emmons and Alfred in Davis County, Missouri, near Gallatin. After three or four years of light crops, and much sickness and the death of Alfred's wife, he had them return to Indiana, in April, 1861. The following August his daughter Sarah Ellen was married to Willis S. Gott, who lived on a farm near Center Point, Iowa. In October of the same year he accompanied Alfred to Iowa and settled him on one of his farms. Emmons moving on to an Indiana farm, near which New Market has since been built."[2]

Elizabeth Jane Busenbark was born October 17, 1859 in Hannibal as Emmons and Anna were making their way to Iowa in a wagon. Our family still has the little cane-backed chair that she sat in on her way to her new home.

Thus, due to the good fortune of one Montgomery County farmer, James Busenbark was able to buy farms and relocate his five sons in Iowa and Missouri. Daughter Sarah Ellen married and relocated to Iowa. The only remaining children of James and Elizabeth in Indiana were Emmons and his wife Anna and their youngest son Samuel Landis (1837-1917).

Why did Emmons and Anna and their family move back to Indiana in 1861? I have visited Emmons and Anna's farm in Davis County, Missouri. The land is pretty, but it is extremely hilly with poor soil. It has an ample supply of water since a reservoir is nearby. However, while the land appears to make nice pastureland, there were no tilled fields nearby. Therefore, it appears that Emmons, like his brother, may have been the victim of a poor crop. I also wonder if the Kansas-Missouri border wars (1854-1858) and the instability of Missouri even into 1861 might have had an effect on their decision to return to Indiana.

William Allen

William Allen is somewhat of an enigma to me as I found his letter copied in the 1938 handwriting of my grandmother Clara Van Cleave Coons. Both my grandmother and her brother, William Edgar Van Cleave were very interested in the genealogy of the Van Cleave family and they carried on a correspondence about it with each other. When Mr. Allen was in Siskiyou County, California, he wrote a lengthy letter to his brother in Montgomery County, Indiana and described his trip on the Oregon Trail. It appears that either Mr. Allen was a friend of the family or that he was related in some way to the Van Cleaves. He was from Johnson County, Indiana and he or someone in his family may have known my third great grandfather Daniel Van Cleave when he lived in Johnson County a short time before moving on to Parke County, Indiana. The 1850 federal census identifies a William Allen who may be the same as the author of this letter. He was age 25, teaching school, and was living in Johnson County's Ninevah Township with the Dunhand family.

Mr. Allen's account of his sojourn on the Oregon Trail plus his journey across Oregon and down to northern California is a fascinating document that describes the major landmarks along the way. The hardships caused by cholera and the perilous river crossings are also described along with frequent encounters with the Indians. The letter is included in its entirety and is unedited.

William Allen's travel account of 1853

Ureka, Siskiyou County, California
November 26, 1853
Dear Brother,

Many a month has passed, many changes have taken place; and I have traveled over thousands of miles, since I last saw you – but I have not forgotten you: And now, since I am settled for a few months, at last; I will spend a few hours in preparing for your perusal, some information concerning myself, which though it may come unexpected; I trust, will be of some interest to you.

Doubtless, you have heard ere this, by some of our relatives in Johnson County – that I have left that region, for Oregon. Taking this for granted, I am led to the belief that you, as well as the rest of my kin, in Montgomery, would like to know something of my whereabouts. Consequently, I deem it my duty – yes and I undertake it, as one of the greatest enjoyments that I am capable of entering into, under the circumstances by which I am surrounded at present. How pleasant it is even to <u>write</u> this to a friend, where the space of 2000 miles, lies between us. Though I <u>may</u> never see you again, in <u>this</u> life, yet I have the means of holding conversation with you <u>here</u>, and the <u>hope</u> that in another state of existence, I shall meet you, in a <u>better</u> world, where we shall <u>no more</u> "take the parting hand." With these remarks, for an introduction, I will proceed to give you, briefly a short history of myself and this country.

On the 16th day of March 1852, I left Johnson County, Indiana, traveled by stream to Iowa to where my brother-in-law, James S. Waggener lives; where

I staid till the last day of April – and then started with a company consisting of about 150 souls, 500 head of animals, mostly cattle and 29 wagons. I engaged to work my way through, to Oregon, with James Long my second cousin, by marriage. He was married to Ann Bond, cousin John Bond's daughter. By the way Cousin John and his son George are Missionary Baptist preachers. I had but little acquaintance with them but from what I could learn, they are both very good men. The whole Bond family intended to come to Oregon in 53. I have not heard whether they have come or not, but I presume they have. James Long had a good team of cattle; a good load of provisions, and a large wife and two children to haul – a daughter and a son – the son was the younger, six years old. I drove the team part of the time and Long drove when I was not driving. When I was not driving the team I was driving loose cattle; sometimes on horseback and sometimes on foot. We traveled from 16 to 30 miles per day, according to the road. We traveled through Iowa to Council Bluffs – 200 miles. The emigration was exceedingly large. The ferries at the different crossing places, and there were three or four were crowded, so that we had to wait 12 days before we could get across the Missouri River. That delay put us back to about the middle of the emigration; so we were crowded nearly all the way. Grass was scarce in a great many places, having been eaten by forward animals and sickness was very bad in some places.

The country from the Missouri River, to the Cascade Mountains with the exception of a few skirts of timber, and they are "few and far between", is <u>one</u> <u>vast</u> <u>Prairie</u>. Some of it is very level, as far as the eye can reach. The sod for hundreds of miles is good teeming with grass, herbs, and flowers of many colors; presenting to the eye, the most beautiful, natural scenery, that the mind of man can conceive. Animals in great varieties and numbers, inhabit the Plains; unnumbered Rattlesnakes lie in the grass – and thousands of Indians roam over the country, with bows and arrows, in pursuit of their own lawful prey. The sun sends down his rays with power, and the land is parched with heat – the windows of heaven are opened, and the rain descends to enliven vegetation. The wind is nearly always blowing from the West or N. West. Again there are regions of mountains and valleys. On the mountains may be seen rugged Winter in all her icy forms, and at the <u>same</u> time, in the valleys; mild summer in her robes of green. Coming up Platt River, we had to use the water of the river, which was not very wholesome. The Cholera raged on Platt. Seven of our company died. Some companies were almost entirely swept away by it. Alkali water killed a number of cattle and hard driving killed many more. From the head of Platt to the Cascade mountains we were hardly ever out of sight of a dead animal. The carcasses were all along the road, and the scent of them, was very annoying. The road was traveled so much that it got very dusty, in many places; and when the wind blew and fine sand flew in such thick clouds that the lungs of both people and beasts were almost filled – it was impossible to breath without inhaling a vast quantity of dust; and that for miles at a time. The ground is of such a nature, in many places, that it becomes dry and pulverized so fine, that a gentle gale of wind sends it in thick clouds so thick, a person cannot see through it. I have driven a team of four yoke of oxen, when I could not see my leaders. They followed the wagon next ahead of them. We had but little rain on the whole route. On Platt River, we had a very hard storm of rain, wind, thunder & lightening one night. The wind blew nearly all our tents over and came very near blowing the wagons over. The Indians never bothered us except by begging; but some trains last a good many cattle and horses by them and some were murdered; but not so many as was common or had been common in previous years. Some Indians beg for money & tobacco, some for provisions and clothes, and some for ammunition and fire arms. Any of them will steal whatever they can get. Some of them live on the flesh of wild animals, some on fish & fowls, and some on insects, carrion, and anything they can get. They are poorly clad, with the exceptions of a few tribes and some are almost entirely in a state of nudity. I must get another sheet. After I commence writing, I cannot easily find a finishing place, but I must pass lightly over the plains and hasten as fast as I can to a description of this country. Though on all it may be yet you can gain something from it that will perhaps increase your stock of information on this subject. I kept a journal while crossing the plains, and I am engaged, during all the time I can spare, in taking extract from it and sending a series of letters, on that subject to Ind. I direct them to J. M Woodruff, with the request that all my friends may have an opportunity of reading them, so I will be saved the time and expense of writing to all, individually, which if I were to do, I would not have time for anything else. But I must proceed. There is a great portion of the road that is very good, and there is much that is very bad. It would be almost incredible to tell of some of the places where wagons have passed, over the mountains; suffice it, to say that for miles we had to keep both hind wheels rough locked and make the wheel cattle hold back with all their might; and then we could not go slowly enough. In the mountainous countries we generally had plenty of water, and that which was cold and good. For hundreds of miles we had no wood, except for a kind of brush, called wild sage. It grows from a foot to six feet high, in general, –it spreads out as it grows, has a great many branches, a bark resembling the grape vine bark, the leaves look like sage – the wood is of a resinous nature; it was a peculiar scent, and it burns well. Millions of acres are covered with it, in the country where it grows. Where there is no wood at all; there are "Buffalo

Chips" enough to answer the purpose of fuel. Providence has provided, even in the desert, for the use of the wanderers of the human family, a substitute of the indispensable article – wood.

In the mountains of the West, like those of the East, there are some hot springs. We passed by several which were hot enough to cook meat. There are, also some springs called the soda springs. They are near Bear River. The water is cold and it tastes some like soda and a little like our Small Beer. It is very pleasant and wholesome. In the vicinity of the Soda springs there is a spring called the steam boat spring. It makes a noise like a steam boat when running. It throws the water out three feet high. There are many curiosities in Nature and many signs of an ancient volcanic country in the Plains; and many other things of interest of which I could write much, but time and space forbid me now. Long and his family got through safely but lost some of their cattle. I got to Oregon City 27th of Sept. When I came to the Dalles of the Columbia River I went aboard a kind of keel boat, in which I came to the Cascade Falls, and from there, I rode in a steamboat to Portland, which is 12 miles from the city. The place called the Dalles, is a very narrow place in the river, where the water rolls and falls, over the rock. It is very swift and deep there and is about 100 miles from Oregon City. The river, below there is about three miles wide. The Cascade Falls, is the place where the river runs through the Cascade mountains, about opposite the summit. The river is narrow there, and it has, perhaps 50 feet fall in 100 yards. I makes a noise "like the sound of many waters." No boats dare venture over.

The sun went down when I was on the Columbia and it seemed to set in the <u>river</u>, thus proving that the Columbia runs due west. It is a beautiful river, below the falls, and on each side of it, there is some excellent land. The land is densely timbered along the river. The timber is Pine, cedar and fir, in general, though there is some oak, ash, alder and maple; and a good deal of Balm of Gilead. Pine, cedar and fir grow very large and tall in Oregon. The fir is the tallest, being 150 to 300 feet high. They grow with a gradual taper and perfectly straight from root to top. I have not traveled any on the north side of the Columbia, therefore, I shall not write much about it, but from what I have learned, I judge there is plenty of good land over there. The Willamette River runs north and empties into the Columbia 80 miles from the Pacific Ocean. The Willamette is about 2/4 miles wide at the mouth. Ships come up to Portland which is 12 miles above the mouth of the Willamette. Portland is a flourishing city of about the size of Crawfordsville. Oregon City is about as large, but it is not yet as good a commercial center as Portland. The city is in the rough part of the country on the east side of the River, at the Falls. Willamette Falls are 30 feet perpendicular, in one place, with a considerable fall for a mile before it comes to the steepest place. The water runs over the falls with a great rapidity and can be heard several miles. Salmon fish jump over the Falls in the Spring. There are some good mills there. The Willamette valley is about 200 miles long and 40 miles wide on an average. The largest prairies are pretty well on the river. The timber and prairie is about equal. The soil is very good for all kinds of small grain and grass but it or the climate will not do for corn. I consider Oregon a better wheat country than any other I ever saw. Vegetables can be cultivated there with more success than in any other place I know of. All kinds of stock can live out all the year. Cattle can keep fat. The country is well watered. The climate is no doubt unconsciously wholesome. I have not been sick a day since I came to this country. My health is most excellent. The climate is very mild and agreeable all the year. Sometimes there is some bad rainy weather in the winter, but it never gets very cold. I staid in Oregon last winter about 40 miles above the city. I came to California to dig gold. I left Oregon on the Willamette last March, and came to Rogue River valley to the mines, near the stream and worked there until the 5th of Aug. then came 60 miles farther. I am in the northern part of California about 20 mile from the line, preparing to work a gold claim this winter. I have not made but little yet, but the prospect is good for making money. I expect to leave the mines next summer. This is a rough place. All sorts of wickedness is here. When I leave here I expect to go back to Willamette, take a claim and settle myself for life. I am well pleased with Oregon. I came to Oregon to live there; I would not have come to the mines, but to make a little money quickly. but now am here, and I feel like standing up to the work till I make a raise. Write to me when you get this. Direct your letter to Ureka, Cal. via Oregon. Give my respects to all my friends and tell them to write to me. I have not written half as much about this country as I would like to. But my limits are out. I must say farewell, at present.

Wm Allen.

Chapter 3

War Letters to Wives

○ ○

"Man is the only animal that deals in that atrocity of atrocities, War. He is the only one that gathers his brethren about him and goes forth in cold blood and calm pulse to exterminate his kind. He is the only animal that for sordid wages will march out...and help to slaughter strangers of his own species who have done him no harm and with whom he has no quarrel...And in the intervals between campaigns he washes the blood off his hands and works for "the universal brotherhood of man"

Mark Twain, *What is Man?* 1906

Civil War Letters of Thomas Nelson Baker to His Wife

My great-great-grandfather is Thomas Nelson Baker. My grandfather, Judge Frank Nelson Richman wrote a brief biography[1] about him:

"In *Bartholomew and Jackson Counties* published by B.F. Bowen, 1904, is a biography of Charles S. Baker, p. 456,[2] it states Thomas Nelson Baker was 6 months old when in the fall of 1831 Samuel and Jincy moved from Lexington, Davies Co., N.C. to farm 1 mile east of Azalia where they, (Samuel at least) lived the remainder of their lives. Also, it identifies Thomas N. Baker as member of Co. F, 39th Reg. Ind. Volunteers, and afterwards the 8th Cavalry. It states: "At the battle of Stone River, Tenn., he was temporarily in command of the Second Battalion, Pioneer Corps, and at a critical point in that bloody engagement, when the Confederate forces flushed with what seemed certain victory, were making a determined attack upon the

28

Union lines the Second Corps successfully resisted the assault, held their ground and turned the tide of battle to victory for the Federal Army. Maj. Baker, then only first lieutenant, was in advance of the battalion, urging and inspiring his men to victory, and in the official, account of this battle, which is given in, "War of the Rebellion," Official Record of the Union and Confederate Armies issued by the government, he receives honorable mention for his gallant services.

Commissioned Second Lieutenant in the 37th Ind. Reg., Oct 1,1863, he was promoted to major in Feb. 1865, mustered out with his regiment, then mounted and called the 8th Cav. in the last week of July 1865, and "died at Indianapolis, Ind. August 14,1865, aged 34 years, 5 months and 13 days," so reads the inscription on his tombstone in Azalia Cemetery. On p. 448 of History of Bartholomew County (in Public Library at Columbus),[3] it appears that this regiment was in the battles of Shiloh and Corinth, in the pursuit of Confederate Gen. Bragg's Army through Kentucky, and at the critical battle of. Stone's River, and later with Sherman on his celebrated "march to the sea."

His prior life has been shadowed by his military record. When he volunteered he was teaching the Azalia one-room school which was located a short distance south of the cemetery. I spoke in that school house many years later and was introduced by David T. Newsom, Quaker teacher who knew and spoke highly of my grandfather as a teacher, soldier and as a man. Somewhere I got the information, perhaps from his brother, James P. Baker, that after the war he intended to study law. That was the choice of his son, Charles S. Baker, still living at the age of 97, one of the distinguished lawyers of southern Indiana.

In the possession of my mother, now 95, are letters written to her by her father during the war.[4] She was 8 years old when he died. Having escaped death many times in action, he died of "army fever", an acute dysentery, at the end of the war, still about 50 miles from home. (Note by FRJ, 1982: I have these letters, plus the love letters he and Ril wrote to each other both before their marriage and during the war.[5] Also his Honorable Discharge papers from the Army, and his picture as well as hers."

Thomas Nelson Baker Company F, 8th Cavalry, 39th Indiana Regiment Volunteers

Military records of Thomas Nelson Baker indicate that he entered the service as a Second Lieutenant of Company F, 8th Cavalry, 39th Indiana Regiment Indiana Volunteers in Indianapolis, Indiana on August 29, 1861. He was promoted to Second Lieutenant on September 2, 1861, Captain on October 18, 1863, and Major on May 4, 1865. He was discharged on July 20th, 1865 in Lexington, North Carolina.[6]

Because he was detached from his original regiment for part of the Civil War, Thomas' letters to his wife, Love Aurilla, and his service record from the National Archives reveal a far fuller record of his service[7] than the official records of his original regiment.[8] On September 6, 1861 Thomas was in Indianapolis giving a deposition in his mother's divorce from David Vanskike. [9-10] He was on sick furlough from August until October 1861 so he must have missed his unit's departure for Kentucky in early September. His unit was in Kentucky until they marched to Nashville, Tennessee in March 1862. On April 6th and 7th Thomas and his unit engaged in the Battle of Shiloh at Pittsburg Landing in Tennessee and then on April 29th-30th were in the Battle of Corinth in Mississippi. On July 26, 1862 they were in Bridgeport, Alabama. From August 1862 until April 1863 Thomas was detached to the Pioneer Corps, Army of the Cumberland. He appears to be back with his unit in May, 1863. On September 29th and 30th 1863 his unit participated in the Battle of Chickamauga in northwestern Georgia. He was on courier duty in December, 1863 and on February 3, 1864 wrote his daughter Ella from Caldwell's Farm in Tennessee. We find him on sick leave in March and April 1864. In November 1864 Thomas is in the Field and Staff, 1st Brigg, 3rd Cavalry Division, Army of Georgia. From December 1864 through March 1865 he is with the 1st Brig Cavalry Corps, Military Division of the Mississippi. In April 1865 he is with the 1st Brig, 3rd Cavalry Division, Department of North Carolina. After he was mustered out, Thomas arrived in Indianapolis during the last week of July 1865. He died in Indianapolis of dysentery on August 14, 1865. Overall, out of about 2500 men on its rolls, the regiment lost nine officers and 138 enlisted men in combat and one officer and 250 enlisted men by disease.

There are a number of items of interest in Thomas's letters to his wife, Love Aurilla. Quite a number of officers and enlisted men are mentioned including his brother, William Ira, who was wounded in the thigh.[11] It appears that his brother Samuel may also have been in his unit although I have been unable to locate his service records. In his letters he mentions his cousins, Oscar and Edwin Shumway, as well as his brother-in-law, Frank Thomson.

Although Thomas did not mention Quakers in his unit, cemetery records from the Bartholomew County Sandcreek Friends Cemetery indicate that at least four men in Company F of the 8th Indiana Calvary were Quakers. These men include Walter Cox, Levi Newsom, and F. and J.P. Nicholson.[12] For an exhaustive review of Quakers in the Civil War, the reader should consult Nelson's *Indiana Quakers Confront the Civil War*.[13]

An interesting postscript to Thomas's Civil War service was provided by his son Charles Samuel Baker (1855-1956), a Columbus, Indiana attorney. Uncle Charles, as he was known by my mother, was told by his mother, Love Aurilla, that Thomas was accompanied back to Indiana by his horse and a young African-American assistant. After Thomas died in Indianapolis, this young orphaned boy of about 12 years of age accompanied Thomas' horse on the train back to Azalia, Indiana. The town folks, who obviously must have included some Quakers, would not let this young man off the train despite the protestations of Love Aurilla. In the end, she had to pay the young man for his effort and send him on his way.

The Civil War letters of Thomas Nelson Baker are unedited to preserve their historical nature and context.

Letter 1

Camp Pittsburgh Landing April 1862
Aurilla

My dear wife I embrace another opportunity of writing to let you know where and how we are   We are still encamped on the field of battle but I hope we may soon leave it as I fear the stench will affect our health   I am fully as well as usual...better by far than I should expect after such exposure   The boys are all up. Ira is not very well & he is still grunting some   he has sore eyes   Willis and all the rest are <u>bully</u>   our tents came up yesterday   I think we will fare better our whole brigade were on picket guard yesterday & last night   we saw nothing of interest   I think we are in no danger from attack the enemy have retreated to Corinth & perhaps beyond our scouts say they are very much scattered and demoralized   My opinion is though they will fight us again at Corinth.

If we had been able to have followed up our victory I am satisfied they could have never made another stand but it was utterly impossible owing to the state of the roads and the want of transportation   We have crippled them very badly   As it is all their field Batteries are in our hands   as to details in reference to____foes & C I will refer you to the papers   I will just say though our loss though in killed wounded & missing will not fall below 15,000 men   our wounded are all up   Isaac Nicholson was not hurt so badly as we first thought   he is back with the Co The loss of the 39th Reg. Is some 35 - The entire loss to the service is not more than 12. the rest being slightly wounded   we were under a heavy fire for three hours but we had the advantage of the ground which accounts for our small loss   as I wrote you before Jim Spurling fell on Sunday morning pretty soon after the fight began. He fell like a brave man in a noble cause I have found quite a number of old friends among them two of the Gilbert boys from Iowa (Ira & Frank) David Smith (James Smith' son) Pat Duko & many others that you would not know   Lieut G.W. Hays is visiting us today   I have no doubt I could find Edwin Shumway if I knew what regiment he is in. I was so glad to hear that Bob Newsom had got home   there has never any thing hurt me so bad yet as leaving the boys behind sick unable to any thing for them   I feared

Bob would never get home. I just received your letter of the 5th   I was so glad to hear from you the children & friends   May God bless you all. I have a new suit   you would hardly know me   I was looking very hard before I got it   I send a Kiss to you & the children   Be of good courage trust in god & all will be right   My love to all

    Yours forever

    T.N. Baker

Letter 2

Camp of 39th 1862 Nov 22nd

Aurilla,

    My very dear wife I Received your very welcome letter by the hand of John Pasley I was very glad indeed to hear that the children still keep well   I had been feeling some uneasiness since you wrote that the Scarlet fever was in town   Knowing that is so fatal an enemy to part of my dearest treasure my family -

    My health is about the same as usual - not very well. I still have that pain in my side Samuel is well   he is building a chimney to our tent this evening he is very useful and a great deal of Company to me   I would not do without him for anything   I think he is well satisfied   He was not so until I came to the Regiment   Willis is better and has gone on picket   Ira Madison has mumps but does not complain any. Ike Peel is very stout   The rest all well there is nothing new to write -

    I have been thinking this day how very glad I would be if this war was honorably ended so that I could return to my dear ones at home and how different home would be from what it has ever been.   Aurilla my dear wife I feel that I have increased Reasons to prize you a thousand times more than I ever did before. Indeed I feel that you have never been yourself till of late. When I was a boy I loved you of course (you never doubted it then) but more because I could not help it than otherwise later in life   I loved you as my partner & the mother of my children but now I love you for the past as I loved in the past but Oh how much more now for the noble womanly patriotism you have shown the sacrificing devotion you have displayed & the high proof you have given of your ability to enter the great struggle of life for yourself.

    I am no love sick one and I knew you would not be when your true character developed You love me a thousand times more for going boldly forth to discharge my duty to my country than you would if I had stayed at home and been nothing but fondness kisses and caresses every day now don't you   We have seen some unhappy days since we were married but it was all because we did not understand each other. We have each looked for happiness in a way that was impossible to find it   I see the mistake now   Selfishness is the grand secret of more unhappiness than is generally attributed to it

And now Aurilla you frequently give me advice   let me give you a little Recollect that Religion consists not so much in doing great acts of good as in doing a thousand little acts of good such as forgetting little injuries speaking well of neighbors preserving the temper.

If I don't get better soon I am going home before long   supper is ready and I must quit writing. Good by my dear girl

your affectionate Thomas

Letter 3

Murfreesboro Tenn, May 8th 1863
Aurilla,

Dear Wife I just Received your letter of the 5th and hasten to write a few lines in Reply. I have not as yet sent you any pass. I do not see that you can come if I should do so. I know it would be very inconvenient to bring the children with you so much so in my opinion that I shall not ask you to do it and besides the inconvenience the cost would exceed what we are able to pay You could not get here with the children and back home at less cost than $100. and glad as I would be to see both you and the children I do not feel that I can afford to pay so much for pleasure   We make our money too slowly to justify it   I shall not however entirely abandon the idea of your coming. Circumstances may favor it more after while. I know you would take great pleasure in making me a visit and are particularly anxious to do so because you think it would gratify me but then what you can't do you can't and I know it. I will make an extraordinary effort to get home for a few weeks sometime during the summer and I don't see why I can't succeed. other officers get to go home. there is no a train leaves here but that carries 50 officers to the north and not one returns but that brings as many back who have been home for no other purpose than to see their families. We are very anxious today about the final Result of the great Battle that is progressing between Hooker and Lee our anxiety has increased as the news today is not so favorable as yesterday. We hope Reinforcements may yet reach Hooker in time to obtain a glorious victory and prevent the Retreat of the Rebel army. We are on the flank still here awaiting developments at other points   I am still grunting as usual   Ira and Samuel are well, the other boys are well   I have received my commission as 1st Lieut   I want you to send immediately my old commission. I believe it was in my trunk   send it the fastest way. I can not be mustered into the new Rank without it and until I am mustered I will lose the difference between a 1st & 2nd Lieutenants pay.

If any of our people want to visit this army I can send them a pass. I have not heard from Willis since Parker came down the last time. Wm Havre is badly crippled from the kick of a mule it is feared it will lame him for life, as the knee cap is shivered   He will probably get to go home.

We Rejoice to hear that Ballanchigham is arrested   We would be happy to know that all such men were arrested by a shortness of Rope about 4 ft above "Terra firma."

Bully for your garden and chickens.

My love to all. Your Thomas

Letter 4

Murfreesboro Tenn, May 23rd 1863
Aurilla,

My brave and noble wife   Although I have written since I received any letter from you I can not resist the temptation this quiet evening to devote a few moments to your interest. I have not been well for two or three days The friends are all well. Almost the half of Bartholomew County is down here and on the road. Edee is arrested and will at least be sent back home without time to dispose of his goods   he may lose them altogether   This climate is not regarded healthy for Knights of the Golden Circle. and Capt Wiles is determined that this class of valuable Citizens shall not endanger their precious health by remaining here to speculate off Soldiers   I fear the consequences for others of our fellow Citizens. It seems as though the black cloud of Treason still thickens in the North. I fear the Enemy in our rear now much worse than in the front   I have serious apprehensions that a large body of Wicked and ignorant men in the North are bent on the ruin of the country, to accomplish a party purpose. I regard the Secret conventions in new York and Indianapolis as decided by ominous   God grant my fears may be causeless. The 39th participated in a spicy little fight yesterday morning at daylight they rode all night and perfectly surprising the Rebel camp, captured 200 - prisoners 400 horses and destroyed 600 stand of arms   scattered the remainder of the Brigade in confusion and Returned to camp without the loss of a man. It is regarded as a brilliant dash. The boys enjoyed it hugely.

Continue to pray for the salvation of our country. Our best service now is in the prayers and patriotism of the noble women of the Loyal States   If the union element can check the traitors of our own States the Struggle will soon be over. My love to all   a kiss for you and the children

   Yours affectionately
   Thomas
   please write soon as this come to hand

Letter 5

Chattanooga Tenn, Dec 3rd 1863
Aurilla

Dear wife

   I am again on courier duty on the old line unless our army advances I shall probably remain here for some weeks   the Co. Is quartered in houses on the "line" As soon as my baggage gets over from the vally I shall be able to make myself quite comfortable   my clothes none of them have come from home. I need them very much   my boots are worn out. I have no under clothes at all There are none here to buy. I get no pay this pay-day which I have no doubt will disappoint you worse than me. I had to borrow fifty dollars for my own use. I could not be paid because I had been Commissioned and not mustered as Captain. I have now more than $800.00 due me in this Department. If I can't get it I can't spend it so I presume I shall lose nothing by it. You must try and collect or borrow what you need until we are paid again. I collected the $100.00 from Dr. Palmer and paid my debts here. You inquired in one of your letters how much I made on the clothing I expected to bring through - in answer I would say that I could not get any through

   I am not in as good health as I had been   my side hurt me for the past few days. The Co generally well. I only have ½ of it with me   the remainder is yet in the valley under command of Lieut Snyder. Ira will perhaps start for Indiana tomorrow   if so I will send this by his hand   I hope indeed he may be able to recruit a company   I don't think a man of his age and vigor can honorably remain at home while the country is involved in war. and I should be glad he could get a position to compensate in part for the disappointment of not being able to get his profession   It is not necessary for me to attempt to detail the news or try to give you the results of the recent Battles in this vicinity you have had better opportunities to learn than I have   It is foolishness for me to write long letters in reference to the movements of the army because you can see the letters of men who have more time and ability. and sooner than mine can possibly reach you   When I get home I intend to whip the old woman and all the children for you gave me the ILCH while I was at home (I'll bet this makes Ella laugh)

Give my Love to all

Yours

Thomas

Fragment of a letter 6

…services in the Field   I shall go there by all means. But so long as I can serve my country to acceptance and the interests of my family to advantage I think I ought to do so. It would truly be very agreeable to be at home now and remain all the time perhaps more so to me than any one else as I would avoid many hardships that I now have to endure in addition to the pleasures we would equally enjoy. I am happy to hear that the children are learning so fast. I am very proud of my whole family (only I wish my little wife wasn't so stingy). I am much pleased with the prospect of a large increase of the population the only thing I can regret about it are too many girls and none of them mine. Time enough for that biineby (as the song goes. I think you might have written a little more about Ira wasn't the children glad to see him. I hope to hear in your next that Father is improved in health. If you have to neglect your own business I want you to see that he has proper attention and has all he needs for his Comfort. Christmas Gift to all of you, and a happy New Year, when it comes. Give my love to every body, and believe me ever

Affectionately

Yours

Thomas

Letter 7

[The original letter has been lost. The text was copied by
Frances Richman Johnson]

Headquarters 1st Brig 3rd Cav Div K.D.M.
Durham Station N.C. April 21st 65
Aurilla

Dear Wife

You will know long before this reaches you that the war is terminated. Genl Johnson has surrendered to Genl Sherman and Breckenridge as the

Representative of the Confederate Government has stipulated the surrender of all the Confederate Armies. The terms of capitulation have not been made known but they will no doubt be acceptable to our people and the Government at Washington. Genl Sherman in announcing our triumph to his soldiers says their valor has secured final and lasting Peace from the Potomac to the Rio Grande. The whole question has been referred to the authorities at Washington meanwhile their decision can be obtained. We will remain here. It is generally understood that the army will march across the country to the most convenient point for giving security to the large amount of Government property in our possession. The most probable point is Harrisburg Penn. It will require at least one month to march there with our immense trains. It will require another month to muster out the army. We can not be home before the 1st of July. You may look for me that soon. I would come at once but that I shall get 3 months extra pay for remaining. If you get impatient I can afford to pay your expenses to Harrisburg. We have heard of the death of our President. Universal gloom pervades the whole army. It the direst calamity and greatest trial of our patience at this time could be imposed. God only knows what will be the issue. I can not write now. I will soon be at home and if I retain my speech I will tell you what I omit in writing.

I am well as also are the boys

I am anxiously yours

for speedy union

Thomas

Harold Coons – World War II Letters

My father, Harold Coons, was born on July 31, 1911 in New Market, Indiana and died on September 11, 1999 in New Albany, Indiana. He was the son of Merle Fuson Coons (1887-1940) and Clara Leona Van Cleave (1889-1967). He graduated from Wabash College in Crawfordsville, Indiana in 1932 and received his LLB from Indiana University School of Law in Bloomington, Indiana in 1936. On April 9, 1938 he married my mother, Margaret Louise Richman (1913-1998) in Columbus, Indiana. He served in the Army during World War II and retired as a major in the United States Army Reserves. For most of his working career he was an insurance adjustor, first in Indianapolis and later in New Albany, Indiana. During the latter part of his career he practiced law and was a Floyd County Superior Court judge in 1978. He was the chairman of the Floyd County Republican Central Committee from 1968-1976.

When Dad was in the Army he carried on an almost daily correspondence with my mother from February 1944 until his return to the United States in February 1946. This series of letters is a family treasure trove. The entire series consists of a first set of 163 letters written stateside from February 9, 1944 to November 28, 1944 prior to my father's shipping out to the European theater. Most of these letters are written from Fort Bragg, North Carolina and Fort Rucker, Alabama. Some of these letters appear in Chapter Six. The second series of 354 letters extends from late November 1944 when Dad shipped out on the *HMV Britannic* until February 13, 1946 as Dad was leaving England to return home.[14] These letters are edited to take out extraneous material of less interest to the reader, but include material related to the war and various recreational leaves.

This second series of letters covers Dad's trip to Europe aboard the *HMV Britannic*, his short sojourn in England before being deployed to France, the sinking of the *S.S. Leopoldville* as his unit was crossing the English Channel on Christmas Eve 1944, his unit's assignment to guard the submarine pens at St. Nazaire and L'Orient in Brittany (since their original unit had been decimated by the submarine attack), brief assignment to guard a displaced persons camp near Baumholder, Germany after the war ended, reassignment to Arles, France to prepare for transfer to the Pacific, final assignment to the Criminal Investigation Division in Paris, France, and a number of leaves while in Europe.

Dad was a member of Battery A, 870 Field Artillery Battalion, 66th Infantry Division (Black Panthers). A number of excellent sources document the 66th Division's service during World War II. [15-17] Alan Andrade's book, *S.S. Leopoldville Disaster: December 24, 1944*, is an excellent account of the sinking of the S.S. Leopoldville[18] as is Sander's, "*A Night before Christmas.*"[19]

I know that my mother also wrote my father a series of letters during the war because he repeatedly refers to them. I believe he shipped their letters home because he shipped home numerous souvenirs. Unfortunately, these letters must have been destroyed by my father or mother, since they were missing when I went through Dad's possessions after his death.

Harold Coons, Battery A, 870 Field Artillery Battalion, 66th Infantry Division

Voyage to France aboard the HMV Britannic

The letters written from sea and letters written during Dad's initial sojourn in England and France are written via Victory Mail. This so-called "V-Mail" consisted of micrographed images of the original censored letters. These images were then placed on a reel and shipped to various regional centers in the United States where they were printed at one-quarter original size and then delivered to the addressee. Thus, the weight and volume of mail was drastically reduced so as to allow the military to reserve valuable shipping space for war materials.

During WWII all mail was censored so as to protect the troops in case the mail was interdicted by the enemy. My father's mail was rarely censored since he was a compulsive attorney who knew what would and what would not pass. In addition, he and my mother agreed on a "secret" code before he shipped overseas so that he could inform her where he was stationed. My mother's letters to his mother detail the precise nature of this code in Chapter Five.

These letters are edited so as to leave out extraneous non war-related material. Both my parents numbered their letters consecutively so they could tell if there had been missing letters. . "Steve" or "Stevie" mentioned in these letters is my brother, Stephen M. Coons, ages 3 to 5 at the time of these letters, and now an Indianapolis attorney. I am referred to as "the baby" in letters after my birth in the summer of 1945.

[November, 1944] #1 At Sea [V-Mail]
Dearest,

I'm at sea in more ways than one. So far I haven't been sea sick however my stomach feels confused. The weather has been almost perfect thus far however it is rough enough to make the ship pitch and roll constantly. I'm settled at a long table writing and my weight slowly shifts from one side to the other. Our particular troop compartment is large and is almost packed with men - to say it's crowded is an understatement. We eat and sleep and exist in the same compartment. I have a hammock and have slept much better than I expected. There is a gentle motion conducive to sleep. In rough weather this motion might be conducive to sickness.

We are allowed on deck for fresh air, a smoke, exercise, and just to stand around and watch the other ships. I prefer it forward or aft as the pitch is more noticeable especially at night at the stern rail.

I can't help but think that hourly I'm going further and further away from you both. I think of you often and hope and pray you are both alright. Give Stevie a great big hug for me, honey. All my love to you both, always.

Coonie

[November, 1944] #2 At Sea [V-Mail]

We had mail call today – mail taken aboard before we left. I received four letters from you written the 23rd, 24th, 26th, and 27th. These are the last letters for a while and knowing they were makes me a bit homesick…

It's rough today but I'm not sick – yet. I hope you continue to feel good, honey. All my love to you and Stevie, sweetheart.

Always, Coonie.

[November, 1944] #3 At Sea [V-Mail]

Dearest,

When I went to sleep last night my hammock swung constantly and sometimes rather violently however this morning the sea was calmer and it was warmer on deck.

We are fed twice a day which is enough considering our limited activity. Even as army food it's only fair however realizing the number of men fed and the crowded facilities for preparing it they are doing an efficient job. From the canteen we are allowed to order as many as four candy bars a day so that satisfies between meals hunger...

...All my love always.

Coonie

[November, 1944] #4 At Sea [V-Mail]

Dearest,

Although yesterday was rather rough today is almost perfect. The sun is out and it's warmer. There is however a strong breeze and the salt spray sometimes blows over the bow drenching the fellows on deck.

Due to the crowded conditions things are constantly being lost. I placed your letters and some I had written with some of my equipment and it was apparently moved, at any rate they are missing so if you fail to get a letter you'll know the reason...

I've been reading a collection of short stories by Ellery Queen - it helps pass the time and it's going rather slowly now since the novelty has worn off...

...All my love to you both, always.

Coonie

[November, 1944] #5 At Sea [V-Mail]

Dearest,

Thought I might make an effort to clean up. Salt water showers are available but it's a matter of standing in line and waiting. They have a special salt water soap however not having any I don't know how clean I might have been. From our experience after the hurricane you will know how successful I was in my attempt. At any rate I went through the motions and I feel refreshed. Hope I'm not boring you with the details however everything else I might write about which is interesting is of course taboo because of security reasons.

We had codfish and I'm still wondering why fishermen go to all the trouble to catch them. I'm sure that is one seafood that I'll steer clear of in the future.

After my shower I went on the forward deck. The sky was clear and though the stars were out it was very dark. The breeze was strong and I frequently caught some salt spray. Looking over the side one could sea phosphorous streaks in the waves. It was quiet and beautiful out there but the ship was headed the wrong way.

Give Stevie a big hug. All my love, always, sweetheart, and good night.

Coonie

[November, 1944] #6 At Sea [V-Mail]

Dearest,

At last I finished a collection of Ellery Queen detective stories. I still have one of the Saint stories which I haven't begun yet. At present I've been refreshing my memory on a foreign language. I'm surprised that I can recall as many phrases as I do. An old language shark like you could help me lots. My reading knowledge is much better than my speaking or my hearing ability. Maybe with the addition of sign language I could get by if necessary.

Today is another bright and sunny day, also the coldest day too. It's such a swell day I'd like to go swimming but I fear the water would be slightly cold. It would be a swell day to take some color movies. I hope that whenever we arrive that we'll be allowed some freedom of action. Though this is definitely not a cook's cruise I expect we'll be able to do some sightseeing at times.

Give Stevie a big hug for me. All my love to you both always.

Coonie

[November, 1944] #7 At Sea [V-Mail]

Dearest,

Perhaps you wondered why my letters aren't dated. As long as we're at sea I won't be able to for security reasons. Since one day is so much like the preceding one it's difficult to keep track of each particular day. Time seems rather meaningless. Some days I haven't written a letter to you and some days I've written more than one. You'll likely receive a fairly good stack of mail at once...

The V-mail folder including your letters and the one I wrote to you finally were recovered today...

All my love to you and Stevie, sweetheart.

Coonie

[November, 1944] #8 At Sea [V-Mail]
Dearest,

Today I finished a book of short stories involving the "Saint." There were a half dozen fellows ready to grab it as soon as I was finished...

While working in the message center the editor of the news bulletin asked for suggestions for the name of the sheet promising a carton of cigarettes to the author of the title selected. Well it is now the "Poop Deck News" and I have a carton of Raleigh. I think the title could be improved upon such as the "poop Deck Scoop" however the inspiration is too late as the edition has gone to press...

It must be getting rough as we are rolling quite a bit and it's difficult to write...

...All my love, always.
Coonie

[November, 1944] #9 At Sea [V-Mail]
Dearest,

We have been aboard now for several days and it is becoming rather monotonous.

For the most part it has been a pleasant and interesting trip. There has been some cloudy and rough weather and we have had some rather sunny warm calm weather and I wasn't seasick though a number of boys were. I was assigned to a troop compartment near the middle of the ship and the pitch was not as pronounced as near the stern or bow.

We live, eat and sleep, in the compartment in which are long tables and benches. At night we sling hammocks above and mattresses are placed on the tables. You would be surprised the number of men that are huddled thus in such a small space. I've found a hammock more comfortable than I supposed and fortunately I'm near a ventilator.

We are fed two meals a day and while the food isn't the best in the world it's as good as expected under the circumstances. I could eat a steak or a fried chicken right now but the prospects seem slim...

...Love you always.
Coonie

Letter from England

[December, 20, 1944] #16 Somewhere in England [V-Mail]
Dearest,

Thursday morning Rosenbaum and I started out to see the sights. I'm afraid I about walked him off his feet but having only one day I wanted to see as much as possible. Even so about all I can say is that I've been in London. We took a double decker bus at the marble Arch and rode down Oxford Street and then down Charing Cross Road to Trafalgar Square and got off at Parliament Square. We spent some time around the Houses of Parliament, Westminster's Abby and St. Margaret's Church. Then we walked down Birdcage Walk past St. James Park to Buckingham Palace - then back down the mall past St. James Palace to Trafalgar Square under the Admiralty Arch. On our way down Whitehall back to Westminster Bridge we passed Downing Street - looks like an alley in size. We wound up on the Thames on the Victoria Embankment to Charing Cross and then down the Strand to Waterloo Bridge. By then our time was about up. On a 7 day leave I could begin to see what I'd want to in London.

Oxford Street and the Strand are business districts with stores and shops. Crowds of people were Xmas shopping, The windows displayed considerable merchandise however inside there wasn't much choice and prices were high. Tell you more tomorrow.

All my love to you both.

Coonie

Harold Coons on leave in London near Buckingham Palace, December 1944

Letters from Brittany, France

My father's unit was decimated because the ship containing the bulk of the men from the 66th Division, the *SS Leopoldville*, was torpedoed by a German submarine just outside Cherbourg, France during its English Channel crossing on Christmas Eve 1944. Of the 2500 men aboard, the converted Belgian passenger liner, fourteen officers and 748 enlisted men were lost. Because of the tremendous loss of men, the 66th Division relieved the 94th Division, which had been guarding the Germans in the St. Nazaire and L'Orient pockets which contained the German submarine bases. The 94th Division was then sent to fight in the famous Battle of the Bulge in the Ardennes Mountains in Belgium. Luckily my father happened to be traveling in an LST containing halftracks, trucks, and jeeps rather than on the *Leopoldville*.

Once in France, the men of the 66th repaired their makeshift huts for the winter and settled in to guard the German forces, which numbered approximately 100,000. Artillery duels were frequent during the months that followed before the Germans surrendered in May 1945. For example, in February 1945 alone the 66th fired 1140 rounds a day.[20] Luckily my father was stationed well behind the front and few casualties occurred in his particular company. With the termination of hostilities, censorship ceased.

[Undated, France] #19 [V-Mail]
Dearest Margie,

This Christmas will be one to tell Stevie - and the others - about in years to come. I hope I will be able to have him on my knees and tell him about it next Christmas Eve. And every time retold it will likely be a better story. The reason being that such tales grow better with the years. Then by the time I tell it to my grandchildren it'll be some tall tale. It'll grow like a fishing tale.

I'm sorry that I haven't been able to write for a few days. Sometimes it's very difficult and at present the conditions aren't too good. I'm seated in the back of a truck in the middle of a field which is covered with frost. Our blankets were on a trailer hooked to another vehicle which last night was like the little man who wasn't there. Therefore I slept in the truck with one blanket - Ok except for my feet.

Two cups of hot coffee have warmed me up and the air is peppy so it's OK...

Coonie

1/6/45, France #24 [V-Mail]

Dearest,

Today I worked on my quarters fixing the flooring. Now the next task is to connect the stovepipe to the stove. This promises to be quite a job as the pipe is too small so unless I have a brain storm I may be smoked out. A degree in engineering would be more helpful than one in law right now. On top of that my French is terrible. However I think I made a deal with a garcon who spoke better English than I do French to get some laundry done. Perhaps by the middle of next week I'll be in a position to take a bath - after a fashion - and put on clean clothes. As long as I'm working on the hut it would be a waste of time to clean up and change. Showers aren't available yet and any bath would be a helmet one. The hut is mostly below ground and without heat is damp. When completed it should be fairly comfortable though I always crack my head on entering. It is shared with a lad named Sunshine who is on the other shift so we only need one bed. At present two other fellows are occupying it while they improve their own.

Give Stevie a big hug for me. All my love to you both. I miss you both more than you can know. Always.

Harold Coons standing besides his hut in Brittany

Coonie

France, 4/19/45 #120

Dearest,

...Yesterday I was on pass to Pontivy and purchased some postcards which I'll send to you and Mother. Hang on to them as they'll help me tell Stevie about them in later years...

...Pontivy has a Red Cross recreation center and serves coffee and donuts. It's nice to have someplace to rest in comfortable chairs after walking around. It was a warm day and I walked around taking about half a roll of film. It's smaller than Quimper and not as pretty.

The Château de Rohan was built in the 15th century - it was two huge towers, a high wall, moat, and enclosed courtyard. There is no water in the moat today and cows graze there. You can see a horse grazing there in the picture. To the left just outside the picture [postcard] is a shady park. I purchased a half bottle of cider and ate there - peanut butter and jelly sandwiches which I took along. If the chateau were in the states it would be repaired and be a showplace. I was disappointed to find it pretty well run down - some French families live in part of it and one of the churches runs a girl's school in the rest of it. The stairway is on the inside of the court yard. When I walked in the kids - age five to ten or eleven - were having recess. When they saw me pull my camera out of my pocket they lined up in a group for a picture. I had intended taking a picture of about six sitting on some steps but there were almost sixty by the time I took the picture. They were certainly a bunch of cute and friendly youngsters. When I left they yelled "thank you" and I yelled back "merci."...

...All my love always. Coonie

France, 5/7/45 # 136

Dearest,

Well according to the radio tomorrow is VE day - and that's about all I know. I wondered what we'd do when it happened - and the answer is - nothing. The radio tells of the celebration in New York and London - there's no celebration here - just silence. We're wondering whether it's true - whether all fighting has ceased every where and whether the Germans are surrendering. We're wondering what we'll do next - whether we're headed to the Pacific or will end up as occupation troops.

I don't believe we have completely grasped the significance that the war has ended. The events of the past month - Roosevelt's death, Ernie Pyle, Mussolini, Hitler, Goebbels - crackup of the German voices every where - so many momentous events in such a short time have rather numbed the mind of the realization of their significance. There's a feeling of relief but not complete relief because we realize there is yet another enemy to defeat. I think that is the reason there is no celebration here on the eve of VE day. There is the feeling that we have a long way to go before we see our families and homes. There are so many who have seen more combat and have been over here so much longer that we can not honestly hope to be among those who return early...

...All my love always.

Coonie

Letters from Germany and France

With the termination of hostilities in Europe, the 66th Division was ordered on an occupational mission in Germany in order to establish military government, impound weapons and ammunition, and guard former prisoners of war. My fathers company was assigned to guard a camp of Russians who had been utilized as slave laborers by the Germans. The trip to Baumholder rapidly covered 700 miles through France and Germany. In late May, the 66th was ordered to southern France near Arles where preparations were being made to ship United States soldiers to the war in the Pacific theater.

France, 5/20/45 #146

Dearest,

...Since the termination of hostilities we had been down in the pocket guarding the German artillery positions. We were in two different locations the week we were there. The first place had small arms dumps and light artillery while the second place was primarily a costal position at Port Louis across the river from L'Orient. I picked up a nice German Mauser army rifle and a couple of leather ammunition cases as well as a bayonet but was not among the fortunate few to find a Luger or P88 pistol.

Yesterday we left and are at present enjoying a truck trip. We came thru Ploerwal, Rennes, Vitré, la Val, La Lune and spent last night just outside Le Mans. That was a rather long day of about two hundred miles. Today we drove thru Nogent-le-Rotrou, Chartres and we camped just outside Ramboiullet which is about 30 miles east of Paris. I doubt if we traveled over a hundred miles today and we camped early about 1 pm. This evening I think about 20 of the fellows may go in to Versailles. I want to see it but I'd rather wait and take a chance on a three day pass to Paris when I have more time to look around.

...Since censorship has been lifted I can tell you some of the things that happened in the past.

We left Camp Shanks the night of the 30th of November and went aboard the Britannic pulling out of the harbor the following morning. As I recall it was a 12 day trip and we landed at Southampton before going to Blandford. I think we left there the 23rd at night going to Portland where we were loaded on LSTs pulling out the next day. It was windy and rough - so much so that the LST was tilted at crazy angles and almost everyone was sea sick. I was almost but managed to prevent it by staying on deck in one of the trucks secured to the deck. In the evening we went below to try and sleep and was suddenly awakened and ordered on deck. I supposed it was just a drill and took my time - had to because of the ladder we had to climb. Upon getting on deck I found all guns were manned and a sailor told me we were under attack. I saw nothing although a sailor claimed that two fish [torpedoes] had just missed us. The crew had been in on D day and said that this was lots more than they ran into then. It was a clear moon light night and though cold I spent the rest of the night sleeping off and on in the truck. It would have been a death trap below. They did get a troop ship carrying part of our infantry and lost lots of men. The clipping you saw referred to that. We heard rumors about it Xmas day while still aboard but didn't learn much about it until later.

Apparently we were headed for the Bulge but due to the loss of so many men we headed for Lorient and St Nazaire sectors. We landed at Cherbourg and traveled south thru Rennes by way of Coutances and Avranches to Châteaubriant where we spent several cold and miserable days camped out on a huge airport. There was a little snow on the ground. Then we headed over to watch the Lorient sector and camped in orchards - still cold and the ground covered with snow - for a few days until we could move in and replace the outfit we were relieving. That outfit headed for Germany in our place and took a beating. New Year's Eve was cold and I swore I'd never spend another like it if I could help it. During all this time we spent most of our time trying to keep warm around camp fires. That night I tasted my first Calvados - something like rot gut in my opinion but very warming - tastes like gasoline. Up until the end we were near the village of Arzano which is about 6 miles or so southwest of Plouay. I doubt if you can find either on a map.

Well, honey, that just about takes care of where I've been up to date. I'll continue the letter as we go along because there is no way to mail letters until we reach our destination…

5/23/45

We arrived last night. Monday we came thru Versailles, outskirts of Paris, Meaux, Laferté, Montmiral, Champaubert, Chalons, St. Menehould and camped outside of Verdun. Yesterday we came thru Etain, Longuyon,

Longwy, Luxemburg, Trier and are now south and east of Koblenz. I don't know the name of the village - it isn't large.

We are billeted in large houses - part of the battery is across the street in what was once a private hospital while we are in a large house which one of the local Nazi big shots lived in.

Today we've been busy cleaning the place up and cleaning our own stuff. After a trip across France we were pretty dirty. The last two days it rained and was rather chilly. I think it will be easier here than where we were in France.

Just what we will do here is not definite. There is a nearby camp with several thousand Russians and Poles and we may help guard and get them started on their way home. Apparently there are few men in the village - all of military age being in the army and now prisoners. Just because we are here does not necessarily mean that we will be permanent occupation troops - time will tell.

This part of Germany is beautiful - hilly like our Ohio River region - many hills heavily forested with pine trees. The smaller villages have not been damaged to any great extent but Trier for example is bombed and badly burnt out leaving just shells of buildings.

The people seem deeply humiliated - instead of looking at us they look down or turn their heads. I suppose they hate us quite bitterly but I failed to observe any evidence of defiance in their glances - just humiliation I would say. They appear to be well fed and very well dressed. Of course all the rest of Europe has been feeding and clothing them...

...All my love always.

Coonie

P.S. The town we are in is Braumholder [Baumholder] and I seriously doubt if you can find it on a map either.

France, 6/3/45 #155

Dearest,

...You are likely wondering why we are in France - so are we. It had been rumored for several days that we were making a move. I was hoping it would be Austria but it's France and I think our destination is Marseilles. No I don't think we're shipping any place as rumor has it we'll be there a while.

We left Baumholder this morning and came thru Hamburg entering France near Sarragrcemines and coming down thru Plateau Salins to Nancy where we are in a bivouac area tonight.

The scenery was beautiful practically all the way - long rolling hills - fields plowed in patches on the contours - small patches of pine woods on the tops of the hills and in the valleys visible by their tile roofs and the spires of their churches. The villages off the main highway appeared undamaged by war but those on the highway were piles of rubble from shells. The larger towns were blasted by bombs. Nancy does not appear to have been so hard hit but there is considerable damage along the river. It's strange how along a street two houses will be blasted into piles of rubble with not a wall standing while the houses on both sides will be relatively undamaged except for broken windows and scars where fragments have struck. Were it not for the fact that all the houses and buildings are built of stone with walls several inches [thick] I think the damage would be much greater. Covering the stones is a mortar with a rough finish which in most cases is painted a tan or a buff. The roofs are mostly all a red tile while in Germany there were many black slate. You see no solitary farmer's houses in the country as in the states. They all live in villages - the living quarters and that containing the farm animals are all in one building. I don't like the odor but I suppose they're used to it and don't mind it where the war hasn't struck the villages are neat and clean. The window panes and white lace curtains are spotless.

The camp we are in has large tents with eight army cots in each. They have a mess hall and German PWs do the rough labor and all the work.

I can't understand why we went into Germany and after such a short stay are on our way back into France but I'm not objecting - I like to see the scenery.

Monday 6/4/45

Today we came through Neufchateau and Langres to Dijou where we are spending the night in a bivouac are similar to last night - a tent city served by PWs. The scenery today was similar to yesterday - long rolling hills - deep grassy meadows with some of the finest cattle I've ever seen.

We aren't far from Switzerland and I certainly would like to detour far enough to see it. I suppose though that we'll go thru Lyon and follow the Rhone River on down.

Well the latest rumor is that we'll spend a couple of months in Marseille and then head for the states. That would suit me but it's just another rumor and I'm not counting on it any. I think we're still in the 15th army but they could put us in some other army without much trouble.

Tuesday 6/5/45

Last night we went into Dijou - seemed like a nice city but every thing was closed and we saw very little except other GIs.

Today we came thru Chalou-s-shone, Macon, Lyon and stopped on a former airport near St. Rambert D'Albon.

Lyon is a very large city where the Soane and Rhone rivers meet. The rivers wind thru the heart of the city and it is beautiful with many trees along wide streets and several side walk cafes.

An outstanding item of the scenery are the fields of scarlet poppies growing wild in profusion. We entered the fruit section today - acres and acres of grapes both in the lowlands and on the hillsides. There were numerous cherry trees and we had three different varieties at one stop- small sweet ones, large red ones and black ones.

The French are very friendly - children from infants on up to elderly people held up two fingers in the form of a V and waved their hands.

The Rhone Valley has very beautiful scenery. The valley is from a mile to ten miles or so wide with a high range of hills on both sides. It is heavily populated - one village after another. The fields are mostly all small and though they raise some grain, grapes and fruit trees seemed to predominate.

Wednesday 6/6/45

Today we came on down the Rhone River thru Valence, Montélinar, Douzere, Avignon, and are now in camp near Arles...

Thursday 6/7/45

...I'd recommend the Rhone valley for anyone who wants a beautiful motor trip. - hope we can take it together sometime, honey. We followed the Rhone for some distance today and saw tall mountains on our left which must have been the Alps. Near Avignon the valley broadened out into a broad level plain covered with fruit trees and grape vines - it must be dry because there were numerous irrigation ditches. Where the land was irrigated the grass was green and the trees all lush and fresh though where not irrigated the land was dry and desert like...

...All my love for ever and ever - Coonie.

Letters from Arles and Letters from Passes

After returning from Germany my father was stationed just outside of Arles, France. His outfit was assigned to process soldiers through the port of Marseille from the European theater to the Pacific theater. With the capitulation of Japan after the bombing of Hiroshima and Nagasaki, this job was no longer necessary.

The long monotonous wait to return to the United States began. Soldiers returned home based upon a "point system." Each child a soldier had counted twelve points. Medals were worth five points each and the soldier was awarded one point for each month overseas.

6/10/45 #157

Dearest,

Yesterday I went on pass at 1 pm until 11 pm to Nimes which is about 30 miles distant - we had to detour to cross the Rhone since the bridge is out at Arles. It's as large or larger than Quimper. Being Saturday the stores were all closed. The sidewalk cafes were open and I spent most of my time relaxed watching the people pass. One café had an orchestra and quite a crowd was there. I was surprised to find so much evidence of Roman civilization - an arena, public gardens, and a temple - the latter in excellent condition and housing a huge coin collection of modern and ancient coins...

...All my love to the sweetest girl in the world – always.

Coonie

6/11/45 France # 158

Dearest,

...I went on a pass to Arles and saw the bull fights. It was held in the old Roman arena. There were a half dozen engagements - no bulls were killed - they play around and get the bull mad by sticking barbs with paper streamers into the bull's front shoulders - usually five or six. Half the crowd was American soldiers and to a man they were for the bulls. Matter of fact I'd say the bulls had the best of most of the matches - the horn of one ripped the seat of one guy's pants and a few minutes later tore his shirt sleeve and brought blood. Personally I don't care much for the sport nor do I think many of the Americans liked it. It was interesting to see one though and get some pictures. The bull fighters engaged the bulls on foot and also on horseback ...

...All my love for ever and ever.

Coonie

France 6/17/45 #164

Dearest,

...we moved into the chateau. It doesn't look like our conception of a chateau nor like the fancy ones in Brittany. This one looks more like the house of a prosperous farmer - large, square with three stories. I don't know how many rooms there are in the main part - seven or eight up here on the third floor, however most of them are pretty small. Sgt. Huber, Cpl. Hurtz and I share one and it's rather cramped. But the larger ones are just as crowded and have as many as eight or ten. Then there is a wing of two stories which accommodates fifteen or twenty fellows in three or four rooms. On the second floor are four or more master size bedrooms while the first floor is a huge hall, living room, dining room and kitchen...

...All my love, sweetheart, always.

Coonie

France 6/30/45 #174

Dearest,

...Marseille is a big town with a smell, Paris is cleaner. Marseille is a rough tough port and I certainly wouldn't want to be in parts of it after dark. It was a nice drive. We went by the way of Salon and came down the last side of the Et de Bene - guess it's a salt water bay - we've had a pass truck go up there to one of the beaches. Between here and Marseille the land reminds me some of the buttes in eastern Colorado - dry rocky plains with high outcroppings of stone formations - very few trees except where there is irrigation in the valleys. The hills aren't shaped like the buttes but they are all stone and treeless. We were on one high ridge and could see the Et de Bene like a huge lake.

We drove out south along the beach from Marseille along the sea. The coast is rocky and the road winds along the edge sometimes a hundred feet or so above the water and then drops down to the water's level where there is a narrow beach for a mile or so. Houses are perched all over the cliff between the sea and the highway and also on the cliff behind the highway. Every so often there will be a small beach of a hundred feet or so between the rocks and there you will see people bathing and lying in the sun. Some will be perched on the rocks. I can imagine that the Riviera is similar only on a grander scale...

...All my love for ever and ever. Coonie

Arles, France, 7/2/45 # 176

Dearest,

Well I have a new job - don't know whether it's a demotion or promotion, probably the latter and anyway it's more to my liking. I'm Capt. Hubben's assistant - he's the investigating officer. We'll be investigating the more serious types of cases - vice, black market, assault, rape, cases of violence, etc. He has only one jeep now so we'll take turns using it - one investigates while the other writes up his report. As soon as the Col. gets another jeep and driver for me I'll be riding around in style. I'm glad of the change as the desk Sgt's job was getting to be routine and mostly an information and file job. This way I'll be out in the open working on my own. The experience may stand me in good stead whenever we get back to the states on redeployment - may enable me to transfer out of the artillery into the MPs.

Last night they brought in a guy who had been identified by three French civilians as having been the one to threaten them with a gun in an argument over his laundry. He was almost half drunk and it was a circus. We found an empty holster on him which he couldn't satisfactorily explain - he claimed he'd had a small automatic but he'd given it away two months ago to a French boy. I never saw such a collection of junk as he laid on the desk when he emptied his pockets - everything under the sun almost. These guys wander all over camp at night, lost. They never know where they belong....

...and all my love to the dearest and sweetest girl in the world – always.
Coonie

France 8/6/45 #206
Dearest,
...Huber got a jeep so the five of us could go sightseeing up in the mountains north of here.

We just visited the old village of Les Baux - Roman and medieval ruins of castles right on top of one of the peaks. It must have been some place in its day with a grand view of the whole surrounding country - on a clear day the sea can be seen. After climbing over the old ruins, on to the top of the castle walls, we left and crossed the mountains over to the village of St. Rémy. The French were having an open air dance at a café on the outskirts and we sat and watched for a long time drinking some very good vin rouge. They ran out of it while we were there so we started driving again and stopped in all the little out of the way villages and sampled their wine. We lunched in another village not even on our map, called Molleges. They were really having a celebration and dance in the middle of the street. I guess it - whatever the celebration is - lasts for three days - today and tomorrow. These French have more holidays and they all last two or three days - I never saw the like...

...All my love for ever and ever.
Coonie

Paris, 8/9/45 # 209
I started to write this letter as soon as I arrived in Paris and just as I said Rod came back and here I am in Marseilles and it's the 13th. I'm so sorry I haven't written in the meantime and there isn't any really good excuse except I was either sleeping or sightseeing all the time. Please try and forgive me, honey. I hope you haven't been worried.

Thursday morning they took me to the airport at Istres. They had cancelled their regular liberty flights (pass flights) and I waited around and at noon was told they'd have a trip to Orleans and Creil, the latter being about 35 miles north of Paris. We took off about 2 pm and landed for a moment at Orleans to let a major off - then a short hop to Creil which included passing over Paris at about five thousand feet - beautiful hardly describes it. As companions I had six Wacs going back to the states - guess they'd flown quite a bit before as they spent the time sleeping. I kept my nose glued to the window like Stevie probably does because it was such a grand view of the countryside. It was a bright sunny day with large white clouds and part of the time we flew below and sometimes above - going up to fourteen thousand feet once. Most of the time the ground could be seen - village after village with their red-tiled roofs, irregularly shaped fields and forests, winding roads and rivers and canals. The climax was Paris - as beautiful from the air as on the ground.

We landed at Creil at about 5 pm and I caught a pass truck at 6:15 pm arriving at the Place de la Concorde about 7:30 pm. I walked up the street a couple of blocks past the church of the Madeliene to the Red Cross Club at Rain Bow Corner. Just as I was going in I met John Maloney from Crawfordsville - Mother will know him - we talked for a little while and he gave me a ticket enabling me to get a meal there. Then I walked up the Champs Des Elysees to Rue du Coliseé and quickly found his hotel. He was leaning out his window yelling at one of the fellows as I came up. He's the same old Rod - he promptly opened up a bottle of scotch and we proceeded to down a few - then took a tour of Paris before dark - came back and had a few more and talked and then visited two or three different bars and came back and went to bed about 1 am. He didn't have to work Friday so we slept late and then I saw his boss in the afternoon - very nice interview - did some more sightseeing that evening and got to bed about 11 pm.

Saturday Rod had to work so I got up at 10 am and walked around until noon and then after lunch I took the metro over to the Left Bank and walked around the Sarbonne - crossed to the Ile de la Cite on which Notre Dame is located - on over to the Right Bank and down the Quai & picked up some small etchings of the places I'd visited from the vendors who have their open air shops there. All in all I saw most of the points of interest but didn't have time to linger inside and was dead tired that night from all the walking and went to bed early.

Sunday morning we went around to see about getting a way back and about noon I made arrangements to leave at 1 pm by train. I got into Marseille about 7:30 am after spending 19 hours on the Paris-Marseille Express Via 2nd class. I thought of how Hollywood played up the Paris-Marseille Express in a movie I once saw - romantic, cosmopolitan, etc. I can assure you it isn't - not now at least. Its speed and comfort reminded me of the Monon and I was covered with cinders when I got off. Fortunately I got about seven hours of cramped sleep.

I waited around the Provost Marshall's office and caught a ride back here at 11 am and got back to the battery at 3 pm...

...All my love for ever and ever – always.

Coonie

Pass to Switzerland

#230 Mulhouse, France 9/5/45

Dearest,

It's about 2 am and after the trip up here I feel in need of a rest –what a joint – WOW! I left the battery about 8:30 AM yesterday morning for the HQS of 262 Inf. Regt. at the camp. We pulled out of there about 9:30 in two large trucks for Marseille arriving about noon and leaving about 1:30 PM for Lyons. The three car diesel express was fairly good being cleaner than a regular train. About 3 PM we passed within less than a quarter mile of the battery and on thru the camp into Arles. That's like the army – six hours, a long truck ride, a train ride and pass thru the place you started from.

About 8 pm we arrived in Lyon and during our layover of about two hours we had coffee and donuts. While we weren't looking some French civilians or someone hauled off with three cases of K rations we intended eating going up and returning. We went without breakfast this morning except for a half an orange that two nurses gave us – but the lunch more than made up for it.

We were lucky and grabbed some first class accommodations– six to a compartment rather than eight as in second class. There were two nurses in the compartment – generous souls they had three oranges. Even first class is not as comfortable as the seats on the Riley – not enough leg room. We all slept after a fashion and arrived here about 10 am. The center consists of a large group of buildings, once part of a French country school. Everything is for the GI's comfort and convenience.

We have been processed – paid $35 for the trip and another $35 for 150 Swiss francs. We leave early in the morning. There are four trips and I had a hard time selecting one. One is very long and the other three not so long so far taking one of the shorter ones and spend more time at each place with side excursions.

I took a little of everything with me – Swiss francs, French francs which aren't worth a tinker's darn in Switzerland, a couple of English pounds, a few American dollars, a money order and some travelers checks. I'll be lucky to spend any except the Swiss francs I guess as even the pound and the dollar are not worth full value there.

Tomorrow we get up at 5:15 AM – pretty early to start a furlough isn't it? I'll try to give you a running account as I go along, honey –

Lots and lots love to you all. Give our little boys hugs and kisses for me. I love and miss you an awful lot, sweetheart – always, Coonie.

Thun, Switzerland 9/6/45
Dearest,

Sorry but I didn't get this off before we left and we have to use the Swiss postal service and since sending an airmail is almost one franc I'm not sending a letter every day because Swiss francs are almost impossible to get and I'm looking around before I get any souvenirs. It's absolutely heartbreaking here with all these stores full of watches, fine jewelry, silverware – the loveliest things you ever saw to buy and just 150 Swiss francs to spend. Excellent watches can be purchased for 100 francs – they start as low as 30 to 35 francs. French francs are worthless – a 1000 franc note which is paid to us and pegged at $20 is worth about one eighth that here. English money is pretty good and even the dollar is only about three-fourths its pegged value. It's supposed to be worth about 4.29 Swiss francs but I guess they'll only give about 3 for it. Well I'm saving until I'm about thru the trip and then I'll get us something nice in Zurich.

We turned our watches back an hour in Basle and left by electric train for Berne arriving in about two hours. We had about two hours to sight see. Without question the Swiss cities are the tidiest and cleanest in the world. After the filth of France it like heaven – flowers in the windows of hotels and apartment houses – clean people – cleanliness everywhere.

We saw the capitol building and their famous white clock was constructed several hundred years ago. Stevie would have loved it – a rooster crows, animals run around, and father time turns an hourglass over and a blacksmith painted in gold hammers a gold bull – and this every hour and the children that live here like to watch it. Then we saw the bears in the bear pit – they eat peanuts and carrots and are so comical when they beg by holding up their paws and crossing them. One even caught peanuts by leaning over backwards.

We arrived in Thun about noon and are staying at the Bellevue Hotel right at the head of the lake – there's a grand view of the Alps but it has been cloudy about all day and the peaks haven't been visible. It has rained three or four times – a shower about 2:30 kept us from catching the boat down to Interlaken but we're going tomorrow.

I'm really dead tired tonight having walked around and window shopped so much so I'm going to go to sleep. I've been lying here since before 9 PM between sheets writing. You can't imagine how soft and wonderful it is – oh my, what luxury. And, honey, I want to show you Switzerland sometime – the rest of Europe isn't worth seeing – but here it's heaven.

Thun, Switzerland 9/7/45
Dearest,

This morning I got up about 8 am – impossible to sleep late surrounded by such beautiful scenery. After breakfast I went downtown and window shopped for awhile. Then we went up to the castle and spent some time in the museum – suits of armor, pikes, shields, old guns and crossbows. It was very interesting and there is a splendid view of the city and all the surrounding countryside and lake.

This afternoon was a beautiful trip on the lake – Thunersee – The boat, a pretty little excursion steamer with side paddles, made several stops at all the resort villages on the way to Interlaken – stops at Oberhofer, Guten and several others on the north side of the lake and then Spiez on the south side. The scenery is so gorgeous I'd give anything to have my camera with rolls of color film so I could bring back some of the beauty I'm seeing. I'm getting postcards but it takes color to really picture it.

Interlaken is built on land between Thun Lake and Brienz Lake. Both lakes are long and narrow and the mountains tower high on both sides. – the highest peaks on the south including the Jungfrau which is covered with snow and up which we are going tomorrow.

Interlaken is a beautiful resort city but not as large as Thun or it didn't seem to be. It has shop after shop of souvenirs – wood earrings of all kinds. One shop had nothing but ivory carvings, beautiful pieces of art, copies of famous sculpture figures and ivory of animals – very expensive though. Some of the wood carving is rather crude but some is just beautiful. There are so many lovely things to buy and I've so few francs to buy with – it's hard and as a result I haven't been able to decide what to get yet. The last day in Zurich I'd really like to go to town.

We got up at 5:30 AM for tomorrow's trip and as I'm tired I'm going to end this though it is only 9 pm. Lots and lots of love, sweetheart. I wish you here with me to see all this beauty.

Thun   9/8/45
Dearest,

We were awakened about 5:30 by the lady who runs the hotel – she opened he door and said "Got morning – are you going to see the mountain?" Well it was early to go see a mountain but up we got, had breakfast and were at the station and pulled out at 6:40. At Interlaken we changed and then changed again at Zweilütschinen. Here we really started up hill on the cogwheel railway. The next village was Grund, high up almost at the top of a valley surrounded by alpine meadows – cows grazing on the steep sides and ringing their bells. The changed cars again and this seemed even steeper going up to Scheidegg which is just above the timber line. We had two hours there, eating lunch in a hotel and leaving about noon. The view from the hotel dining room was beautiful and at each stop the view was more thrilling and stupendous.

Now the cars were even smaller and the grade steeper. The rest of the ride is thru a tunnel over five miles long which goes through two mountains – the Eiger and the Mönch and ending at a point called the Jungfraujoch which is at the top of the Aletsch glacier, the largest glacier in Europe – it stretches away into the distance for fifteen miles or so – beautiful. All in that direction is ice and snow – the glacier in a valley with snow covered peaks on both sides. On the way up there are two stops made at stations called Eigerwand and Eismeer – holes have been cut out and the view from these places are wonderful too but not until one reaches the top and then takes an elevator to the weather station still another 400 feet or so is the whole laid out in the most awe inspiring scene I've ever witnessed. While I've mentioned the ice and snow on one side – in the other in the direction we've come – one sees the opposite – here are the valleys and the lakes and beautiful alpine meadows.

We were up on top for about two hours and started down about 3:30 PM – I sent Stevie and mother cards from the highest post office in the world. Well I thought the scenery going up was beautiful but coming back it was even more so. At Scheidegg where we had lunch we changed trains again and came down a different way around Wenger Alp which is a good sized mountain by itself but is of course dwarfed by the three peaks I've mentioned. The last stop was Wenger, a small village with many beautiful hotels – I want to stay there when we come for a couple of days. I think it has the most beautiful view of any of the villages – it's about 4500 feet up. We stopped there for about fifteen minutes. The next village was at the base of the mountain in a beautiful valley – narrow with high sheer cliffs on both sides and a beautiful waterfall coming down from Murren high up on the cliff and reached by the steepest cog wheel railway – just goes straight up. Wenger is on the other side on an alpine slope than breaks and forms the other cliff of the valley. This valley ends up again the high snow covered mountains and the view of it from Wenger is just gorgeous. From Lauterbunnen we went down the valley following a mountain stream to Zweilütschinenand have completed the circuit around Wenger Alp – then back to Interlaken and to there getting in about 8 pm. It was a full day alright but the most beautiful scenery I've ever seen or hope to see. I'd have given anything for my camera and several rolls of color film because only that could catch the beauty.

Well, honey, it's 10:30 pm and I'm tired so I'm going to bed. I intend to finish this in the morning and mail it. I want to show you this someday, honey. Good night and sweet dreams – I love you with all my heart – Coonie.

Thun   Sunday 9/9/45
Dearest,

This morning we awoke to find it raining – not a hard rain but wet nevertheless. We leave early this afternoon for Lucerne, about a four hour trip by the electric. It's supposed to be a very beautiful trip but if it doesn't clear up soon the beauty will be hard to see.

We are there Monday and Tuesday until about 2 pm when we take a lake steamer to Brunneau and then by rail to Zurich. We leave Zurich Wednesday afternoon and go to Basle for the night and then leave there for Mulhouse Thursday morning.

Darn it the trip is about half over – like all good things it must end but I hope we can see it together sometime. Without question this is the best trip or furlough the Army ever made possible and I suspect it is largely the responsibility of the Swiss. They will certainly profit by it because every GI that takes the trip will be a booster for them and want to see it as a civilian sometime.

I hope I can do business with the money order and travelers checks in Zurich – I'd like to bring back a lovely watch for you. I shouldn't even mention it because it's probably unlikely that I'll be able to get it changed and I'd hate to have you disappointed.

The Swiss are so very friendly and most of them speak at least a little English as well as German, French and Italian. Yesterday at a mountain village – Wenger where we stopped for fifteen minutes – a train load of men, women and children sang a lovely song. We applauded and asked for an encore. They started another than then the train pulled out – still singing they waved and we waved. It was just like a musical comedy and you almost expected to see Judy Garland riding down the hill on a bicycle singing.

Give our little boys hugs and kisses for me sweetheart. I miss you so much now sweetheart thinking how wonderful this would be with you. All my love forever and ever.

Coonie

Luzern, Switzerland 9/10/45 # 231

Dearest,

Yesterday it rained all day and was cloudy. We left shortly after one o'clock from Thun and went to Interlaken where we changed trains followed the north shore of the lake east of there and to the end and then care over the pass at Brünig. We were up in the rain clouds there and could see very little of the valley until we were almost down. There were beautiful little villages all along the next two lakes until we arrived in Luzern. We arrived shortly after five and were put up at the Union Hotel – it isn't a resort hotel in the sense that it's on the lake – probably a second class one but fine.

Today it has rained quite a lot and as it was so cloudy and threatened rain all the time I didn't think it worth while taking any excursions though there are a number of nice ones for clear weather.

Consequently I spent most of my time shopping – that is looking and comparing prices and quality. With only 150 francs I'm really taking my time. Thus far I've spent about 25 francs on postcards, excursions and a little extra food and a half dozen beers with Ray Weals – I've cut out the beers now and am on water.

This afternoon I spent about an hour in an old lady's shop – wood carvings, music boxes, etc. She had several lovely fruit dishes with music boxes in the base that played a tune when it was lifted. They played two different tunes and were priced at 22 to 28 francs. She showed me how some were much better carved than others and finally because I'd been in there so long she told me she would fix up that played three different tunes and sell it to me for 30 francs – one tune is the Blue Danube Waltz and the others are lovely too. I'm almost sold on a fine carving of a Swiss cow – cow bell and all – it would look fine in the breakfront or if you don't think so we'll put it out to pasture on the farm. That's another 20 francs. Then there arc two other with Swiss chalets that are toy banks – cutest little things you ever saw – that's another 10 francs - one for Stevie and one for Philip – similar but different.

I've been looking for a musical cigarette box but haven't found just what I want yet – perhaps I'll wait until I get to Zurich and then if I have enough left I've seen some fine carvings of horses – one to go with the cow.

The watch situation seems out of the question here. There is no way to cash money orders or travelers checks except on the black market and you love 35 to 40 percent. Then the prices in some stores have been jacked up.

Luzern   9/11/45

Dearest,

Today it cleared off so we had a nice trip. I made some purchases before we left. At one shop, the lady's, I got a fruit dish with two tunes as the merchandise for three tunes didn't fit. Also a lovely carved cow, with bell of course, but it doesn't ring being of wood – and two chalets for Stevie and the baby that can make nice bands for them. At another shop I picked up a fine carved horse which is the same proportion as the cow. Stevie will probably want to play with them but they are for the breakfront and wouldn't last long in his hands. The banks won't either. Too bad I didn't get him something to play with but he has so many toys anyway. Then at another shop I ran into luck and found a woman who would take travelers checks so I bought a lovely carved fruit dish that plays four different tunes and also an inlaid cigarette box which likewise plays four different tunes when the lid is opened.

We left Luzern about 2 pm on an excursion steamer and for two hours enjoyed beautiful scenery stopping at several small mountain resorts – Hertenstein, Weggis, Vitznau, Buochs, Beckenried, Seelisberg and finally Brunnen. We were there about an hour and then took the train for Zurich arriving about 7 pm. We stayed at a very nice hotel, the St. Gothard, the nicest yet. The waiters were in tails and it was just as nice as eating at the Columbia Club. We walked round the town awhile – Zurich, the largest Swiss city, is a beautiful town and the cleanest large city I've ever seen.

While we were walking, one of the boys asked a man where a street was that he had an address. Several people gathered to help us – one a girl who spoke very good English. They took us to the station and looked up the address. Then she took us for a walk about the main part of town and we stopped in a coffee shop for coffee. She was a Swiss Jewish girl of about twenty-five or so and had studied in Paris and London speaking German, French, Italian and English. I gathered that her people had been well to do but that they lost their money because she was working in a hospital learning to be a technician and also going to night school to learn to type. She was very interesting and wanted to discuss world politics and the Jewish question –guess she was part of the intelligentsia of the town She was typical of all the Swiss we met – very friendly and helping – going out of their way to help the American soldiers. We gave her extra ration coupons as she looked almost hungry enough to eat the stamps.

Well I guess I better go to bed now, sweetheart. Gee, but I wish you were along. All my love forever and ever – give our boys my love and kisses.

Coonie

Balse   9/12/45
Dearest,

   We spent a very nice day in Zurich looking around. I tried to cash traveler's checks in watch places but the only place was one which had jacked up their prices. For example one watch they displayed for 195 francs was 80 francs cheaper down the street. So I decided not to buy any watches and pay New York prices. When I get you a watch I want to get you one which you select and there were none in white gold except a few which were more than I had along in money orders and travelers checks. I decided to save the money so we can take the trip together sometime.

   We left about 3:30 pm and took the train for Basle and got a second class hotel. After eating a very good meal however we took off to see the town which is a combination of Swiss, German and French being right on the borders of the latter two and on the Rhine. It is the second largest Swiss city and seemed filled with refugees. We made a few of the cafes which featured very good swing bands. We all had about 20 francs left – I had bought you a lighter in Zurich, cute as the devil – and we were unable to spend all of our money on drinks – the Swiss insist on buying the drinks.

Mulhouse   9/13/45
Dearest,

   We got up about 7:30 AM ate breakfast and I spent the last few francs on another lighter like the one I got in Zurich for you and some more postcards. We passed thru customs and landed here about noon. We're about ready to shove off now. Give our little boys hugs and kisses for me and all my love to you, sweetheart – forever and ever.

   Coonie

Mulhouse   9/14/45 # 232
Dearest,

   Well were still at Mulhouse. We were scheduled to leave for Lyons and Marseille yesterday at 5 PM. The RTO (rail transportation office) had 250 seats reserved on this train to Lyons and when it pulled in our car was full of French soldiers, officers and civilians who refused to get off. Finally a French captain and a French policeman started pulling them off but here was room only for about 20 and 11 of us spent the night here and are to leave at 5 pm today unless the same thing happens again…

   Last night went into town and drank a few glasses of beer while we listened to a string orchestra play some classical music – very good. After we got back I took a shower and slept on an army cot again. One week of clean sheets and fine mattresses has spoiled me.

This morning the PWs shined my shoes and gave me a haircut so I'm now ready for the dirty disagreeable trip back to Marseilles.

Yesterday's Stars and Stripes had an item in it that Arles Staging Area was closed and that nothing had been decided about what the 66th Div. would do so we don't know what we'll run into when we get back. The first thing I'll do is build a wooden box to send these things as I'm afraid to use a cardboard box for fear they might be damaged.

I think I sent the letter from Switzerland to you at Columbus and yesterday's to Crawfordsville. I hardly know where to send you mail but I expect I'd better start sending it to Columbus now until I hear what your Florida address will be.

I haven't written mother since I left on the furlough but I'll try and send her a letter today and as I don't want to write about the whole trip again I suppose you can send her those two letters describing it.

Give our two little boys hugs and kisses for me. And to you just all a very special kind of love, sweetheart. I've missed you so much on this trip because it would have been perfect with you. All my love forever and ever.

Coonie.

Back in Arles

Arles, France   9/15/45 #233
Dearest,

Well I'm back in the dust bowl - pulled into Arles about 8 am - what a trip. We got on at 5 pm in Mulhouse and though crowded were fairly comfortable for a French train. We changed trains in Lyons about 4 am and the rest of the trip was a bit more comfortable and uneventful. I went to Hqs Btry with the rest and then got over to the outfit about noon...

...Now here is the latest official news. The 66th has been alerted for shipment to the states - but as usual with the army there is a catch. It takes 60 points or more for a ticket and I have 57 - I figure 58 but one point doesn't make any difference. Those with 54 and under are headed for Germany and that is more than half the outfit. From 55 and to including 59 - we will be transferred to Delta Base Section and work here until the port is closed. It probably won't last much longer since the Army is returning all dock space except three births at Marseille to the French so it would appear that the port won't be used much longer - and then perhaps I'll be on my way home. There is a slight chance that I might be able to tag along but it is so slight I can do nothing but hope and pray. The division will be allowed to go back 10% over strength and they will carry certain essential administrative personnel of which I am not a part. Well we'll know in two or three weeks most likely.

We will be moving back to camp this next week and I must build a box or boxes tomorrow and get the gifts off before we move.

Just loads of love and lots of hugs and kisses for our two sweet boys. And a lot of very special kind of love for you, sweetheart - all my love always.

Coonie

Arles, France, Sept. 21, 1945 #239
Dearest,

Well here I sit in the supply tent in the middle of the Dust Bowl. Pete went into the orderly room tent adjoining and apparently became exhausted reading while lying on the cot and now seems to be asleep. What a life, these tents are as hot as hell in the afternoon. I decided to keep busy and try to make the time pass more quickly. I just finished writing Mother a letter....

This morning we had our last parade. The General of the 66th said that it was for us since we were breaking up however I'm quite certain if the decision had been made by the democratic process there would have been none. Instead of walking around the troops when inspecting them as is customary, he rode in a jeep while we all hoped he would fall out on his face.

The news today is good. In the winter the point system will be thrown out and married men with two years service will be eligible for discharge. So January or February should see me out of this here army. Then we'll spend a month or so in Florida and get back to Indianapolis in our little home in the spring. I surely wish I could make it by Xmas but I miss the boat by 3 little points. There still is some doubt about those between 60 and 70 points going home with the 66th but they'll probably make it.

I miss you so much, honey, and wish that I could be on that boat. We're over the hump though on the down hill grade so it won't be too long now. Give Stevie and Philip hugs and kisses for me. All my love, sweetheart, forever and ever, to the sweetest. girl in the world.

Coonie

Arles, France, 9/22/45 #240
Dearest,

Last night #218 arrived. I suppose that now you are planning your Florida trip. I hope and pray you have a safe and pleasant flight. I catch myself dreading now and then about what all we'll do when I get to Florida with you all. We'll play on the beach, swim, go deep sea fishing, get darkly tanned, walk barefooted in the surf, hunt sea shells, take pictures and just play like happy-go-lucky children.

This morning I went over to Div. HQs. to inquire concerning my request for transfer. It together with my personnel card and the cards of others in my situation due to be transferred to DBS are up in the AG section. It seems likely that I'll be transferred to DBS and that my request will go along. Perhaps it will serve to call attention to my qualifications so that I'll draw a good assignment. I am not dejected by the vicissitudes of army ignorance, stupidity and red tape.

After two years I have come to accept them with passive fatality. It is futile to argue. You never know, maybe I'll get home sooner. I wish I had learned of it sooner as I could have applied for a two months school session at Cambridge. It wasn't down my alley though as it was a science course. I do not intend that they will get much work out of me and I will confuse them by applying for every school and furlough and pass that comes up that they will be glad to get rid of a nuisance.

Today's news, the discharge of those not useful in the states regardless of points, certainly has created a furor around here. The army's infantile actions in demobilization has certainly made a mess of things. The idea of discharging men with 15 or 20 points while men sweat it out over here with two and three and four or more times as many points. Some of the boys are so mad I think they'll blow their top. The profanity is a bit scorching and it is hot enough as it is.

Pete took off this morning early with Pierce and Lt. Ralen for Nice or somewhere in that direction. They may be back tonight or tomorrow. Meanwhile I'm in charge of the supply tent, not much to do but sit on my fanny and write letters. I owe Phil and several others, however much as I like to receive letters I find it almost impossible to write more than one or two a day. It's a good thing I unloaded my pistols when I did because a soldier is only allowed to take one to the states as a souvenir and I had three and would not have realized as good prices now. There is, of course, one slight hitch as I have a few more thousand francs than I can presently secure money orders for however I will manage to solve that difficulty soon.

Give our sweet little boys hugs and kisses for me and tell them how much their Daddy loves them. All my love to you sweetheart, forever and ever, honey. I love and miss you so much.

Coonie

Arles, France, 25 September 1945 #242

Dearest,

This mistral wind almost drives a person crazy especially when you are out in it like we are here in this damn Dust Bowl. It has blown now for the last two days and our clothes and bodies are saturated with dust. My mouth feels like I had been eating the stuff and I have as our food gets a liberal covering of dirt. It's almost impossible to do any work, papers blow away and dust covers everything.

Yesterday I went with Pierce to Nimes for a short while in the afternoon. I traded a pair of dark glasses and some other things I would have thrown away when moving for a dozen old U.S. stamps. I'm getting to be quite a trader with the French though not as good as the transactions Pete and I engaged in before going to Switzerland.

Tomorrow we'll be fairly busy. Carbines and pistols are some other equipment is to be turned in while winter clothing will be issued to almost everyone and their records will have to be brought up to date. This poor typewriter is getting full of dust I wonder how it can operate. There is a fine layer of grit covering everything.

The surroundings and the wind are not conducive to writing. The only pleasant place is the sleeping bag and though it's only 6 pm I almost feel like crawling in and covering up my head and going to sleep. This afternoon I placed my blankets inside the sleeping bag with the aid of the blanket pins and should be considerable warmer tonight than I have been the last two nights. I was getting a little ripe not having been able to take a shower since leaving our chateau and since we still have no shower facilities here in the Dust Bowl I took what is known in army parlance as a "whore's bath" using my helmet. What a wonderful invention is the steel helmet. It's used to wash your face, wash clothes, shave in, wash feet in, take a bath, a necessity for sea sickness, sometimes ate out of and now and then it is even worn on the head strange as it may seem. Well anyway I don't smell as much like a goat as I did...

...All my love for ever and ever.

Coonie

Arles, France, 9/28/45 #244

Dearest,

Last night your letter #222 arrived together with one from Phil. From what he said I suspect you got to see him before you left Columbus. Maybe he has been separated from the Air Force by now and is a civilian. He seems to be interested in practicing law. Guess I'll be going back with the Aetna for a while until I see how the wind blows. However I'm not so much interested in what I'll do as when I'll be getting home. My stock went up a bit today, not as regards coming home however. I'm pretty much convinced now that my boat won't leave until after the first of the year.

Lt. Swanson, the I&E (intelligence and education) officer, came around today and asked me if I'd be interested in taking a law course in Scotland. He didn't know what the law course was nor the school except that it is in Edinburgh. It begins Oct. 18th and ends Dec. 21st. The only other one in the 66th eligible is someone in the MPs and he thought that I would probably be selected if I wanted it. So I have completed my application and will now sit back I and wait for development. I'll really be surprised if I am selected but I'm hopeful. Matter of fact I think I would like it better than going to Paris and I'd very likely have more time to my self to look around. You know I said I'd like to go to Scotland and pick up some woolens to send home. Of course it will be the cold part of the year I expect but it'll be cold here and in Paris too.

Honey, I don't know how it will work out- when I do get home but I suspect that I'll get a 45 day leave and then the discharge depending on how fast they are being discharged. They probably won't get down to 58 points until January or February and my main consideration is to find a place with some of the comforts of home until then. I don't want to spend the winter in the Dust Bowl.

Give our two boys hugs and kisses for me and my love to your Mother. I love and miss you so much, honey, all my love forever and ever.

Coonie

Arles, France 9/29/45 #245

Dearest,

The mistral is stronger and gustier today. We aren't crazy yet but this continual wind and dust is getting a bit on our nerves after a solid week of it. Well I'm not going to Scotland, not surprised except that I found out about it quicker than I supposed, even before my application was in. The education program like every thing else in this damned army seems to be run on the basis of whom you know instead of merit. I wouldn't mind so much if my application had been in and given fair consideration but it seems that someone got advance notice of it and was in a position in higher HQs to get it before it got down to the lower levels. Well I'll take any kind of a course to get out of this hell hole.

We sent out twenty-five men yesterday for Austria and I don't envy them their four day trip in box cars crowded in twenty five to the car. We are due to ship out a like number the first of the week. As many new men have come in all with more than 80 points. The shipment yesterday seemed to take the heart out of the outfit. I had some good friends leave.

This old typewriter is so clogged with dust it hardly operates. I spent the morning shaking out the dust from some of the equipment to be issued and getting a little order out of the mess we have in the tent with all the dust and dirt. One tent blew to pieces on us and we had to move a few days ago. Pete and I took a shower yesterday and though cold I managed to get some of the dirt off and was refreshed. I'm just as dirty now though.

We went to our outdoor movie last night although we had seen the show. It was either do that or go to bed at seven as our light plant was on the blink again. It is working now but I thought I'd better write you while it was still light just in case it fails tonight.

Lots and lots of love to you all. Give our two sweet boys hugs and kisses for me and to you, sweetheart, a very special kind of love. I miss you so much and want to get home just as fast as I can. All my love always.

Coonie

The Criminal Investigation Division

The letters that follow describe my father's experience with the Criminal Investigation Division or CID to which he transferred until the end of his time in Europe. He was stationed in Paris. He was discharged in Europe prior to returning home aboard ship as some of the CID men had been thrown overboard by men whom they had arrested previously.

Arles, France, 9/30/45 #246
Dearest,

Well the CID [Criminal Investigation Division] transfer came thru unexpectedly today. The Major told Griffith at HQs that he couldn't understand it because mine was the only one of several request for transfers that the 66th approved. I leave for Paris this Wednesday, the 3rd. The address will be "7th M.P. C.I.D., APO 887, C/O PM New York, NY." I had given up any hope of getting up there and it's quite a pleasant feeling to know that I'll spend the time sweating it out in a hotel instead of The Dust Bowl.

Bad news for most of the other boys in the outfit today. No one with less than 80 points will ship home with the 66th. That means than well less than five per cent of the original men will be on the boat. I swear I don't know why they say the 66th is going home. Over ten thousand will be in the army of occupation in Austria and the rest in DBS. They won't get down to those under 60 points until well after the first of the year.

Now I'll be able to get you that Paris gown if you are still interested and some Chanel No.5 perfume. The time should pass more quickly and pleasantly and I intend to see all that Paris has to offer in the way of the art galleries, museums and libraries. My spare time spent that way should pass rapidly.

I hope I'll get to fly up but I doubt it, probably take the "Express," a reasonable facsimile of the Monon. The day you get to Bradenton I'll be on my way to Paris. I just hope and pray that you have a safe and pleasant flight. You and Stevie are becoming more air travelers than I. Packing will be some problem too. I'll have to sort and throw stuff away because I have to carry everything I take. That includes blankets, bedroll, overcoat, helmet and even the shelter half and tent pegs. I'll really be loaded down.

Give our two boys great big hugs and kisses for me. All my love to you sweetheart, I love and miss you so much. All my love to the sweetest and dearest girl in the world, forever and ever.

Coonie

Paris 10/16/45 #259
Dearest,

The mail began to catch up with me today, five letters from you beginning with #231 written the day you arrived in Tampa to and including #235, also one from Mother, a Time and Newsweek. I'm missing four you sent before you left. What I can't understand is why you haven't received any letters at Bradenton Beach. I began addressing them there one week before you were to leave expecting that you would probably have a letter or two when you got there. It might be that some of our mail is being sent by boat instead of by air. Surely you are getting my mail now. I hate for you to be worried because I know what it is like not to get any mail for about two weeks or so. I was certainly glad to receive all these letters and know that you had arrived safely and had gotten straightened around with the laundry and help situation. Too bad you had trouble getting from the airport to the hotel at Tampa but even so it wasn't likely as difficult and tiring a trip as if you had traveled by train or car. At least it was over sooner.

Well last in, last out, I guess. Phil, Rod and Mac will probably be out a few months before I am. I guess I shouldn't kick though because they were in for a long time before I was drafted though they all had slightly better deals out of this army than I had up to this time. How about Phil, is he out yet! That law school opening sounds interesting -- Prof Phil.

Apparently Stevie is cutting up some. I wouldn't worry, honey, but I wouldn't allow myself to get in a position where it was possible to get locked in. I guess he must be full of vim and vigor though I suspect that it is pretty annoying and trying at times. He'll probably tone down some after he gets to playing with all the other children. I'm so glad the Baby is a good boy. From what you write he must be a darling. Mother commented in her letter how pretty you looked at the airport and how handsome and pretty Stevie and the Baby looked. I'd like to see this lovely family of mine in the worst way. Tell Stevie how fine I think it is that he can use the big Johnny seat now. He must be getting to be a really big boy. Gosh, honey when I think how darned little I've seen of you and him in the last two years it makes me sad and mad at the same time. Well it shouldn't be much longer, one of the boys with 70 points is leaving in a week. Guess there are two or three others going too. My partner, Miller is one.

Glad you like the cottage so well and that it's large enough and comfortable. I want you to have enough help so that you get plenty of rest and have a good time, honey. Then maybe about the middle of the winter I'll be coming down and then we'll just have a wonderful time. When I think about it I get as excited as a little boy. Then come spring and we'll be moving into our home again.

This afternoon I turned our case over to the legal section of the Paris Detention Barracks so I'm without a case right now and am using this spare time in the office to tap out a letter. There isn't much work around here right now, but I guess it runs in spurts. Well it is after 5 pm so I guess I'll head over to the hotel...

...Sweetheart, I love and miss you so much. Always.

Coonie

Paris, 10/18/45 #260

Dearest,

...This morning Miller and I had a messy case handed us. A lieutenant ...committed suicide in his room by slashing his neck in two places, both wrists, and both arms inside the elbow joints with a razor blade. The bed and the floor was a gory mess. He was seated on the floor with his legs crossed and bent over like a yogi. He'd been dead about three days. Hope I don't have bad dreams tonight. He was ...a great big husky fellow a little over thirty with a lovely looking wife and sweet looking boy about two or three. Guess he was worrying about being transferred to Germany but that alone shouldn't have caused a man to blow his top like that. We're checking into other possible motives...how sorry I feel for his wife and boy...

…I love and miss you so very very much, honey. All my love for ever and ever.

Coonie

Paris, 10/19/45 #261

Dearest,

…We continued work on the case today - there seems to be no question but that it was suicide. The motive is the strangest thing though. He seems to have been the victim of his own imagination and shame. A couple of months ago he picked up some French girl and thought he had contracted VD. Tests were negative but he seemed to have no confidence in the tests and thought that every little thing which was wrong was a symptom - a rash which was scabies - an eye irritation, etc. While he apparently worried so much about it, his fear of having gotten something plus his sense of guilt and shame that he just committed suicide. Well I hope I get something besides a death case next time - little tired of stiffs. I've come to the conclusion there is no such thing as a clean murder or suicide - they all stink and I don't like my appetite lessened. I haven't had any nightmares yet so they haven't bothered my sleep.

While such morbid things don't interest you so why do I mention them except that's about all I've done lately. Some of the boys went out to make a raid up in Pigale - some café, for black market activities. They haven't come back yet. Think I'll go to be about 10 pm.

I love you and miss you all, honey, and wish the days would just fly by until I get home. Have a good time, honey, and take good care of yourself for me. Give the boys hugs and kisses from their Daddy. All my love to you, sweetheart - always.

Coonie

Paris, France 10/26/45 # 267

Dearest,

Well I'm on night duty tonight. We came on at 5:30 and it's now 9:30 and this is the first opportunity I've had to even think about writing a letter. There has been a steady stream of MPs and prisoners all evening. I just inspected our store room here in the hopes of finding a pair of civilian shoes, but no luck. Only one pair fit and they weren't in very good condition so I guess I'll buy a pair at the officers PX. Although I don't have my credentials yet Capt. Dermody gave me my officers PX card and I got a trench coat with a wool button in liner today. We have been having brief fall showers now and then and I thought it about time I get something.

So far this evening we sent two gents out with a GI who had just been picked up by the French in civilian clothes with forged French papers. He's a nice appearing Italian boy who married it a French girl and has a baby. He is in a tough spot since he is a deserter by virtue of being in civilian clothes. He is worried and is ready to help us catch some other deserters and AWOLs. Then an Agent from out of town came in with an informer and wanted three or four Agents to help him conduct a raid. And lastly we had to send a couple of agents out to investigate a case of a GI hanging himself. So you see it has already been a busy night, unusual for us to have to send out so many agents. Many nights go by without anyone being called out.

Miller and I spent several hours this afternoon around the Metro entrances at the Place de l'Opéra looking for a GI who sells passes to other GIs who are AWOL and though we have a fairly good description we failed to see him. We can sleep tomorrow since we are of duty but will probably try to pick him up again after lunch at the same place.

This must be the pause or calm before the storm as it has been quiet now for a half hour. Miller and the French girl translator we have on duty until 11 pm just went over to the hotel for a cup of coffee. When he gets back I'll go ever for a sandwich and cup of coffee. About midnight we can expect the MPs to begin bringing in more GIs and this will continue until 2 am or so. I'm getting sleepy right now.

Take good care of yourself, honey, and get plenty of rest.

Coonie

10/27/45

Dearest,

And that's as far as I got on your letter last night. We were busy from about midnight until 4 am. About 1 am a fellow walked in on us. Three of the agents had picked him and while Miller and I were busy with other duties and had a room full of soldiers and MPs he just slipped out the door. The agents who had brought him in had left so he was our responsibility. Now we'll have to help find him. If he's around he should be easy to recognize because of a particular scar on his face.

I slept until about 4 pm and then took a bath shaved and dressed. I'm just a bit hungry since I missed lunch but caught up on my sleep.

There wasn't any mail today unless there is this evening - hope so.

Well I will be glad when they get down to my number. I miss you all so much, honey. It's almost a year now since we were together. You're so sweet and pretty and I want to see you and hold you and love you so badly. And then there's Stevie and the baby. Gee I hope he's cute and sweet and fun to hold. Give our two sweet boys big hugs and kisses for me. And all the love in the world to the sweetest and dearest girl. All my love always.

Coonie

PARIS, FRIDAY, 11/23/45 [#292]
DEAREST,

THIS IS SOME TYPEWRITER, ISN'T IT? ALL THE LETTERS ARE CAPITAL LETTERS. IT'S ONE WHICH WAS RECOVERED IN A RAID ON A FRENCHMAN'S HOME AND I THOUGHT I WOULD USE IT JUST FOR THE HELL OF IT. I EXPECT THAT IT ONCE BELONGED TO A NEWSPAPER CORRESPONDENT. IT'S A BEAUTIFUL MACHINE- A REMINGTON NOISELESS. SO FAR TODAY WE HAVEN'T BEEN VERY BUSY BUT WE USUALLY HAVE THE RUSH HOUR ABOUT 4PM. I HAVE BEEN USING MY SPARE TIME TODAY TO BRUSH UP ON MY FRENCH ASKING THE TRANSLATORS HERE VARIOUS QUESTIONS -- HOW TO SAY THIS OR HOW TO PRONOUNCE THAT. I'M AFRAID I'M NOT THE TYPE THAT PICKS UP LANGUAGE QUICKLY THOUGH. MAYBE IF I LIVED OVER HERE A YEAR OR TWO I COULD GET SO I COULD SPEAK IT.

Well, I have now transferred to the other portable which was picked up. It is a Corona and also a noiseless. I believe that I like it better.

After writing you and Mother and your folks last night I decided to go to a show. It was an American film with subtitles in French. By hearing English spoken and seeing the French flashed on the bottom of the picture it's helpful to both Americans learning French and French learning English. The French translations don't catch all the humor in fast dialogue out its pretty good.

Here it is 4:30 pm and we haven't had our usual rush yet of MPs and prisoners. We get some of the darndest calls. Some officer just called up and wanted us to send an Agent out to investigate a French employee who had been caught stealing two cans of Coca Cola syrup. Bowers told him to discharge him, that we were too busy to handle such petty stuff. Our men have more work than they can do, serious cases such as a stabbing and a shooting last night and then to be bothered by people calling up about petty larcenies.

It has been foggy and cloudy for almost a week now, especially at night when it gets almost too foggy to drive. I suppose that it is sunny and pretty on the beach. When I get there I intend to lie on the beach and just soak up the old sunshine.

A GI we call "Pretty Boy" Mc Clure broke confinement for the fourth time last week. Lingle, one of the Agents, saw him in a café and bought him a drink and talked with him for a half hour but didn't try to arrest him because he was armed and Lingle wasn't. Lingle told him he wasn't working that night when Mc Clure ask him where his gun was. It makes a good story but I take it with a grain of salt. Since Miller left I don't hear as many tall tales.

Give our two boys hugs and kisses for me. Take good care of yourself, honey, and try and get plenty of rest. I miss you and our sons so much. All my love, forever and ever. Always.

Coonie

Le Havre, Wednesday 2/13/46 [#352?]
Dearest,

This is probably the last letter you'll have from me for some time. I go aboard a Belgian ship, *Ville D' Fluvers* (City of Antwerp) tomorrow night and sail Friday morning. We stop at Newport in Wales one day for ballast and then proceed to New York. I expect we'll dock there about the first of March.

Three are about forty of us whom they are shipping back as passengers, four to a cabin on B deck so we'll have much better accommodations than on a Liberty or Victory ship as troops. This seems to be turning out to be a very good deal.

Chapter 4

War Letters to Children

○ ○

"In time of war you know much more what children feel than in time of peace"

Gertrude Stein, *Wars I Have Seen*, 1945

In my opinion, nothing is more precious than a letter written from a parent on the war front to his or her child back home. Chapter Four consists of two sets of letters, those of Thomas Nelson Baker, my great-great-grandfather, and those of my father, Harold Coons.

Thomas Nelson Baker

Thomas Baker wrote a series of five letters to his children[1], Charles Samuel, age eight, and Elma Jane or Ella, age six. Four letters are written to Ella, who was two years younger than Charles. One letter was written to both Ella and Charles. With one exception, these letters are unedited for historical accuracy.

Letter 1 from Thomas Nelson Baker to his daughter, Ella Baker

Camp Clements, June 13th 1863
Ella
My Dear little girl.

I seat myself this evening to write you a short letter

I am not very well but am much better than I have been. Uncle Sammy and Uncle Ira are both well   this is a very pretty morning and the Soldiers are

78

out with their fifes and drums making pretty music. It is now about time for you to start school. Oh! How I would like to see you and Charlie marching out this beautiful morning to the School House with your books and Slates under arms or in your Satchel and hear you talking about your lessons and it would be nice to help you work in the garden and feed your chickens and get nicer by and by to help you eat your peas and your potatoes and fried chickens. You and Charlie must both try very hard to be the very best children at school and to get "head" oftener than any one else. You must mind mother and the teachers - and not be ugly to the little boys and girls. Pa will be home after while and then we will have "lots" of fun. You must learn mother how to spell the word School she uses one S too many. Did you "hug" Uncle Sammy any when he was at home   If Uncle Sammy went to see any of the girls you must write me all about it and I'll plauge him good   You may hug Charlie once right good for me and I will pay you back when I get home   Give my Love to Grand Pa and Aunty and Grand Ma when you see her

Good by Ella. I must go to see the soldiers "march" and you must go to School -

Your affectionate Pa –

Letter 2 from Thomas Nelson Baker to his daughter, Ella Baker

Head Quarters Co F 39th Ind M.I.
Caldwells Farm Tennessee
February 3rd 1864
Ella

My Dear little daughter I have been trying for some time to find leisure to write you a short letter. This evening seems to be a good time to do so. I am pretty well, have plenty to eat good warm clothes to wear a warm Room to live in, and a good bed to sleep on   I have everything so nice I wish you was here to live with me - wouldn't we have funny times way down in Tennessee. How do you and Charlie get along in school? Do you like to go to school? I hope you have learned very fast. I am sure any little girl and boy will try to be very good   I should feel very bad indeed to hear that they were lazy and ugly to their teacher or to mother. Can you spell your name now? Can you read the story books I bought you? When you read them though I must send you some more, or mother must get them for you.

I will be home to see you after while   then we will have a good time. I tell you if mother will let us, may be we will go to see Grand ma...You may just tell Uncle Ira he told a story, and pull his nose in the bargain.

Do you ever go to see India Madison? You must see her and tell her that you got a letter from Pa.

Good bye -

Ella.

From your Pa,

Letter 3 from Thomas Nelson Baker to his children, Charles and Ella Baker

Undated

Charlie and Ella...Pa's little ones   how glad I would be to See your bright little eyes. (The tears blind me so I can't read the lines) and how I would like to See you Strutting in your new copper tipped boots and Shoes

Charlie you must carry Stove wood and help dig the potatoes and pick beans and mind mother and Grand Ma and Grand Pa and get mother to write the next time how many of your A.B.C.s you know

Ella you must help mother cook and wash dishes and be Pa's good little girl.

Good bye my dear ones

Your Pa

Letter 4 from Thomas Nelson Baker to his daughter, Ella Baker

Undated

Well Ella my little white haired Girl pa must write you a letter too. Your pa would like to see your little blue eyes & kiss your sweet lips tonight but I am too far away. I send you a kiss in this letter don't you let mother get it. Pa wants you to be a pretty little girl & not cry or get mad love your little Charlie Brother & kiss him for me. You must help mother wash the dishes and learn to Sew & Knit so you can knit Pa's socks & make my shirts. I am tired and must quit writing. Tell Grand Ma you got a letter from Pa.

let us go to bed

Good bye from your Pa

Letter 5 from Thomas Nelson Baker to his daughter, Ella Baker

S Head Quarters 1ˢᵗ Brig

Durham N.C. April 28ᵗʰ 1865

My Dear little girl how do you do this evening. I hope you are well. I am not very well.   But Preston and jack and the pony are all very well. We have Caught all the Rebels and made them quit fighting and now your papa will soon be at home.   Then we will go to see Grand Ma and may be we will go to Ill. To see aunt Comfort. I think I will be at home in a month. Cant you have some new potatoes and some chickens large enough to eat? I expect you are at school today and I wonder if you a<u>int</u> head this evening. What book do you read in now?   are you going to learn to write? You must be a good girl. When I get home then I tell you we will have fun.   give my love to mother and Charlie

    Good night

    Your papa

    T.N. Baker

Harold Coons

The following four letters were written by my father to my brother Steve while he was stationed in France. The first three letters were written before hostilities in Europe had ceased.[2] These letters are unedited

Letter 1

January 29, 1945, France

Dear Stevie,

    Today I received some letters from Mummie and guess what I found - two colored pictures that I had taken when we first went to Florida. There was one of you in your raincoat the day it was windy and cloudy and the other was on a bright sunny day when you were playing in the sand and Mummie and Kitty were watching you.

    Remember when you slept in a sleeping bag. Your Daddy does now. It has a green covering and two blankets and the sleeping bag inside. I crawl in and then zip up the side so that it covers my head too. Then I sleep just as cozy as a baby in a rug - or maybe it was a bug in a rug. You ask Mummie because Daddy has almost forgotten which it was.

    I hope Santa Claus brought you a lot of nice presents and that you have fun playing with them. I forgot to tell you that Mummie also sent me a picture of you with Meg and Skip and Robert. Do you have fun playing with Johnnie and would you like a baby brother like him or a baby sister. I think you should suggest a name too.

    I miss you a lot and hope it won't be long before we can play on the beach. Give Mummie a hug and a kiss for me.

    All my love,

    Daddy

Letter 2

March 5, 1945, France
Dear Stevie,

Since you liked the other letter Daddy decided to write you another. I would have written before but sometimes Daddy is busy and has a hard time writing Mummie every day. Then of course I have to write to Kitty and Grandpa and Uncle Bruce and Aunt Frances and Uncle Phil and Aunt Teddy sometimes too.

I made a picture frame out of a tin can and put the pictures Mummie has sent in it. There are some pictures that I took of you and Mummie and Kitty on the beach when we first went to Florida and then there are some of you with Meg and Bill and Skippy. They're on the wall where I can look at them and see and know you're safe and having a good time playing in the sand. Right now over here boys and girls find it too cold to play in the sand because it is still winter. The little boys wear jackets and short knee pants which are sometimes patched. You see the Germans were here for about four years and they haven't had new clothes. Some of their Daddies are still prisoners in Germany. They also wear wool knit stockings and wooden shoes. When it's cold their knees are red and I expect they are cold because they stand around and shiver. Because of the war there is no leather to make shoes and therefore they have to wear wooden shoes.

I don't think they have very many toys because when I was in Quimper I failed to find any. If I can find some toys that French children play with perhaps I can send you one but I don't want to if it would mean that some little French boy would have to do without.

Mummie tells me that you have been a very good little boy. I'm glad to hear it. Take good care of Mummie and give her a great big hug and kiss for Daddy every once in a while.

I miss you and Mummie so very very much, son, and I love you with all my heart and soul. Perhaps it won't be too long until we three will be together again and can play on the sand and in the water on the beach. Be a good boy, son.

Love
Daddy

Letter 3

March 29, 1945, France

Dear Stevie,

Day before yesterday I visited a large French town named Quimper. It is an old town of stone buildings and narrow streets. There is a canal which runs through the town and fishing boats are tied up alongside the banks.

The children all wear wooden shoes and they go clacking along the cobblestones of the small narrow streets. They come up and ask the American soldiers for chewing gum and chocolate because the French have neither. I gave chewing gum to three little girls and two small boys who are about your age.

I had some wooden shoes made for you and sent them in a package several days ago. They'll probably be hard to walk in because they don't bend like your leather ones do.

Last Sunday while I was on KP a little girl Meg's age brought her little brother who is five but not as large as you are, over to the kitchen. They lived across the way in a stone cottage with their mother. Their father was in the French army and is a prisoner in Germany. The little girl just barely remembers her daddy because she was three when he was last home and of course the little boy doesn't remember his daddy because he was just a baby then. I showed them pictures of you playing on the beach and they giggled and laughed.

In Quimper I found some toy French soldiers which I got for you. I'm going to send them in a box to Kitty because when the box arrives you'll probably be back in Indiana instead of Florida. It takes almost two months for a package to go from here to Indiana. I also got a pretty and colorful cup with blue ribbons for the baby. I'll bet you think it's the prettiest cup you ever saw and just in case it's a little girl baby I got a couple of little French dolls. I also got a French doll for Judy. When you give it to her you tell her that I sent it to you to give to her.

I hope the war will soon end so that I can come home and rough house with you and play on the beach. We'll certainly have a lot of fun won't we? But until I can come home you'll have to take care of Mummie and help her by being a good boy. Mummie has written me that you have been a very good boy and that's just fine.

Give Mummie a great big hug and kiss for me and tell her how much I live and miss her too. Loads and loads of love to you, son.

Letter 4

May 15, 1945, France

Dear Son,

Happy birthday, son, and may I help you celebrate your next one with many toys. There aren't many toys in France and while I sent you some toy soldiers and wooden shoes, it seems that because of the war the French children have few toys.

I've thought about you lots today because you and Mummie were on your way home and I couldn't be there to greet you. I hope you had lots of fun on the trip.

I know on your birthday you'll have a cake with one candle for each year and I'm so sorry that I missed helping you eat your cake this year as well as the one last year. A little French boy about your size has been playing here while I write. He was singing a song and jumping up and down. Now he's run across the street and gone home. There he is now looking out of an upstairs window with his sister who is a couple of years older. Now he's back with a rubber ball which he's playing with bouncing up and down. I wish that we could be playing ball together - it would be fun wouldn't it?

How long it'll be until we'll be playing together I don't know but I hope it isn't long.

Be a good boy, Stevie, and have a wonderful birthday and lots of fun playing with your presents. I miss you very much, son. Give Mummie and big hug and kiss for me tonight. I'm very proud of you and love you lots.

Daddy

Chapter 5

Letters from the Home Front

○ ○

"We saw the lightning and that was the guns; and then we heard the thunder and that was the big guns; and then we heard the rain falling and that was the blood falling; and when we came to get in the crops, it was dead men that we reaped."

> Harriet Tubman, as quoted by Earl Conrad, *Harriet Tubman: Negro Soldier and Abolitionist,* 1942

The following letters were written from the home front to soldiers in the field. The first letter was written during the early part of the Civil War by Love Aurilla Shumway to her husband Thomas Nelson Baker. The second letter was written by Margaret Baker Seward to her brother Thomas Nelson. My mother wrote the last series of letters to my father in France during World War II.

Love Aurilla Shumway

Love Aurilla Shumway is described in the words of my grandfather, Judge Frank Nelson Richman:

"In a book entitled, 'The Shumways, a Genealogy of the Shumway Family,' compiled by A.A. Shumway of Atlantic City, N.J. and printed in 1909 by Tobias A Wright of New York, an edition limited to 200 copies, on p. 133: 'Grandma Bland's'" name is given as Love Aurilla.[1] On her tombstone in the City Cemetery at Columbus [Indiana] it appears as 'Aurilla L.' She was the only grandparent I ever knew, and her home at 1020 Franklin St.,

Columbus, Ind. was our visiting place many times during the years we lived in Kansas and Chicago. After my marriage we lived next door to her for about a year. While she was helping the young bride stitching curtains she told of her life with Thomas N. Baker and his tragic death in 1865. She was with him when he died, and as she told of it, she cried and said, 'I thought I never would I get over it, and I never have.'

In the meantime, however, she had taken a second husband, Dr. Marion E. Bland, on Sept. 17, 1868. They had a daughter, Bertha A., who afterwards married Will Wetz, and another child who died in infancy, and again she became a widow. She was a lovely little old lady, frequently absent-minded; for instance, looking for her spectacles when they were perched on her head. She was a staunch Methodist and quite disappointed in our choice of the First Presbyterian Church. In her later years when she should have had company or help of some kind she was quite independent and preferred to live alone. She was a victim of the flu, Feb. 13, 1918, at the age of 84."

Love Aurilla Shumway Baker

This single letter from Love Aurilla to her husband Thomas is unedited for historical accuracy.

Letter from Love Aurilla Shumway to her husband, Thomas Nelson Baker

Azalia, Indiana, Sept 3rd 1862
Thomas,

my dear Husband I will write you a letter & start it to you although I have almost no hopes of your getting it the last that I got from you was dated the 18 of last month I hear that the communication has been cut off between Buels army & Nashville. I hear it is so we also heard yesterday that you have been fighting at Chattenoga. this news & the news of the fighting in Ky keeps us as you may know in awful dread I hope and pray that you are safe. we are all well   there is considerable sickness around. none dangerous. Captain Palen is at home on a recruiting furlough he looks well & hearty   he says tell you so & that he wishes you would happen home while he is here Ira has some recruits   Wm Peelle for one   Samuels feet are badly poisoned again   we got a letter from Oscar yesterday   he was at Woodsonsville Ky near Morgan Guerallas   he was well and hearty   there seems to be a calm (by the paper today)   I was in hopes we would hear some good news today there is nothing more said about the fight at Chattenoga   Mary Parker is very bad again   Ellen Thompson has a fine girl   Matt Palen is working there   as I wrote you before Frank Thompson & Jacob Leonard have gone to war & Mary is coming to stay with Mother   RM Patrick was here today   he says I can have his house at two dollars a month   I think I will be a great deal better situated there than here   don't you Annette is going to Jonesville   I would break up keeping house if I could better myself but I don't think I can   all the way I can help make a living here is to save all I can & economize, which I try to do   I have more garden vegetables than I can make use of & expect to sell some at gathering time which will buy my molasses & sugar & e   I have maid three nice flannel Shirts (two grey & one blue) two pair grey drawers & three pairs of socks for you & have not got your jeans pants maid yet. I have you a silk kirshef & linen towel. I paid 60 & 50 cents for the flannel and 85 for the jeans and for the lining   it all came to near 12 dollars. have not got your trunk yet. I wrote the day Ira came home about Charlie getting his arm broke & have not heard yet that you have got the news   it is well now but I still have him carry it in a sling & keep it done up with splints around it for fear of its getting hurt again   Lieut Hays has gone back & Sarah has taken Jimmie over to uncles with her   Mrs Hays is going to Jonesville in Maxwells house   Hannah wants to move over here   Thomas, I am very anxious about you as we do not hear from you & know that you are ___ the ___   if I could get some letters from you tomorrow & hear that you are all safe I would be so glad. & Oscar oh how I fear that he will have to meet with those guerillas before they are drilled   God in mercy protect our friends & save our country I pray   Oh Thomas, God bless God bless you dear one & protect you from harm & oh may we soon meet in peace & safety & how happy I would be. we want to see you so bad but I must not complain if you can only be spared to us.   that you can return when the war is over & our country saved that will do   again I say God bless & protect you my husband   give my love to all of our boys & tell them I wish them well   the children are asleep   do not think they have forgotten you   far from it   they often talk of Pappy as Ella calls you   no more now

your loving wife Aurilla B

Margaret Catherine Baker Seward

Margaret Catherine Baker, sister of Thomas Nelson Baker, was born on December 13, 1834 in Azalia, Bartholomew County, Indiana and died on July 21, 1875 in Lucas County, Iowa. Her parents were Samuel Wilson (1804-1849) and Jincy Ellis (1810-1873). On August 30, 1855 she married Jacob Seward in Bartholomew County, Indiana. They moved to Iowa shortly after they were married. Back in Columbus in 1863, she wrote her brother, Thomas Nelson Baker, about Morgan's raiders being in Indiana.[3]

Much has been written about Confederate Brigadier General John Hunt Morgan and his Morgan's Raiders. Morgan's most famous exploit, Morgan's raid, took place from June 11 to July 22, 1863.[4] This raid covered about one thousand miles from northern Tennessee, through Kentucky and southeastern Indiana, to northeastern Ohio. Nearly 2500 Confederate cavalrymen participated in this forty-day sojourn deep into Northern territory. About 1800 men crossed the Ohio River at Mauckport, Indiana. They participated in the Battle of Corydon in Harrison County, Indiana on July 9, 1863, the only known Civil War battle on Indiana soil, while drinking up local supplies of alcohol and stealing horses to refresh their mounts. Although casualties were light on both sides, Morgan's men prevailed against the town's hopelessly outnumbered defenders. The victors extorted cash and supplies from the town and over the next two days swept through Vernon, Salem, and Versailles. On their way they tapped telegraph lines, sent out false information about their whereabouts, and created panic amongst the residents of south central Indiana. It is clear from Margaret's letter that Morgan's Raider's were successful in their misinformation campaign and ability to spread panic. At the time, Margaret was writing from Columbus, Indiana located in Bartholomew County and only one county removed from the action. Columbus just happened to be a major hub from where defenders assembled and were dispatched into southern Indiana.

This letter is unedited.

Margaret Catherine Baker Seward (sister of Thomas Baker) to her Brothers and Sisters

July the 12 1863 Columbus
at home

Dear Brothers and Sisters I sat down this morning to write you a few lines to let you know that we are all well   As far as I know mother and me are all that are here and we don't know how long we will get to stay here for times are awful here now   The first of last week the news was good   vixburgh was taken and the bell rung all over town and two days after which was Thursday the news came that Morgan was crossing the river between madison and Jeffersonville with 4000 men   then the news was that he had crossed to _____ and then you know it was time for the men to begin to rally   Such times I never saw everything was in excitement and against Friday night they had two companies made up of all armed and ready   Governor Morton sent them arms Friday on the one oclock train and the boys started at five in the morning for madison   The word was that morgan was there and yesterday morning he was at brownstown and Seymour and the men was making companies as fast as they could and going to blockade the roads and then along in the day a dispatch came that he was retreating and that they did not want any more men and then news is that old morgan sent the dispatch himself and then cut the wire So as to confuse our men which it did of course and then there was another dispatch that came that he was at vernon and in a little while news came that old vernon had surrendered and the rebels had the place and that was getting pretty close to home and in the evening there was three trains (these trains were from Indianapolis) loaded and being loaded too with soldiers besides one train of artillery sent to meet him and the news is now that they are fighting at north vernon and the town and bridges here has to be guarded night and day   there was a company of calvary came into town a few minutes ago but I don't know where they are from   it may be they have been out hunting   I can tell you that Such times was never witnsed here before   there was thousands of folks in town yesterday besides the soldiers and I expect there was about three thousand of them for there was three regt of them and they was all made up after they heard that morgan was in the state and I heard them say that there was five Co made here in town and I heard a man say that he was on the car last night that the regt he was in was all made up in brown co after ten oclock Thursday night   The soldiers eat supper here last night   they did not get off the cars   They took them bread and crackers for they stopped here nearly three hours those from Indianapolis I will tell you that james went in the co that went to madison Friday evening and we have had no news from him yet but some of them wrote to their wives yesterday morning and said the rebels was ten miles from there when they got there and we are looking for Morgan here for he was in disguise all the time he has been here twice already. Last week he was in Indianapolis with a load of chickens and let on to be a chicken pedler and then he came here in old Soldier clothes and rode into town on a load of wood and put up at the Jones house all the time he was taking items and after dinner was over he asked his bill they told him that being he was poor old soldier that they would not charge him   So he struck back for the ohio river captured two boats and got his men across the river and then he dispatched to governor Morton what he had been doing and who was at the dinner table and what they had for dinner and all about it and the governor sent a dispatch describing it just as he had the day and everything and they remembered the man and Say things was just as he described them to the governor   A dispatch just arrived a little bit ago that our men had catched up with him and had captured some of his men and horses and was still after him and he was making back for the river as fast as he could but my prayer is that get back for of all the men in the South they say that him and his men are the meanest for he always goes under disguise   he wont come out in uniform like our men do   sometimes he has black whiskers and some times red ones   he never goes twice alike in one place and that is the reason he does so much mischief   we have not heard from the boys very lately but they are in rosacrans Army and he is away in louisana   I Have not heard from Jacob since 26 of June   he was well and he was at vixburgh and since that has taken place I don't know what they are doing   goodson and altha was here Friday   the folks was generally well Now I don't expect this letter for ___ ____ but for all   I want you all to see this letter and then all write whether you have any trouble there or not and give me all the news good or bad

So no more at present
but remain your sister until
____from Margaret Seward
to her friends

Letters from Margaret Coons to Clara Coons

My mother wrote a series of letters, all numbered consecutively, to my father who was stationed in France during World War II. Either she or my father must have destroyed these, because none were present when we cleaned out their house after my mother's death. However, these letters, written during World War II by my mother to my father's mother, Clara Van Cleave Coons, survive.

During the war when my father was overseas, my mother lived on Bradenton Beach, Florida in the winters. My parents had rented out their small home in Indianapolis to make ends meet. During the summer in 1945, when I was born, she lived first with her parents in Columbus, Indiana and then my father's mother in Montgomery County, Indiana.

Margaret Richman Coons at home in Indianapolis

Her letters are gut-wrenching in places. For example, she speaks of the death of her friend Tilla's husband, a Captain with the 99th in Europe. She speaks of a "code" that she and my father devised before he shipped overseas. This code allowed him to secretly tell her where he was stationed during the period of strict war censorship. Mother expresses her displeasure with the

Army's point system, which was established to determine when soldiers were to be shipped home from the front. She dryly jokes that she would need to have quadruplets to give him enough points. There are humorous anecdotes, including one of my family's favorites where my brother hopped out of his bath and ran stark naked through the Bradenton Beach neighborhood to announce the cessation of hostilities in Europe.

Sharp readers will wonder what a hurricane had to do with my conception. It has always been a family joke that I was "conceived in a tempest." Actually what happened was that I was conceived in a Bradenton hotel during Hurricane 11, which hit Bradenton in southeastern Florida on the night of 10/18/44. This occurred on my father's last leave before he shipped overseas.

These letters have been edited to include only material about World War II.

December 25, 1944
Dear Clara,

The best present of all came this afternoon - 5 V-mails from Harold! That was the first news. They are numbers 1, 2, 6, 8, & 10, all written at sea. I can't understand why the other numbers are missing but am only too grateful to have these. I was feeling a little desperate when I wired you but after this I expect we'd better keep our own letters so we can show them at the post office for requests he makes for packages...He really must have been at sea for a long time - to have written at least 10 letters there. In the 10th one he hinted at being close to England.

...So far, I think it has been an interesting experience but I certainly hate to think of him being on the front now with things so bad there. Tilla's husband is in the 99th Div and was in England two months but now is with the first Army...

Jan. 2. 1945
Dear Clara,

Coonie sent me a code letter yesterday so I know what town in England he's in now. Be sure you don't tell a soul...It's Blandford. But I can't find it on any map I have & I tried to buy a big map of England today but I couldn't even do that. It must not be far from London as he got there in a half a day. But I guess it's a pretty small place...

Monday night   (undated)
Dear Clara,

Since I wrote you before I found a big map of England to locate Blandford so if you haven't here's the dope. It's about 10 mi south of 51 ⁰ Lat. & 7 mi west of 2⁰ Long. It's in Dorset County about 15 mi from the English Channel & about 100 mi from London as the crow flies. Pop is 3371...

Thursday night
Jan. 18, 1945
Dear Clara,

A little jackpot today - got 3 V-mails written Dec 28, 30, & 31st. I suppose you got some too...Each of their letters had a code message in it. The first one spelled out Cherbourg - so I know that's where he landed in France & then the next one was Lorient and the last one was "send dollars" so I'm sending him a postal money order for $50 tomorrow.

I decided to confide in Col. Bowen who is retired & very discrete as he fought in France in the last war. He told me that Lorient was one of the places on the coasts still in German hands, though they were surrounded. It is a former submarine base too. He says there wouldn't be any fighting there now - they just have to keep troops there. So I was relieved to find that out. I had feared he'd have gone directly to the fighting front- of course, he probably will later, but I imagine they get some more training at Lorient...

...He couldn't tell what happened on Christmas except that it was a tale he hoped to tell Stevie next year & his grandchildren for years to come...

Monday night
Jan. 22, 1945
Dear Clara,

...A tragic thing happened on Saturday & something I was afraid of with so many Army wives here. Tillas's husband was reported as missing in action as of Dec. 17th the day after the big German push. He is an infantry Capt. In the 99th Div. She's due to have her 2nd baby in 3 weeks has one about 2 ½ - Skip. Fortunately she's being with her brother. She certainly is taking it bravely & firmly believes he's either wounded & hasn't been found yet or a prisoner. We were all terribly shocked & couldn't get over it. If I hadn't heard from Harold on Thursday I'd have really been in a sweat as Tilla & I had our last letters about the same time...

Well, I don't know when you're reading this, but hold on and prepare for a shock! Yes, I'm gaining weight - four pounds already, but I'm also bulging at the seams of my clothes for I'm 3 ½ mos. Pregnant!.. Harold knew, too, before he went overseas, in fact at Tallahassee that weekend he knew I was a week late. It's a good thing he did know as one of the girls tells me they are soldiers going across if their wives are pregnant before they go & if they say no & later have a baby they receive no government aid. You know we didn't plan to have one till after the war, so it must have been the hurricane that did it. The date is July 14ᵗʰ. Steve is thrilled to death at the prospect, so some one in the family is tickled any way. He's planning to take complete charge of it, it sounds like - change diapers, feed it, bathe it etc. The only thing is when we go for a walk with it in the baby carriage he's going to ride his tricycle & have a "parade"...

Saturday night
Feb. 3, 1945
Dear Clara,

   No, I couldn't find any code I the V-Mail you got from Harold. The code he used on mine was the first letter of the second word in each sentence in the first paragraph, I tried several other systems in that letter, too, but no results. I wrote him tonight & mentioned that you thought there was hidden meaning in #8 and I couldn't find it either - so we'll see...

   Stevie pulled a fast one this evening - he wanted to know how the baby got out of my tummy & I told him the doctor got him out and he said but how, "does the baby have a key?" You can tell he's really putting some thought to this business...

Monday night
Feb. 12, 1945
Dear Clara,

   Your letter enclosing the clipping about the 66ᵗʰ Div. came today. I was glad to get it & I sent it on to Coonie. I've never seen any mention of it in the papers & I can never buy Time or Life on the news stands. So since I've been without the radio or the local paper is about the only way I have of keeping up...

Monday night
Feb. 19, 1945
Dear Clara,

   ...I got a letter from mother today saying that Pete Burns who is in the Inf. of the 66th was wounded on Jan. 29ᵗʰ. That was pretty fast notification & just bears out what Harold said in a recent letter that the Germans shelled them occasionally. He said he was far enough back to be out of danger, thank goodness.

One of the boys from Columbus brother's called mother & told her that her son (in the 66th) had written that they were in a serious accident X-mas Eve in which some of the boys didn't come out of it. Mother said it sounded like a ship-wreck as she knew they must have been moving them. It just conformed what I already suspected as I thought Coonie made a lot more to do than normal over Christmas Eve & saying that if he had been able to write his letters would have been? Etc. I had seen about Jan. 25 an article in the paper telling about a troop ship being sunk in "European waters" by submarine the latter part of Dec. & thought that might have been when he crossed, so on Jan. 28th I sent him that clipping & told him I thought that applied to him & wanted him to refer back to it.[6] I haven't gotten a letter in answer yet but since brother wrote about this other I know he was in it. And, oh my, I certainly did have cold chills when I knew for sure to think he was safe & what a close call we had that time. The article in the paper said that there were 2200 men on the ship & that 1400 were saved & the others dead or missing! Harold has hinted other things recently. I'm sure about that - he asked if I'd heard from our neighbors in Alabama. I hope nothing happened to them...You should have heard little old Stevie saying, Oh, I'm so glad my daddy was saved." Its funny but I have worried about his being lost that way - it was always if he got to the front. I certainly hope we don't have to wait till he gets home to hear all the details...

Tuesday night
March 27, 1945
Dear Clara,
    ...Yesterday I got 5 letters from Harold & one envelope contained 3 letters - one was for Stevie. This was his second letter from his Daddy & he was thrilled to death - I've already read it to him a half dozen times...

Friday night - April 13th, [1945]
Dear Clara,
    Your letter of the 10th came yesterday but with all the excitement of Roosevelt's death last night I didn't write any letters except to Coonie.
    I was the "Paul Revere" of the neighborhood in conveying the news. June said when I came over to tell them she thought I was coming to say the war was over. I only wish I had. I'll bet Stevie will remember this occasion... Stevie was so excited when he went to bed that he didn't go to sleep till 9:30

& woke up twice & then bright & early he rushed and was telling the other kids "President Roosevelt died yesterday"...

Saturday night - Apr. 28, [1945]

...We got the premature news of Germany's surrender just as Stevie was getting out of the bath tub. Both Mrs. Jackson and Mrs. McKnight came to tell us. Stevie came in and ran around yelling "The war's over. Germany has surrendered unconditionally." Then he ran out the door over to June's stark naked! I went along after him but stopped and talked etc. so he ran around that way for 15 minutes before I got him back home! Then after I put him in bed I found out it wasn't time! What a let down. I hope the real surrender news comes through soon...

Friday (undated) [1945]
Dear Clara,

...I was certainly disappointed when I heard how the "point system" would operate. I figured up Coonie's points including this baby & he only has 52 - needs 85 - so unless I could produce quadruplets it looks like it'll be a year from next fall before he gets 85 points. I think children should count more than 12 pt. apiece, don't you. He gets 5 for that bronze service star he recently got...

Thursday night (undated) [1945]
Dear Clara,

I've had two letters from Harold this week from Germany dated the 28th & 29th of May. I can tell by the numbers that there are two missing between the 18th & 28th which will surely show up soon. He's in a village called Baumholder, which we haven't been able to locate on the map... Sounds like it's in Bavaria as he talks about the foothills of the mts. He said they had a pretty nice set-up there. He goes on guard for 6 hours and is off 18. - and that's the regular routine. They're guarding a Russian camp and have to check the passes of the Russians going in and out. He said these Russians were formerly slave laborers of the Germans. I suppose eventually they'll be sent home...

Chapter 6

Travel by Train

"... more and more I like to take a train I understand why the French prefer it to automobiling, it is so much more sociable and of course these days so much more of an adventure, and the irregularity of its regularity is fascinating."

Gertrude Stein, *Wars I Have Seen*, 1945

Elizabeth Lapp

Elizabeth Lapp Bowman was born on March 23, 1879 in Story County, Iowa and died on May 7, 1965 in Paradise, Butte County, California. She married Alva Edward Bowman on July 19, 1908 in Los Angeles, California. She moved with her parents Jacob Lapp (1844-1912) and Amy Alward (1847-1929) from Iowa to Oregon in the early 1890s and then on to Orange County, California in 1898. "Lizzie," as she was called wrote about her family's move from Oregon to California when she was in her late teens. Elizabeth's husband was born in 1876 in North Manchester, Wabash County, Indiana. The boy Arthur who is mentioned is Elizabeth Lapp's brother.

Elizabeth's account is unedited.

Our Trip from Oregon to California - 1898[1]

Sunday Morning,

We are still in Ore. We will cross the line about 12 or 1 o'clock. Ma didn't sleep much last night but I slept fine. We have eaten our breakfast and everything taste fine, the Porter made us some coffee he is a colored man but he is just as accommodating as can be, the country around here look a great deal the same as around Salem. Ma is in her glory, she run across a baby. There is a little girl in the car six years old she is going to Sacramento all alone. Her name is Reta, she is sitting on Arthur's lap playing. We have just passed a rock a great deal like table rock where the Indian and white men had a fight, the Indians were on the rock and the whites in the valley. We didn't stop to see which licked. Ha.

We have just eaten our dinner, we are up in the mountains and have a big long train with three engines on and when we go around a curve we can see all three of them. We have crossed a tressel 76 ft. high and have gone through a tunnel it took eight minutes to go through.

1 o'clock P.M.

We have just crossed the line and are now in Cal. There are three soldier boys and one sailor boy on the train the soldiers are going to Manila.

It is a lovely day the sun shines so pretty and bright but it dos'nt seem a bit like Sunday some of the passengers are playing cards.

5:45 P.M.

We have passed Mt Shasta, we came in sight of it this forenoon and it has been following us up ever since, part of the time it would look like it was way ahead of us than after while we would get ahead, and that is the way we chased each other all afternoon. It is a beautiful sight and right near it is a rather high peak called Black Beaut. We have passed the springs they are just on this side of the mountain the cars stopped there ten min and we all got off and drank soda water. I didn't like it very well but drank some. For all of you and when I got around to myself it taste pretty good but didn't "taste for more." I filled my little bottle with it, the springs are beautiful, at three different places the water spouts up 50 or 60 ft. and we could look up the mountain 7 or 8 hundred feet and see the water running down over the rocks and through the timber. The springs are on the side of the mountain and the water that comes down from them form a creek, at one place in the mountains there is a small dwelling house built on a high peak and it is about 8 or 9 hundred feet high the mt. Is so steep and we could see no road or possible way for them to reach it, I guess they had an elivator.

Monday noon

We have crossed the river on one of the largest ferry boats in the world, they run the whole train on. I got out of the car and down on the boat so I could get some fresh air and see a little, there are two high mountains on the other side of them it is a pretty place.

10:30 A.M.

We have just eaten our breakfast we hadn't time before we changed cars. We crossed the bay on the fary to Okland and got our tickets to Los Angeles. Er [Earl] took the car to the ticket office and got back across the bay just in time for the train. When we were going back across we saw the battle ship Iowa anchored in the bay. Today is the first time we have seen so many flowers, the orchards are in bloom and everything looks nice. We are now at a little station called "Byron." I guess people die down here once in a while for we have just passed a funeral procession it must be something unusual though because there is such a long string of teams there must be forty or fiefty.

7:30 P.M.

There are five salvation army girls just got on the train. They are all young girls and are all dressed alike in red dresses with a white cross worked on the front. They seem to be enjoying themselves the best kind. Our sall. Girls didn't stay with us long but before leaving, they sang us a song and played on the violeen. The band was playing at the place they got off so we raised the window they played some lovely pieces. It was so dark we couldn't see but I think they were holding a concert.

We reached Los Angeles Tuesday about 8:30 A.M. Pa met us at the depot and after getting us some breakfast and "rubbering" around a while we took the car and went out to the Thomases where we spent the rest of the week and had a very pleasant visit. They took us to the ocean one day but it was so stormy and the sand blew so bad we didn't enjoy it very much. It is a grand sight though.

Sunday morning

Mary took us to Campton where we took the train for Long Beach, on the road there we saw the residence of Gen Rosecrans he died there about a year ago.

Pa met us at Long Beach with the wagon. It is a very pretty little station. They have kind of a side walk built so one can walk out about a quarter of a mile in the ocean. We ate our lunch on the beach, that Aunt Becca sent with us and then we started for Gearharts. We had a ride of about eighteen miles in the big wagon.

We stayed two days with Gearharts. We are now comfortably settled down in our little home by the sea side, and the gulls play around the house.

the end.

Harold Coons

Forty-five years after Elizabeth Lapp Bowman traveled from Oregon to California by train and ferry, train travel was faster and more comfortable, even for troops about to go overseas. My father wrote my mother about two troop train trips in 1944.[2] The first letter from my father describes his trip by train from Fort Harrison in Indianapolis to Fort Bragg, North Carolina. The second letter describes his train trip from Fort Rucker, Alabama to New York City just before he embarked on the *HMV Britannic* on his way to England. These two letters are unedited.

Troop Trains

Leaving Indiana

Wed - 2/9/44

We lined up ready to ship at 2:45 pm and left Fort Harrison at 4 pm. We waited on a siding at Union Station until 6:45 when the train finally pulled out on the N.Y.C. for Cincinnati. Although we changed over there to the C. & O. it didn't take long. There was a 100 in our outfit in 3 pullmans. Though … I shared a lower bunk I slept well and was getting up when we stopped at White Sulfur Springs. I recognized Charlottesville from the university buildings. About 2 pm we got into Richmond and upon a siding until 6:30 or so when we transferred to the Atlantic Coastline and finally got into Fort Bragg at 3 am in the rain. There were no more sheets on the pullmans so they were made up with blankets and I slept with my pants and shoes off - slept like a log again.

A troop train is an experience, the place most free of smoke was the smoking room. The pullman was frequently like a poolroom. There were a number of Kentuckians in the outfit and their speech was picturesque and profane.

It was raining and cold when we arrived at 3 am. Some of the boys were lucky and had a covered truck. I caught an open job and it wasn't over a half mile with raincoats and helmets we kept dry. We slept until 6 am and then spent a couple hours waiting in a rec hall in raincoats and our luggage. We never found why we were waiting but finally about 1:00 am we marched back to one of the barracks in the rain - went to chow and then we split up and assigned to barracks.

The basic is 17 weeks but doesn't have much walking since we usually ride. Speed marches of 5 miles is the rule. The battery trains with 105 mm howitzers. The last two weeks we go on a problem and are out in the open - late spring so it should be good - better than the boys who just finished.

If it wasn't for the rain and mud I think I would like it - rather think it won't be so bad.

We are quarantined for 2 weeks and I won't be able to telephone you until then most likely confined to our barracks except when on duty or training.

All my love to you and Stevie. Write more later.

Coonie

Train to New York

Wednesday, November 22, 1944
Dearest,

This letter may be hard to read due to the train's jolting. Like all troop trains there are assigned to the Pullman section - one above and two below - and drawer lower - not the best manner of sleeping but I slept pretty well. We've been traveling through Georgia all day - mostly hilly and wooded though I see off in the distance what are apparently foothills. The hillsides are very colorful in their autumn foliage - not so heave pine trees. Passed some pecan groves, however for the most part it appears to be a rather poor section reminding me some of Brown County.

It's been fine weather for traveling - bright and sunny all day, like Indiana in October.

Unlike the other troop train trip I went to Fort Bragg, this time we don't eat in diners but have our own kitchen car. We file through having our food served on paper plates and then back to our seats where we eat with wooden forks. Breakfast and lunch were both good and of course the coffee hit the spot.

What to do is a problem. Some read, some talk, some play cards and others just sleep. I finished Time this morning and have spent the afternoon watching the scenery.

I can't help but think that each minute takes me further and further away from you and Stevie and I hope it is a journey that will soon be over. I guess it is a trip I have to take before we'll be together again. It'll be a great day when I have that return trip ticket in my hand.

We may spend Thanksgiving Day on the train. Maybe we'll have turkey.

Friday, November 24, 1944

Thanksgiving day was spent on the train and for a while it looked like no turkey however when we arrived in camp we had the traditional turkey with all the fixings - dressing, mashed potatoes, sweet potatoes, cranberry sauce, celery, peas, ice cream, pumpkin pie, peaches, and coffee. In addition we were given a package of Camels and a sack of nuts, oranges, apples and candy. It was the best meal the Army has furnished - but of course it lacked the family touch.

When we got in we walked quite a distance to our barracks carrying our field bags and blanket rolls. By the time we reached the barracks my back was numb and the load weighed a ton.

Everyone is looking forward to receiving passes and seeing some new scenery after the hills and small towns of Alabama. It seems colder than it really is because we aren't used to it. Fellows who never wore long underwear put them on last night and are still wearing them today.

As I don't know our APO I can't send this out yet.

I love you so much, sweetheart, and I miss you and Stevie like the dickens. Give him a big hug and kiss for me, honey. Love you. All my love always.

Coonie

P.S. Our APO continues to be 454 but it is care of Postmaster, New York, N.Y.

Chapter 7

Love Letters

○ ○

"The frankest and freest product of the human mind and heart is a love letter; the writer gets his limitless freedom of statement and expression from his sense that no stranger is going to see what he is writing."

Mark Twain, *Mark Twain's Autobiography*, 1924

Love Letters from Thomas Nelson Baker to Love Aurilla Shumway

Thomas Nelson Baker, whom we have met before, attended school in Azalia, Bartholomew County, Indiana. From September 1853 until April 1854 he taught school in Alexandria, Madison County, Indiana. These are his love letters to Love Aurilla Shumway whom he had met in Sandcreek Township back in Bartholomew County.[1]

One of Thomas' first cousins on his mother's side was Margaret Ellis who had moved from Rowan County, North Carolina with her parents, Ira and Frances Starr Ellis, when she was but an infant. It is this first cousin's wedding to Thomas Norris that delays the return of Thomas to his home in Azalia, Indiana at the end of his school term.

I am continually amazed at the wonderful prose evident in love letters written in the nineteenth century. One of my distant Baker cousins was so enamored with the poetic nature of these letters that he lifted some lines for use in the courtship of his prospective bride.

These letters are unedited to preserve historical accuracy.

Love Letter #1

Azalia Ind- July 17th 1852
Miss AL Shumway

May Virtue modestly & of every other femaleness grace that makes a female worthy & useful afound not only with your intercourse with others but also with your private walks of life & may you preserve unsullied & unsustained a character free from repraach & that knows no influence

May God keep and Bless you
Th.NB

Love Letter #2

Alexandria September 2nd 1853
Miss A.L. Shumway,

D.r. girl for the first time in my life do I attempt to hold this species of converse with you. & permit me to say that it affords boundless pleasure to be thus highly honored: But it would be a source of infinitely more pleasure to converse with you face to face.

Ri1. separation cannot sever the chord of affection; next to my Creator you are the object of my adoration, & I fear that too often you Reign supreme in my affections. yes Ri1, this evening, though miles intervene between us my love is as ardent & devoted as on that night I pledged eternal love. I have lightly loved before, But never until I thought my affection toward you was fully reciprocated could I experimentally define the passions

This subject is pleasant, & one I like to dwell on, But with the hope that our affection may be undying & that we may live to enjoy all the blessedness it imparts I leave it with you.

We all arrived safely at our destination, & since our arrival I have enjoyed one of the Best Camp meetings that ever was enjoyed. God poured out his spirit on the people and scores were made shouting happy in the love of God.

I am now unwell, insomuch that I can hardly set up & write. I think my indisposition has arose altogether from exposure on the camp Ground & is only cold.

I do not know positive yet that I shall get a school But I think I shall. So you must not look for me until you know I have come.

Answer quickly.

You shall hear from me often. Remember to pray for me Ril. Send me a kiss.

Yours in love forever.
T.N. Baker

Love Letter #3

Alexandria Oct 1st 1853
Miss A.L. Shumway

Dear girl I again resume my station to write you a few lines   I received your very kind letter which relieved my mind of not a little anxiety for, like you, I labored under suspense for one week longer than I expected   But it came at last & with it came joy & those modest simple declarations of constancy and eternal love lit up my anxious and desponding heart with hope of future bliss and abiding happiness.

Ril I would like to see you   I would like to tell you again how deeply and devotedly I love you but I will see you again. Separation will not last forever & then our happiness will just have a beginning. …that kiss Ril   I unconsciously looked for it before I thought & I should have felt myself disappointed and not your disavowal of disinterested love more than overbalanced the momentary pleasure of a kiss   I shall desist writing at present.

Write soon and give me a history of the procedure since I left   I forgot to tell you I had got well   Miss Margaret Ellis is also well

Send another kiss   that was so sweet

No more now

Yours forever

TN Baker

Love Letter #4

9 o'clock
Alexandria Nov 23rd 1853. Saturday night
Aurilla

Dear girl I at this late hour of the night Resume my station in order to give you additional evidence of the affection I bear for you   Your last letter gave me more than ordinary pleasure on account of its unaffected simplicity & its positive declarations of an abiding love

Like you I once thought you would never make such admissions as you or to say the least of it I feared you would not. But the surprise has been the most agreeable of any I ever met with

Ril I do not know how to write in any stronger terms than I have written heretofore or in other words I do not know how more plainly to manifest my love in a letter than I have done   if I could master a more implicit style I would adopt it. However permit me to make another protestation of changeless love for I do emphatically declare that no time place or circumstance (without your desire) can lessen my affection for you. Forgive me all the anxiety I have ever caused Rill & believe me it was not willful   Still be plain in your letters Rill & reveal the sentiments on every subject for you can not conceive the infinite joy the faithful declarations of your heart imparts

Remember that I love you tenderly ardently passionately   Remember that I pray for you daily earnestly

Be faithful to all the obligations you have taken upon yourself

Give Ada my respect and kiss her for me

I forgot to tell you I was well in fact I can say that I enjoy more than ordinary at this time. My school only lacks two weeks of being out   I do not expect to continue idle many days   I shall teach another school   no more now

yours in love forever
T.N. Baker
can't you send another kiss

Love Letter #5

Alexandria 21st 1854
Aurilla

Dear girl I seat myself this morning to pen another testimonial of my Regard and affection for you   your last letter Ril gave me more than ordinary delight   It made me so glad to hear that you were happy & that you placed implicit confidence in me. May my Right arm be Palsied when I willingly forget you   you Reverted Ril to your feelings one year ago   I almost knew you loved me & I have been sorry many times that I treated you so & I hope that in a life times devotion I shall be able to prove the sincerity of my declarations

Live in hope Ril for I love you still with the same ardor and devotedness that I have hitherto declared.

You spoke Ril of my Short letters   you must Remember that I have not so good a chance to write long letters as you have because I have not things to write about unless I about something that would be of no interest to you take good care of your self   Encourage Ada all you can. Give my respects to all you wish   I will be home as soon as I can now

I am so cold I can not write any longer   Excuse the manner in which this is wrote for I have a bad chance.

Yours truly
T.N. Baker

I wrote to Jonesville the day before I got your last letter.

Love Letter #6

Alexandria January 12ᵗʰ 1854
Miss A.L. Shumway,

Dear girl though I have received no letter since I wrote to you yet I feel in duty bound to write again   Supposing that my last letter has been detained in the office at Jonesville owing to the absence of Silas or to some other unavoidable cause for Ril I never can attribute such disappointments to any negligence of yours for when I can consistently woe is me.

Ril the same passion still burns in my bosom that I disclosed for you & I look forward with pleasure to a happy realization of my most ardent anticipations to a life of bliss I trust Spent in the light your Soul irradiates.

Ril I want you to tell me in your next letter whether you think your parents would be willing to our union   you need not ask them yet but you can tell what you think   I am getting almost homesick Ril   home seems to have a double meaning   I want you to prepare to set one night & watch the stars about the middle of March   write as much as you can Ril   tell me all the news   oh Ril you must plauge Em. I seen a letter directed to Miss Emely Polen the Last Saturday. Give my Respects to Ada again   be a good girl Ril

yours forever
T.N. Baker

Love Letter #7

Alexandria February 5ᵗʰ 1854
Miss A.L. Shumway

Dear Girl I only seat myself to write a few lines merely to inform you that I am still alive. I am just getting so I can set up after having the measles   they made me pretty sick   But I have got through tolerably well   but let me tell you Ril it is a right severe way of punishing Sinners.

my School has been detained two weeks   consequently I shall Be here some longer   we have the Small Pox in our county seat   but they are taking great pains to prevent its spread Excuse me Ril for my Brevity for I can not write   next week I will write a long letter

yours forever
T.N. Baker

Love Letter #8

Alexandria Feb 27ᵗʰ 1854
Ril

Dear girl I am glad that I once more have the privilege of addressing you even in this way But I much prefer addressing you face to face   I addressed you Ril at the time I promised So that the fault of you not hearing from me was not mine   I have not been permitted to answer your last as Soon as I desired on account of having the Rheumatics in my arms   But I hope that when you do hear from me it will do you the more good   I got over the measles in good order leaving my general health I believe better than it was before. Do not believe Ril that I could wilfully break my pledge   nothing but the common leveler of our Race nothing But the cold and palsifying hand of death can ever intervene to prevent the performance of all my vows   all I ask of you Ril is to be a good girl and be faithful

I have been immediately under the influence of Revival power for two or three weeks & you may guess that I have felt a little of it   we are in the midst of a fine Revival in town now & my soul is happy while I write   I wish you could enjoy as good times as I have the last two days I was glad to hear that there would probably be no objections in your family   I used to think in my boyish days that I would like to Steal my wife   But I have got Bravely over it.

There is many things I would like to write   But I shall desist as I want to write my mother Before meeting time and it is now four o'clock   goodbye the Lord be with you my dear girl

T.N. Baker

Love Letter #9

Alexandria April 14ᵗʰ 1854
Miss A.L.S.

Dr. girl it is with no small degree of pleasure that I announce that my school is ended that my stay in this place is concluded for I have become weary of so long an absence from you

My school closed this evening   But I do not expect that I can possibly Be at home before ten days as I have to close my account of Both Schools yet   if I was Ready to start home now I do not know whether I could get off or not for cousin Margaret will not consent for me to leave until I See her married which will be in about eight or ten days   The name of her intended is Thomas Norris a merchant of this place a widower by the Bye   Ril my visit home done me no good in extinguishing my desire to see you for I believe

I want to see you worse than I did before I went   Ril I look forward to the time with delight when we shall be as one when our Interests Shall be united never to be Separated until death Shall Sunder our embrace.

April 15th

I feel tolerably well this morning. I forgot to offer an apology for not writing Sooner   the reason was that I found that I would be detained longer than I expected and I thought I would wait until about half of the time had expired before I wrote

I assure you. Ril it was from no disrespect, on the contrary I love you Better than I have ever told you. I will see you as Soon as I can. This is probably the last time that I Shall ever write that I love you no more.

Yours

Tom

Chapter 8

Work

"Travel is fatal to prejudice, bigotry and narrow-mindedness."

Mark Twain, Innocents Abroad, 1869

William Edgar Van Cleave

William Edgar Van Cleave was my great uncle. He was born on November 3, 1877 in Montgomery County, Indiana and died on October 26, 1946 in McAlester, Oklahoma. He was the son of Daniel Brewer Van Cleave (1852-1928) and Anna Elizabeth Reynolds (1855-1940). On April 4, 1906 he was married to Catherine Gunkle (1884-1972) in Crawfordsville, Indiana. He graduated from the Kentucky University Medical Department in Louisville, Kentucky in 1905. For most of his career he served in the Indian Health Service. From 1916 to 1943 he was and Medical Director and then Superintendent of the Talahina Indian Hospital in Talahina, Oklahoma. He wrote an article about his experiences in the Indian Health Service.

William Edgar Van Cleave as a new graduate of
Kentucky School of Medicine, 1905

Here is how he describes himself in a letter to another Van Cleave
genealogy researcher:

"I was born and raised near Crawfordsville, Ind., and while
waiting to make up my mind as to what trade or profession I would
follow through life, taught school for seven years in Montgomery
County. After deciding on medicine, I spent four years in the Medical
Department of Kentucky University, at Louisville, Ky., graduating
in 1905. Practiced general medicine at New Market for a couple of
years, then accepted a position as "Physician" in the Indian Service,
from the Government, through Civil Service. This was in November
1907. I became 65 years of age about the time I completed 35 years
of service, which gave me full retirement privilege, which I accepted,
since I had a heart attack (coronary thrombi) in June 1940, and during my last two years of service with the Government had to slow
down. I was given retirement November 30, 1942.

I had always planned to go back to Indiana after retirement, but my heart condition, made it more advisable to stay out of long cold winters, so I decided to stay with the "Okies," and am here in McAlester, Okla., where I have lately opened up an office, and doing special eye work and refraction, only."[1]

Dr. Van Cleave practiced medicine with the Indian Health Service; most of his time was spent as physician and then Superintendent and Medical Director of the Talahina Indian Hospital in Talahina, Oklahoma. Prior to going to Talahina he was Indian Health Service physician at Tohatchi, New Mexico from 1907-1910, Indian Health Service physician at the Sioux Indian Reservation in South Dakota from 1910-1912, and then medical supervisor of Indian schools in Oklahoma and Kansas from 1912-1916.

Here is how he describes his experience in Talahina:

"My introduction to the Choc-Chick Sanatorium came in February 1916, while I was Medical Supervisor of Indian Schools in Oklahoma and Kansas, I was ordered by the Government to proceed to Talahina, where a Govt San. for Indians was under construction, and to make a list of all items of furniture, instruments and other equipment necessary for furnishing and equipping the institution, ready for operation. I was also directed to give the office a. list of subsistence and other expendable supplies sufficient for one years operation.

As there was no road out to the San. I hired a liveryman to drive me out through the woods to the foot of Buffalo Mountain, where I found the hospital building, and the power plant in a clump of tall pines.

Five months later I was ordered back to Talahina with the explanation that as the supplies and equipment were being shipped, I should take charge of the same as it arrived, and make the hospital ready for operation at the earliest possible date.

By November first, we were ready to receive patients but the incoming was very slow, as hospitalization of Indians, was a new thing for them, most of them preferred to let the other fellow try it out first.

To go back a little, the Choctaws and Chickasaws had talked for some time about a hospital or home for old Indians, and it was largely with this idea in mind that they voted to give $50,000 of their tribal money with which to start the institution, $35,000 corning from the Choctaws and $15,000 from the Chickasaws. This amount was just sufficient for the construction of the main building and the power plant. No tribal moneys have since been used in the operation of the hospital, nor in any of the additional construction. The present support is entirely from annual gratuitous Congressional appropriation, known as "Relief of Distress and Prevention of Disease among Indians"

Patients came in very slowly and skeptically, and changes were frequent. The old people did not take kindly to hospitalization, for the reason they had always been free agents, lived an irregular and indifferent life, and disliked the ordinary routine and rule which is necessary in any hospital. The women fell into line with less objection."[2]

Further description of the physical grounds is provided in this document containing no source or date:

"The next few years might be called a pioneering period. Here was a new hospital set out in a small cleared space among tall pines, at the base of Buffalo Mountain, three miles from Talahina, post office and railroad point. Timber had to be cut and the dense woods about the hospital thinned to let in the sunshine. Much grading, drainage, and landscaping had to be done, and this gradually followed up with grasses, flowers, and shrubbery. Doctor Van Cleave induced his mother to send him two barrels of flowering bulbs, roots, roses and shrubbery from his home in Indiana. Another free shipment was obtained from the U. S. Botanical gardens at Washington. The three mile trail to Talahina wound around here and there through the woods and across three creeks which always became unfordable for a few days following each heavy rain. This meant grading, drainage, and general improvement, and gradual hewing out of a survey line."[3]

Dr. Van Cleave wrote an article on his experiences in the Indian Health Service, which was published posthumously in the Tobucky News.[3] This article is largely a description of the practices of the old Indian medicine men and the use of herbals and other native medicines. The practices of the medicine men included the use of singing and chanting, magic, prayer, exhortation, fetishes, suggestion, massage, bloodletting, scarification, sweat baths. Herbal remedies included the use of twigs, bark, leaves, seed, or flowers, which were usually mixed in a tea-like brew and were administered in the morning. Snakes, crickets, spider's eggs, and lizards were also used in healing practices.

I will quote a few passages from his paper to illustrate Dr. Van Cleave's first-hand accounts of his experiences.

Dr. Van Cleave was an Indian Health Service physician among the Navajo at Tohatchi, New Mexico from 1907-1910. He says of the Navajo superstitions:

> "When an Indian died in his tepee or hogan, they believed that the evil spirit which caused the death, still hovered about the home, so for that reason the home was immediately destroyed or torn down, and no one would live in or near that place again."

He then described a case of paralysis in a Navajo policeman whose face was paralyzed when he awoke after lying out in a chilly plain overnight:

> "A medicine man was sent for. He ordered a "sing" to be held for three nights to drive away and destroy the influence of the moon and the ghost who had, while the man slept with his face uncovered, blown his breath over, this part of his face, causing this spell. They called this the moon disease."

Dr. Van Cleave was an Indian Health Service physician at the Sioux Indian Reservation in South Dakota from 1910-1912. He says of the Sioux:

> "...there were fewer medicine men, for they depended more upon white man's medicine. During epidemics, such as smallpox, Indians were rounded up like cattle, and compelled to undergo vaccination. Those having smallpox were under police quarantine."

From 1916 on Dr. Van Cleave was an Indian Health Service physician and then Superintendent and Medical Director of the Talahina Indian Hospital in Talahina, Oklahoma. He says of a couple of Choctaws that he treated:

> "One old Indian likened life in a hospital to, 'Living just like a machine.' Another old Indian who did not understand hypodermic medication reported me to Washington for sticking a needle in a very old sick Injun two or three times a day, just to see if he was dead yet."

Edith Rogers Richman

My grandmother, Edith Elizabeth Rogers Richman was born on February 24, 1885 in Ottumwa, Iowa and died on August 20, 1968 in New Albany,

Floyd County, Indiana. She was the daughter of Lannes Edgar Rogers (1851-1914) and Nancy Alice Wilson (1849–1936). On December 24, 1908 she married Frank Nelson Richman in Studley, Kansas. She accompanied my grandfather when he went to Germany in 1947 to be a judge at the Nuremberg Trials. Her diary written that year describes her experiences.

Edith Rogers Richman

The Nuremberg Trials consisted of a series of post-WWII trials of prominent members of the German military, political, and economic leadership during World War II. The most notable trial was that of the International Military Tribunal which tried 22 of the most prominent military leaders. This trial was conducted from November 1945 through October 1946. A series of 12 trials of lesser political, military, and economic leaders was then held from December 1946 through April 1949. All trials were held in the Palace of Justice in Nuremberg, Germany. Judge Richman was one of the presiding judges at the Flick Trial, which lasted from April 19, 1947 until December 22, 1947.

At the time he was appointed to the Nuremberg Court, Judge Richman was teaching law at Indiana University School of Law in Indianapolis, Indiana.

Edith Richman's diary is heavily edited. It is quite lengthy and contains much material describing various side trips from Germany, dinners and luncheons, purchases while abroad, and various illnesses. These excerpts contain only what pertains to the Nuremberg Trials and two side trips to Hitler's Eagles Nest redoubt and his bunker in Berlin.

The Richmans stayed in a hotel for a couple of weeks before they found suitable housing in Nuremberg at 17 Novalia Strasse.

Due to a serious automobile accident, which left Mrs. Richman totally incapacitated for two weeks, Judge Richman took over the diary writing from September 24 through October 10, 1947.

Nurnberg Diary[6]

January 8, 1947

Frank was called by Judge Battzel about 10 a.m. who told him Col. Gunn of Washington wanted to see him about a matter of interest to him, Frank went to see Col. Gunn at Judge Battzel's office, heard his proposal, invited him to have lunch with him at the Columbia Club [in Indianapolis, Indiana] where they talked over the proposition until 2:30.

The proposition was that Frank become a member of the court to try German industrialists accused of mass murder & enslavery of displaced persons etc in Nuremberg. Time, a minimum of 6 months, maximum of 18 months. Privilege of a general officer. Family to be transported overseas. House & couple of servants and a car to be furnished. Salary ten thousand a year.

Sounds very exciting and Frank agreed to go if university could give him a 6 months leave of absence.

Deans Witham and Gavit agreed that he could not refuse such an offer: that it would reflect credit upon the university so the final decision was passed back to us.

We weighed the advantages and disadvantages and were both in favor of accepting the challenges of the big adventure.

Col. Gunn had spoken of the chance to travel to other European countries at small expense which made the offer even more tempting.

January 21

Announcement of Frank's appointment carried by papers[8] and heard over the radio…

February 11

…Ate lunch at 11, back at quarters awaiting pick up by the bus at 12:15 - 6 bus loads drove to the Staten Island Ferry; then over to the island and on to Pier 12 where we ascended the gang plank, received our pass port, table sitting and APO numbers. Cabin 202…it was roomy but short of hooks for hanging clothes…Spent the time looking over the ship…had to take table next to the galley…Sat on lounge in the evening…must be on deck when ship sails at 10.

February 12

Slept well and awoke enjoying the ship's roll. A fine sunny day. Yesterday we were told we had to take the same table sittings we had before, so we seem stuck with the table next to the galley. Meet on deck for a good walk right after breakfast - Air cold but pleasant. Attended orientation talk later had a boat drill, lunch, took a short nap & reported for volunteer service. Got stuck with German teaching…A good many are sick.

Stayed on deck quite a while out of the wind and in the sun. It was remarkably pleasant…Time changes at midnight.

February 13

During the night we were conscious of a more decided roll… Have a slightly better table in the room for meals. Was quite worried about the German class but it wasn't too bad. On A deck this morning. It was cloudy with long waves & the ship was rolling more. Still feel OK.

The meals are pretty good and we have learned to ask the waiter for only as much as we want so we don't have to look at a full plate…First edition of "Barry News" [ship's newspaper] is out this evening.

February 14

Valentine's Day. I suppose the children at home eagerly watched for the postman today…This has been a most wonderful day. I tried to study a little for the German class in the lounge but too many people would drop down to visit for me to get much planned. There weren't so many people there today and there were some new ones…I went to the orientation meeting but didn't learn a lot in which I had much faith. A Red Cross Center is in each location

& we are invited to its parties. Not so cold today & about as it has been. We are all traveling comfortably. A community sing is scheduled for 5 p.m.

Saturday, February 15
A very fine day indeed with the sun shining more than it did yesterday. Out of the wind and in the sun, it is pleasantly warm, delightful for walking on deck or sitting if one is wrapped in a blanket. I only had six or eight in my German class but it was easier to teach on that account. We tried some sentences in conversation. Had my last typhoid shot this afternoon.

Have a cold, which is a follow up on the sore throat I have been having ever since last Monday at Fort Hamilton.

...Set clocks ahead.

Sunday, February 16
...Felt alright this a.m. except for some cold & sore throat. Mild on deck, but rain, drove us down. Saw a rainbow.

At 8:00 quite a show was given in the lounge by the passengers...A lot of horseplay put all the passengers into a good humor. Church services at 3 conducted by a Catholic chaplain. Only thought he gave was our responsibility to live so that people would respect the American way of life.

Monday, February 17
Another fine day. My cold has almost disappeared. Took a brisk walk on deck shortly after breakfast. German class was interrupted at 10:30 for fire drill.

Played bridge for over 3 hours...Took a turn on deck before dinner. An especially good dinner of soup, lamb chops, roast potatoes, salad & Boston cream pie.

Went to a show which was terrible...I didn't sleep very well and was conscious in the middle of the night that the ship was now rolling up and down instead of side to side.

We made good time today and are now going north...

Tuesday, February 18
I awoke to find myself ailing...Went to breakfast & up on deck but it began to wring. It is quite cold and blustery as we approach England. They saw this weather will be normal from now on. Spent the rest of the morning on my bunk. No German today.

Felt bad all day...I did go down for meals but ate nothing much except for supper...

Wednesday, February 19

Felt better this morning...Reported for German class but it was so cold and so few came we gave it up...

Went for a brisk walk on deck - very cold wind. Should have seen Land's End this afternoon but it is too cloudy. Saw a ship off stern. Listened to the chaplain at orientation...Another 4 times around deck...Feeling much better.

Went to a church service. Saw lighthouses.

Thursday, February 20

At 9 A.M. we reached the breakwater, the Castle, the White Cliffs of Dover and took the pilot aboard to take us through the mine filled channel. Everybody on deck. Raw and cold. Sat in the lounge writing until I was warm...Packed...Attended orientation...Passed a cursory medical inspection.

...Next to a horrible murder show and then went up on deck...Clock advanced an hour.

Friday, February 21

...Took pilot aboard about 5:30 to take us down the river. Great cakes of ice with water flowing between slowed the ship to a very slow movement. We docked at 10:30 at Bremerhaven. It was bitterly cold on deck so that we could not stay out for long at a time. We had seen the submarine base of Withelmshaven on starboard side.

Lighthouses, buildings and houses had a distinctly foreign look but church spires here and there looked like home. We were boarded by navy and army personnel around noon & many girls were met by their husbands. Were processed about 2 P.M. receiving railroad tickets, berths an scrip...

Monday, February 24

...All German's in the military zone look well fed and warmly clothed altho' their garments are of old unattractive style...

Tuesday, February 25

Went to the Palace of Justice this morning to obtain permanent pass. Saw Frank's temporary office, which he shares with Judge C. [Judge Curtis Shake?] Obtained PX card and a day's pass to the trial being conducted in Court 2. A doctor who was second in command in the LuftWaffe and who was indicted for complicity in the horrors of Dachau testified that he was never a member of any political party & took no interest therein, that his life was so filled with important matters as supervision of all hospitals in which all people were welcomed for care & treatment with participation in all sorts of cultural, intellectual and scientific interests, with handling of great masses of details that he had no time to know anything about anything except such exemplary activities as the above, so that he was completely innocent of all wrong doing. He disavowed any connection with Hitler, Goebbels, Goering, and Himmler. He was asked directly what connection he had with Dachau and at that interesting moment the court recessed.

March 3

Went to the Palace of Justice and spent the morning listening to the trial of Dr. Gaugodin, who was accused of responsibility for the use of inmates at Buchenwald for experiments. Many were inoculated with typhus virus. He claims that his entire responsibility was with the production of vaccine and he knew nothing of such inhumanity. He described his visits to the concentration camps which, according to him, were models of comfort & sanitation. Mr. Hardy, the prosecutor, conducted a very poor cross examination of the witness. He told us that he had been on a "party" the night before and had a blinding headache. Someone ought to tell him why he is over here.

Last night we went to hear Dr. Kempner tell about the reaction of the U.S. to the Nuremberg trials. He was a former prosecutor for Goring in 1933. Was fired for lack of sympathy for Nazism and later conducted the prosecution of Goring. He called these trial an experiment in education both for Germany & for the world...

Wednesday, March 5

Went to Court III for its opening today. 15 justices are being tried. Judge Marshall provided Oehers, Blair, Braud, and Harding. General Taylor opened the prosecution with a very able address. He is a Harvard man and speaks excellent English meaning his choice of words. His youth surprised me for he must be in his late thirties. Mr. LaFollette spoke only for a few minutes before noon recess...

Thursday, March 6

At 10 Capt. Marshbanks and her German driver, Hudson Halgan, arrived to take us to see the Hilton house. It is small, compact, cheerful and warm. Maids seem friendly. Pauline is the owner: Frau Pfeffer is a maid. We decided to take the house. - 17 Novalia Strasse...

Richman home while in Nuremberg, 17 Novalia Strasse

Monday, March 17

...Frank reported that an additional criminal industrialist had been apprehended and would be arraigned soon thereby delaying the opening of their trial by at least two weeks...

Wednesday, March 19

At 9 this morning we were taken by the Christiansons (because our car was out of commission) to the opera house at Furth where we heard two people talk for two hours on the military occupation - its objectives, methods, and the history of the German people, especially with reference to their manner of thinking - their ideology as a result of the history of the last 300 years. We had been told by the first speaker that a responsibility rested upon us to "sell democracy" to the women of this country. The second speaker suggested the possibility that Germans might indoctrinate Americans with their ideas since they were in the habit of excusing themselves from responsibility for the war and its secrets...

Thursday, March 22

Went to the second period of orientation - discussion of what U.S. has accomplished in Germany since the war, the education of youth with an appeal to the women for aid to the girls. The third speaker began by insulting the dependents "luxurious living" and bad behavior but he gave some suggestions by which we might profit...

Palm Sunday, March 30

...In the p.m. we went up to see the ruins of Hitler's house, the V.I.P. guest house - the less important one, Goering's house, Bormann and above the road to the Eagle's Nest, Hitler's Tea House which Bormann built at a cost of 12,000 & gave to him. Inaccessible until the middle of May, two days before the end of the war. R.A.F. bombed Hitler's house at 1:30. At 3:30 the S.S. troops burned it and at 5:30 the French arrived, magnificent view of Saltzburg, Austria thru window of council room.

Bombing damage to buildings in Nuremberg

Friday, April 11

...We reached Berlin about 10 a.m. Were met by Capt. Rugola in whose care we had been placed during our stay as well as by a general and several important members of the legal division...

Sunday, April 13

...We went sightseeing in the heart of Berlin with Dr. Diekman as our guide. He had fled Berlin in 1938, warned 6 hours before the Gestapo appeared to get him. He came to the U.S., studied law at U. of Penn, taught at Princeton & is back there with the legal division. He wants to return to teach in the U.S. in the fall. His wife is a Czechoslovakian doctor.

We went...and saw the flooded bunker where Hitler and Eva Braun's bodies as well as Goebbels were supposed to be found...

April 15

Monday morning. Left the house at 8:40 for the airport where we boarded a C47, Gen'l Clay's private plane. 15 passenger size - a perfect day. Major Concannon was the pilot. Smooth taking off - circled Berlin for 10 min. then took an hour and a half to fly to Furth airport. Flew at 6000 feet at 170 miles per hour - not a bump & very smooth landing...

Monday, May 5

...Went to hear a Czechoslovakian laborer give evidence about his treatment in a labor camp. On cross examination he contradicted himself so he wasn't too strong...

Monday, May 12

Went to listen to the doctors' trial for the first time in several weeks. Heard a cross examination and re-direct examination of a doctor who was supposed to have had much to do with "mercy killings." He had admitted a knowledge of the killing of some hundred children, but on this day nothing of particular interest developed.

Monday, May 19

...Went with Mays to a lecture on the psychology of the German woman under the Nazi domination given by a woman who read a chapter from her book in broken English as we could not understand it. Questions followed which showed the German thinking to be to abstract for our American minds to grasp. Heard that Judge Shake is coming to be a member of Tribunal V.

Wednesday, June 4

I went to court this morning but it was very boring.

Tuesday, June 10

I went to court this morning. The defense asked for a six week interval in which to prepare their case. The court took it under advisement & will determine the length of the recess. The Belgian witness who was on the stand could not be shaken on cross examination. He was clever as well as staunch and did the defense no good.

July 31

Went to court this morning. Steinbrindt was on the stand but his testimony was not very interesting...

Tuesday, August 19

...Hurried on to trial going in at 2:45. Heard closing judgment on Brandt.

Friday, August 22

...Heard...that Flick trial is deferred to Sept. 8th or 9th. Also that Flick trial is not expected to end before December.

Wednesday, August 27

Went to the opening of the Farben trial.

September 24 [Entry by Frank Richman]

Edith & Irene Merrill left 8 AM for Munich and Augsburg. At 1700 got message that both seriously injured in auto wreck near Augsburg, being taken to 98th General Hospital Munich. She was in Ward B2 shock room. Skull, pelvis, ribs fractured. Auto skidded off temporary bridge, flipped in air and landed 25 feet below on hard ground. Given blood plasma. Went downstairs October 19. Sat outside October 21. Went to hospital October 25 for exam.

Friday, October 31 [Mrs. Richman's entries resume here]

...Went at 4 o'clock for a drive and picked up Frank at a little after 5. Court held until then to complete testimony on Berger. Gen. council were told any time spent on documenting now would be taken from the 2 weeks recess when they prepare their arguments. Result documents are not so important.

Monday, November 3

...Went with Bud to get Frank. Court held until 7. Prosecution promises to finish this week. Frank wrote all evening.

Tuesday, November 3

...No court tomorrow because of a hitch in prosecution's plans but Frank will work as usual.

Friday, November 7

...Frank came home quite depressed because the prosecution had introduced 20 books into rebuttal which he felt was part of the main case in fairness to the defense they should be allowed to answer and that will drag out the case at least a week. In spite of holding court until 5 each day and all day Saturday, the prosecution will not finish this week as agreed...

Saturday, November 8

...Frank came in happy because the prosecution had finished their case by the time court closed at 5. Only two questions asked by defendants. Two weeks of recess.

Saturday, November 29

...have tickets for Bud and me to go to court for what we hope is the final session.

Sunday, November 30

Frank got home at 6:45 last night from his long session in court...

Saturday, December 6

...Frank went to work at the usual time...Frank came home for a one o'clock lunch but worked most of the afternoon. He is working on the opinion on all counts but one which Christianson wrote and had accepted.

Sunday, December 7

...Frank has been working on his opinion all day. Seems to have doubts and difficulties...

Wednesday, December 10

...Frank came home with the word that we are due to sail Dec. 26th so they are not planning to give the judgment until the 20th...

Friday, December 12

...Frank called up to report that the ship which should have left the 23rd had been advanced 2 days and we would be unable to catch it - that the next one was a slow one, sailing the 29th and the one after that was the Barry, sailing the 3rd...

Judge Frank Nelson Richman
Nuremberg Trials – The Flick Trial

My grandfather, Frank Nelson Richman, was born on July 1, 1881 in Columbus, Indiana and died on April 28, 1956 in Indianapolis, Indiana. He was the son of Silas Tevis Richman (1852-1938) and Elma Jane Baker (1857-1953). On December 24, 1908 he married Edith Elizabeth Rogers in Studley, Kansas. He obtained his JD degree from the University of Chicago Law School in 1909. He began the practice of law with his uncle Charles Baker in 1908 in Columbus, Indiana. He was a judge on the Indiana Supreme Court between 1941 and 1946 and a judge on the Nuremberg Trials American Tribunal IV in Nuremberg, Germany in 1947.

Frank Nelson Richman

Judge Richman wrote *Log of the Big Dipper*, an account of his trip from Madison, Indiana to New Orleans with Clessie Cummins. He also wrote about his experiences as a Nuremberg Trial judge, as follows below:

Summary of the Flick Trial[8, 9]

The court on which I served at Nuremberg dealt only with war crimes. I shall have something more to say about that. Like most laymen, lawyers have difficulty in defining a war crime. Most of us think of war itself as a crime. And certainly the planning and waging of an aggressive war is a crime by any standard. The Kaiser, Hitler, Mussolini, the Japanese at and before Pearl Harbor, the leaders of the North Korean and Chinese invading armies, all were guilty of this crime. So also many others, whose wars of conquest blacken the pages of history. Few of them, however, were ever brought to trial.

War breeds criminality and when a war is being waged, as a matter of course other war crimes follow. Some of them are well known, for instance, the massacre of the inhabitants of the town of Lidice, the deportation and slaughter of the Jews of Poland, Germany and other European countries. These are some of the grosser crimes. But of course there are individual crimes and criminals. Rape, torture, wanton killings of defenseless civilians by members of the armed forces or by bandits in the train of the army, fall into this class. With these the Nurnberg courts had little or nothing to do. They did bring to trial top men in the Nazi criminal conspiracy.

Most of you remember something of the first trial, widely publicized. The court was called the International Military Tribunal, commonly shortened to I .M. T. There were over 20 defendants, including Goring, Hess, Ribbentrop, Admiral Raeder, Schacht (the banker) and Von Papen. Four judges sat, each with an alternate, representing France, Russia, the United Kingdom and the United States. The trial, conducted in four languages, began 20 Nov. 1945 and ended 1 Oct. 1946 with the conviction of 19 defendants, 12 sentenced to death, 3 to life imprisonment, 4 to lesser terms and 3 acquitted, including Schacht and Von Papen, with the Russian Judge dissenting. He wanted them executed.

Before this trial was begun, Britain, Russia and the United States, in conjunction with Belgium, Czechoslovakia, Greece, Luxemburg, the Netherlands, Norway, Poland and Yugoslavia began plans, later approved, by a number of other nations, including France, to bring other less notorious Nazi leaders to trial. These plans crystallized in December 1945, when the four occupying powers, United Kingdom, Soviet Russia, France and the

United States, acting through the four zone commanders, promulgated Control Council Law No. 10 which authorized each power in its zone to set up courts for the prosecution of war criminals... other than those dealt with by the International Military Tribunal, then in session.

France tried a few defendants, one just recently. The British tried a few more. Russia, so far as we know, tried none or if there was a so-called trial it was merely perfunctory. They used some German leaders in their own war preparations. Those whom they could not use were sent to slave labor camps or liquidated. No one will ever know what happened to many of them.

The United States, living up to its obligations under the Moscow Declaration of 30 Oct. 1943 and the London Agreement of 8 Aug. 1945, set up six courts called American Military Tribunals (but in fact International Courts manned by American civilian judges) each court having three judges and some an alternate judge. These courts tried 185 defendants in 12 cases. Four defendants committed suicide, four more were too ill to stand trial, 35 were acquitted, 98 were given terms for year's, 23 were sentenced to life imprisonment and 24 were ordered executed. The last group included 7 doctors, tried in Case No.1 for inhumane experiments on living occupants of concentration camps, 3 officials of the SS for murders and other crimes against inmates of concentration camps, and 14 defendants in what was designated the Einsatzgruppe Case.

These were officials of various Nazi organizations, branded as criminal by IMT, who had planned and executed the slaughter of all Jews in occupied areas and some other racial groups, including gypsies. Thus far, I have given you essential background information. I come now to the organization and functioning of these six American Military Tribunals. A serious problem was the selection of judges. Discarded was the idea of using federal judges because there had been much criticism of Mr. Justice Jackson's long absence from the Supreme Court. The Army was running the Zone so the Army selected the judges. Col. Gunn was given the job. Where he got his names I do not know except as to the three Indiana judges. Upon their selection they were appointed by the Zone Commander, who in February 1947 was General Lucius Clay.

My selection came like a bombshell. I was sitting in my office at the law school in Indianapolis preparing to teach full time beginning the second semester. The phone rang and Judge Baltzell, of the U.S. District Court told me that Col. Gunn was in his office with respect to a matter in which I would be interested. I had never heard of Col. Gunn. But I went down to see him and was given a few days to accept. In less than two weeks I was on my way. Later I learned that Prof. Fowler Harper, then at Indiana University, now at Yale, had suggested my name. The F.B.I. investigated me. Judge Baltzell added his blessing and thus, without an election, without endorsement of a political committee without senatorial approval and with no designation by the President, I became a judge of an international court, trying a case in two languages in a court room of the Palace of Justice in the famous old town of Nurnberg. General Clay signed my commission. Later the President issued another commission, but, when the matter was tested, it was held that the effective appointment was that of' General Clay acting on behalf of the four occupying Powers. It now seems a long way for an Indiana County seat lawyer to have traveled.

I left Indianapolis 2 Feb. 1947 and got home 8 Jan. 1948. With me were my wife and 18 year old daughter then in her sophomore year at Bloomington. She missed one semester returning in September. On the ship also sailed a New Castle girl who had been my secretary on the Supreme Court and served me in similar capacity in Nurnberg.

After about a week we were assigned a small comfortable house, five miles from the courthouse with two servants and a Chevrolet army painted car and G.I. driver. We lived under the same conditions as a General Army Officer which did not set too well with some of the lesser Brass whom were outranked. So for almost a year I was a V.I.P. But when I got home I was deflated.

There were 32 judges in all, about half being judges or former judges of state courts of last resort, about one third trial judges from state courts and the remainder lawyers and one dean of a law school without previous judicial experience. Indiana had three. The others were Judge Shake of Vincennes, my former associate on the Supreme Court of Indiana, whose name, incidentally, I suggested to Col. Gunn, and Clarence F. Merrill, a leading Indianapolis lawyer who went over at Judge Shake's suggestion as legal adviser to the court but was assigned as alternate judge in the Farben case over which Judge Shake presided. Judge Merrill died recently.

Our court was the American Military Tribunal IV of which the presiding judge was Judge [Charles B.] Sears formerly of the Court of Appeals of New York and the associate judges William H. Christianson, formerly a judge of the Minnesota Supreme Court and myself. For several months Judge Richard Dixon of North Carolina sat with us as an alternate but when they needed him to replace a judge of another court who had gone home, they asked us if we thought we would live through the trial and being assured Dixon left us to sit on the other court. Both Sears and Dixon have since died. Christianson is an elected district judge in Minnesota.

Listening to opening statement of General [Telford] Taylor, Chief of Prosecution in Tribunal IV, United States of America vs. Friedrich Flick, et al., on Saturday April 19, 1947. Top row left to right, Judges Richman, Sears, Christianson, and Dixon; bottom row left to right first two unknown, Secretary General Charles E. Sands, Colonel John E. Ray, and Captain Carl I. Dietz.

We tried the Flick case, the first of the three industrial cases. The others were the Farben and Krupp cases. We had before us only six defendants, the smallest number, except one, of all the twelve cases. In some there were over twenty defendants. Five of the six were employees or former employees of Friedrich Flick who, born on a farm, cultivated a unique genius for corporate organization and became the head of an industrial machine that produced 5% of the coal and 5% of the steel for the German economy, besides a few other allied products all of which mines and factories at their peak employed about 250,000 persons. The names of his companies appear in the last 2 pages of the indictment which I am passing to you for inspection.

The defendants had very able German lawyers of their own choice paid by the United States in the first instance but charged as a part of reparations to the German economy. Four of the lawyers had been counsel for defendants in the IMT case and were thoroughly familiar with the procedure and the character of evidence that was produced in our case. Each lawyer had one or more assistants and adequate stenographic help.

The prosecutors were young American lawyers, some of them not long out of law school, and with little trial experience. That was not too great a handicap since the trial was not under the technical procedural rules common to United States courts. One or two of these young lawyers succumbed to some of the bad habits of the German counsel without adopting their good practices.

Dr. Dix, chief counsel for defendants, was a man of great culture, but much inclined to airing his learning in long dissertations not vary much in point. One of the young Americans was somewhat of a copy cat, but he lacked the learning to make his speeches effective. Over 10000 pages of evidence were introduced, many witnesses examined and cross-examined, some of the defendants themselves testifying for as much as a week at a time. The trial actually began 19 April and ended in the judgment 22 December. This large book contains the indictment, opening statements, part only of the evidence, the closing arguments and judgment. It was edited by a lawyer who was one of the prosecution staff and does not present as fairly as might be the point of view of the defendants.

We sat from 9:30 a.m. until 4:30 p.m. Monday through Friday, with three short intermissions, one larger than the others, for lunch in a restaurant in the Palace of Justice. When Americans were speaking we could lay aside our head phones but for days on end we sat with them pressed against our ears, and by the end of the week were thoroughly tired. For relaxation on week ends we made sightseeing trips in Bavaria, the most beautiful part of Germany.

There were five counts in the indictment - none charging the planning and waging of aggressive war. The first was what we called the slave labor count in which the defendants were charged with procuring and mistreating foreign nationals including prisoners of war. To this charge the defense of necessity was held to apply. Under compulsion of threat and fear of concentration camps or worse, the defendants were compelled to accept the production orders and to take the labor sent by the Nazi Labor Government. There was no substantial evidence of mistreatment. Four of the defendants were found not guilty but Flick and his nephew Weiss, knowing that they would be assigned prisoners of war labor, voluntarily asked the government for additional orders that they might run one of their plants more efficiently. This we held, took away from them the defense of necessity, as to this factory.

The second count charged all the defendants with spoliation, i.e. plunder of occupied territory. The proof was weak. Flick only was found guilty because, as head of his organization acting as trustee for the Reich, he deprived a French owner of the use of his steel plant during the German occupation of Lorraine. The French owner came from England to testify. He said that they had blown up the plant when they fled before the German army and when he returned after the Germans left it was in much better condition than when he left. It was shown that none of the production went to Germany and Flick's group plowed all the profits back into the plant, taking nothing for themselves. He did have a hand, knowingly in depriving the owner of the use of his property which we held was a violation of the Hague Convention and so he was found guilty.

The third count took at least two months to try. Soon after the evidence was begun I tried to convince my associates that our court lacked jurisdiction but they felt, and I acquiesced, that we should get the whole story. It was charged in this count, as a crime against humanity, as well as a war crime, that by the exercise of anti-Semitic influence, exerted directly and through the Reich, Flick and two of his associates had acquired for a very small price the controlling stock of several industrial corporations held by Jews. When the evidence was in it appeared that the Jews had gotten out while the getting was good - before 1939 - and that Flick's deal was with British and American financial interests. It also appeared that the transaction had been completed before the invasion of Poland, a dated fixed by IMT as the beginning of the war. Because it occurred before the war it could not be a war crime, we were not commissioned to try any except war crimes and therefore held that our court was without jurisdiction. But we also said, recognizing that it was mere dictum, that crimes against humanity as theretofore defined covered crimes against the person, not against property. We recognized that the transaction might be set aside, because of duress, by a court of Equity but said it was not a crime against humanity.

In the IMT trial the court held that certain Nazi organizations, including the SS of which Himmler was the head, were criminal and that continuing membership in or support thereof, with knowledge of the organizations' criminal character was also a crime. Flick and Steinbrinck were so charged in the last two counts of the indictment. They denied knowledge or that their money went to the SS contending that it was paid to Himmler for cultural purposes. While the evidence of their guilt was weak we felt that the operations of the SS were so notorious that with their opportunities for knowing they must have known. So we found them guilty. I might add that on very similar evidence one of the other courts found certain defendants not guilty.

I think that you will have concluded from this review that these defendants were not guilty of any heinous offenses. At least that was our conclusion.

The judgment freed three of the defendants, one of them Flick's lawyer, gave Flick 7 years, Steinbrinck 5, and Weiss 2, crediting each with the years spent in jail awaiting trial and judgment. Weiss was out in about a year, Steinbrinck, ill on the date of judgment, died in prison. Flick, after going to three courts, the District Court of the District of Columbia, its Court of Appeals, and U.S. Supreme Court, was unsuccessful in his contention that the judgment of our court was void for lack of jurisdiction. In a general amnesty a year or two ago he was released from prison.

Neither the court nor the parties had any procedural problems. Almost any evidence having probative value including hearsay, was admitted. The only important test was relevancy. Objections on the ground that the offered evidence did not tend to prove or disprove any of the issues, often started a long argument which the court terminated with the statement that the evidence would be admitted but if, upon consideration, we determined that it was irrelevant, it would be disregarded. There was no jury, of course, to be misled, and the judges were accustomed to sifting the wheat from the chaff ignoring the latter.

Many affidavits were admitted. If the affiant was available for cross-examination he was called. If not, and there was objection on that ground, some of the courts excluded the affidavit. We had no problems of this kind.

There were no surprise witnesses. At least 24 hours before a witness was called, the opposing party had his name, address, and the general subject of his testimony. The court liberally permitted recalling of witnesses for further questioning.

After the indictment was read to the defendants and their lawyers had been appointed, they had at least 30 days before the opening statements. Recesses were not infrequent to enable translator to catch up on translating German documents into English. After the prosecution rested, defendants had two weeks recess to get ready to present their evidence. There were two weeks between the close of all the evidence and the closing arguments. All in all the case was leisurely conducted and neither prosecutors nor defendants could complain that they had, not had a fair trial, with adequate opportunity to present to the court any evidence or any argument which they thought material to the issues.

The credit for devising the procedure under which all the courts including IMT operated goes to Mr. Justice Jackson, who collaborating with British, French and Russian lawyers so harmonized the varying procedures to which they and the German lawyers were accustomed as to prescribe a simple form of procedure retaining the fundamental elements of what we lawyers call due process.

The following language, which I wrote into the very beginning of our opinion, has been quoted as fairly representing the principles which guided our Court, and the others at Nurnberg:

"Facing this Tribunal are private citizens of a conquered state being tried for alleged international crimes. Their judges are citizens of one of the victor states selected by its war department. There may well be misgivings as to the fairness of such a trial. These considerations have made the judges of the Tribunal keenly aware of their grave responsibility and of the danger to the cause of justice if the conduct of the trial and the conclusion reached should even seem to justify these misgivings. To err is human, but if error must occur it is right that the error must not be prejudicial to the defendants. That, we think, is the spirit of the law of civilized nations. It finds expression in the following principles well known to students of Anglo-American criminal law.

1. There can be no conviction without proof of personal guilt.
2. Such guilt must be proved beyond a reasonable doubt.
3. The presumption of innocence follows each defendant throughout the trial.
4. The burden of proof is at all times upon the prosecution.
5. If from credible evidence two reasonable inferences may be drawn, one of guilt and the other of innocence, the latter must be taken.

"We cannot imagine that German law contains concepts more favorable to defendants. Any less favorable, we, as American judges trained in Anglo-American criminal jurisprudence, would be reluctant to apply even though this is not an American Court, but a special tribunal constituted pursuant to a four-power agreement administering public international law."

I also quote, to cover up a common misconception, one paragraph written by Judge Sears:

"The Tribunal is giving no ex post facto application to Control Council Law No. 10. It is administering that law as a statement of international law which previously was at least partly uncodified. Codification is not essential to the validity of law in our Anglo-American system. No act is adjudged criminal by the Tribunal which was not criminal under international law as it existed when the act was committed."

I have often been asked concerning the reaction of the German people to these trials. I have no good answer. We sensed resentment by many Germans to our presence but I think this attitude was directed, not against us as judges, but against the occupying army. Allied personnel had good food and plenty, purchased, of course, outside of Germany, whose people were then on a very meager ration. Many of the better residences were occupied by the Army Officers from Generals on down to Sergeants. The owners were not happy, particularly since these transient occupants did not take too good care of the properties. Americans were riding where they wished, in army and their own American cars while the Germans could not buy gasoline except for urgent business. Put yourself in their place. You would not be happy.

Through the years since our return, as their living conditions improved so that instead of worthless marks Germany has the hardest money in Europe, and as they found the Americans sympathetic and helpful in their rehabilitation I am sure that whatever resentment earlier existed has largely subsided.

I never did know of any common reaction to the trials which opened the doors to German visitors and were well reported in the German press. I do know that many Germans, who had lived under the Nazi regime with their eyes shut and ears closed, were astounded by the revelations of brutality brought forth by the evidence in some of the cases.

What was the cost of the trials? I have never seen any figures. The IMT case was much more expensive than any of the others. For our six courts judges' compensation alone came to more than $300,000. And the judges were only a minor part of the elaborate organization of lawyers, investigators, translators, reporters, secretaries, typists etc, who were necessary to operate the court

Were the results worth the cost? I have made talks like this to groups like your own as many as fifteen times, most of them soon after my return from Germany, but I have never yet hazarded such an appraisement. After six years, however, I have reached certain conclusions. You are at liberty to disagree.

In the first place the trials were necessary to make good the promises of the allied governments to the world and their warnings to the malefactors, that when came the armistice there could be diligent prosecution in courts of justice of all those in high places responsible for mass murders, persecutions and other war crimes that were then shocking the sensibilities of all civilized people. Some of the agreements and pronouncements of the Roosevelt - Churchill - Stalin triumvirate have proved to be unwise. But it must be said to the credit of the American people that they have fulfilled their commitments, and kept their promises of their president, and in so doing, have kept the Nation's self respect. Whatever the cost in money, it was well spent to maintain our national honor.

Secondly, these trials and the others in France, the British Zone and Japan, have made a very substantial contribution to international criminal law. When I started to Germany I knew little or nothing of any branch of international law. I took some books to read on the ship and consulted all available texts in the meager library at Nurnberg. I found that there had been protests and denunciation by American presidents and others in high places of racial persecutions such as occurred many years ago in Armenia. There had been treaties denouncing in general terms war crimes. There were, of course, the Articles of the Hague Convention of 1907 and the Geneva Convention of 1929 dealing which treatment of prisoners of war. But of litigated cases in which crimes were defined and the law applied to facts, with final judgment, there were amazingly few precedents. The IMT blazed the main trail but there were many subsidiary questions which our court and the other five had to decide upon reason and without precedent. Ours was the first industrial case. Our opinion was cited as authority on several points raised in the Farben and Krupp cases. That is the way international law grows following the same process by which our common law was developed. I have no doubt that in future war trials the judges will profit by the labor which went into our decisions.

These opinions not only defined the crimes, applying the law to the facts but also set forth a procedure which future courts can follow from the framing of the indictment down through the trial to the judgment and penalty. Remember that no legislature nor any other authority had prescribed the sentences for guilty defendants. That was entirely within our discretion. The only limitation upon our authority was in the Military Governor of the American Zone who could reduce, but not increase, the penalties by us imposed. He had no say as to guilt and no other reviewing power.

This absence of review put a great responsibility upon the American judges. I am sure that all, save perhaps one, of some of whose courtroom conduct the rest of us were ashamed, fully appreciated their obligation to be fair and to be judicial and to the best of our ability tried to measure up to the task before us.

The trials had other minor benefits. But these seem to me to be important and justifying the expense.

At the conclusion of our case I was asked to stay on as presiding judge to try the last case then about to begin. It would have been profitable financially for we were able to save a good portion of our compensation, but money is not the only good thing. Before I went I was told that we would be through in six months I had made my plans accordingly. The trial dragged to almost a year. I felt that I had done my duty. It was a great experience, but enough is enough. We lived comfortably in Nurnberg but there is no place like our Indiana home.

Those interested in reading more about the Flick Trial and the other trials involving Hoosier judges should consult references 10-14 for this chapter.

Wayne Arthur Van Cleave - Florida Gig

Wayne Arthur Van Cleave was my father's first cousin. He was born in New Market, Indiana on March 5, 1903 and died in Crawfordsville, Indiana on July 31, 1984. He attended Wabash College in Crawfordsville from 1920 to 1924 and while there was a member of the Wabash College Glee Club and played the clarinet. On June 23, 1925 he married his beloved "Betty" or Autumn Alleen Hester (1904-2007). They had steadily courted each other during his time at Wabash.

Wayne was a man of many talents and went on to have a distinguished career as teacher, band and choir director, bank president, and farmer. For two years he taught English and history at New Ross High School in west-central Indiana. From 1927 to 1937 he was Band Director at Normal Illinois Community High School. He and Autumn then returned to near New Market, Indiana where he farmed. Over the subsequent years he won many local, state, and national awards for corn, wheat, oats, and soybeans. In 1958 he was the Indiana State Farm Corn King. He was a trustee of Scott Township in Montgomery County and served on the New Market School Board. He was director of the choir at the New Market Christian Church.

Wayne Arthur Van Cleave

From November 1924 until sometime in early 1925 Wayne played in an orchestra at the Seminole Lodge, a up-scale dinner club, in Hialeah, Florida, just south of Miami. The following letters to his parents, Joseph Warren and Viola Armstrong Van Cleave, detail his train ride down to Florida on the Dixie Flyer and his subsequent gigs over the next two weeks.[15] He undoubtedly wrote his future wife from Florida but none of those letters survive. His other letters to her do survive and they date from June 1921 to August 1924 and are deposited in the Wabash College Archives in Crawfordsville, Indiana.

The letters Wayne wrote to his parents from Florida detail a wide-eyed young man, son of a framer, who had never traveled out of the Midwest before. At the time, Miami was just 28 years old having been first incorporated in 1896. During the early 1920s Miami was prospering due to the Florida land boom. Construction was going on all around and millionaires had just begun to play there.

November 25, 1924 [aboard the Dixie Flyer, Chicago-Jacksonville Florida]
Dear Dad and Mom,

Just a line while we are riding. Just left West Palm Beach a few minutes ago. Will get too Miami in about 2 ½ hours. We are running on time. Certainly had a wonderful trip today from Jacksonville where we left at 8:30 AM eastern time. Have seen worlds of orange orchards, palm trees, pine apple fields, grapefruit trees, yellow root patches, banana trees, etc. The air is wonderful. We have been traveling near the coast all day. Could see the ocean once in a while. Saw some lighthouses. We get a refreshing breeze off of the ocean all of the time. The train is bouncing too much to write. I will probably drop you a line in the morning so you will know that I arrived safely.

Love,
Wayne

November 25, 1924 [Vereen, Miami Florida]
Dear Folks,

Just a line. Arrived O.K. The piano player's wife, a girl from Danville, met us at the train. We are staying here in a new hotel until we get rooms. Everything is wonderful here. Must go meet Joe King.

Love, Wayne

November 29, 1924
Dear Mom and Dad,

I just came from downtown and have a little while to write. I noticed in the paper that there was a lot of snow in New York so I imagine you have had some cold weather. Well we have both windows clear up here and I am going around bareheaded and in shirt sleeves. This sure is a funny old county down here. Everything looks old, Spanish type houses, just a world of thin concrete block, stuccoed. This is a terrible city for automobiles. They drive rather fast and blow their horns and the first one to the corner wins. The atmosphere must be close here cause the horns sure sound loud. You can hear one all over town. One can't begin to describe the sights down here.

I am sending a clipping from a paper advertising the place where we work [Seminole Lodge]. It is a high class dining place and of course lots of them dance between courses. The place is outside of Miami about six miles at Hialeah. We ride out free in a Cadillac sedan.

We don't start work until about 8:30 or nine unless it is on an unusual occasion like Thanksgiving, etc. Rich families have dinner parties there. Thanksgiving night everything was sold out. One party numbered forty. We have a nice elevated place for the orchestra, covered with three carpets which you sink your ankles in. A brass rail draped with plush goes around the orchestra stand. Every night about 11:00 the orchestra and two or three singers have our table in the dining room. We sit down and fill up. We are privileged to the soda fountain too. They certainly treat us fine. The boss advanced us $20.00 before we ever played any. They are well satisfied with the music. Sometimes we work overtime and any portion of an hour counts as a whole hour. We get $2.00 per hour over time. We play apiece about every 15 to 20 minutes on an average. Night before last tips amounted to $2.20 apiece. One fellow gave us $10.00 to play one piece. "Murf," the piano player was the only one who knew what he wanted so he led off and the rest of us faked it getting over $2.00 apiece.

We worked quite a bit overtime Thanksgiving night, so our earnings are above average, $19.50

I got two letters from Betty yesterday. It was the first mail I have received.

I saw "Chic" Little yesterday. He graduated from college last year, was on the glee club.

Here in Miami they are building all of the time. In the down town districts they are working day and night constructing new buildings. It is a sight. Nearly every other door along the streets down town leads to a real estate office. A hundred foot corner was listed at $25,000.00 in one place. As you go down town men here and there in groups are always talking about houses, lots, additions, etc.

I want to get a letter out to Betty now so I had better stop. Am feeling fine, eating lots of grape fruit. They sell for 15 cents a dozen and some for 50 cents a basket, one of those great big bushel baskets. Have had some real good fish down here too. Well bye for now.

Love,
Wayne

December 4, 1924
Dear Mom and Dad,

It seems like quite a while since I have heard anything from you. So far I haven't received any word from you. Betty has rewarded me with six letters. Two came to Joe King and the lady didn't understand. Sent them back to the post office. I inquired but haven't found them yet. Four, however, got to me. One came today, the first one to the new address.

From the papers I see it must be cold up at New Market with quite a lot of snow. One night it was cool here. Almost threatened to frost. Today though it is real warm. I am sweating here now while I am writing. It is always just a little cooler at night. Last night a balmy breeze made the clouds go hurrying past the moon. The air is fresh and balmy from the gulf stream two miles away.

A Mr. Sleight came to see me yesterday to play in his band for a concert on Sunday afternoon. I accepted. It pays seven dollars for the two hours. He wanted me to play second chair clarinet. He is formerly from Indianapolis. He organized and started the Indianapolis Military Band. Arthur Pryor starts Sunday too I guess. In the park where he plays there is of course a world of benches to sit on. In one section there is a bunch of long tables with chess and checker boards painted on them . Old fellows by the score sit there all afternoon and play. They have a big horse shoe court in the same section too. It is always occupied. The park is wonderful there, lots of flowers, palms etc. It is about 200 feet from a bay and on out between two stretches of land you can see the ocean tossing up and down and see the big white caps as the waves break.

You might be interested to know that the income of my first full week, which ended last night, amounted to $102.31. I get seven Sunday for the concert and if we make $17.83 last we did last week I will be getting a good start for the week. People sure do spend their money out at the Lodge. Dinners average about $2.50. A bottle of ginger ale was a dollar but they cut to fifty cents. It is just the same as pop and the same size bottles.

A bowl of ice, which is about the size of a half gallon cup, comes at 50 cents. It's a regular hold up place but it is visited by the millionaire class and they don't seem to kind. A fellow will come up and ask for some piece; he will shove over a $10.00 bill. I am going to take some pictures as soon as I can get to it of some interesting things around here and send them to you.

It is clouding up here now. We will probably have a little shower. They just come up all at once and then it clears off right quick.

My, all you can hear around here is automobile horns, hammers driving nails and concrete mixers.

Well I will close now. Hope it don't get too cold for you. If it does you had better come down. I believe I could support you.

With love,

Wayne

December 8, 1924

Dear Folks,

Just a line to let you know that I'm alright. Enjoyed playing in the band yesterday very much. It was concert in real estate interests. It is what you could call very hot down here today. Had a little shower last night.

I am sending $100.00 this time. Made a payment on my horn last month and will have another for this month and then X-mas is coming so I don't know when I will send the next.

I saw some wonderful homes yesterday out on 22nd St. It is just off the ocean. The houses are built of concrete block then stuccoed. Some are built out of coral rock which is very hard. Scotty had thought it would be very novel to have one of these houses up north but when thinking about it we could quickly see they wouldn't look right without the green foliage which they have here.

Well I will close now and mail this as I go down town.

Love,

Wayne

Chapter 9

School

"School days, school days; dear old golden rule days."

Will D. Cobb, Lyrics to *School Days, School Days*, 1907

When children go off to college they often write letters home to their parents. Although I have no surviving letters home from my great grandfather, Silas Richman, we do have my grandfather, Frank Richman's description of his schooling. The second two sections of this chapter include letters written home to my parents from school, the first when I attended the Indiana University Geologic Field Station in the Tobacco Root Mountains in Montana as a high school student and the second when I attended Wabash College in Crawfordsville, Indiana. I have also included an anecdote written by my mother describing an incident when I was in grade school.

Silas Tevis Richman (1852-1938)

Silas Richman was my great grandfather. He did more than his share of traveling to get his education and afterwards in the practice of medicine. The son of Enoch Richman (1800-1882) and Adeline Elvira Gillette (1814-1880), he was born May 25, 1852 in a log cabin three miles east of Hartsville in Decatur County, Indiana. He was the second youngest of five boys and five girls. On October 3, 1878 he married Elma Jane Baker (1857-1953), daughter of Thomas Nelson Baker (1831-1865) and Love Aurilla Shumway (1831-1918).

Silas Tevis Richman just before 1900

My grandfather, Judge Frank Nelson Richman, wrote a short description of the life of his father[1]:

"All of my children will remember their grandfather, although Elizabeth was not quite 9 years old when he died. We were at Pensacola when we learned of his stroke and hastened home. He was then and remained unconscious until his death 3 Jan. 1938 He would have been 86 years old on 25 May thereafter.

He made his own way in life. No one else paid his bills. To get an education he taught one-room country schools in the neighborhood of Hartsville, attending Hartsville college between terms. Somehow he went to Asbury, now DePauw University where he graduated in 1877. While there he joined Sigma Chi fraternity. One of his fraternity brothers was Charles S. Baker whose sister he married 3 Oct. 1878 at Columbus, Ind. (Note by FRJ: I have 2 different newspaper accounts of their wedding, listing wedding gifts and their value!).

They lived for a while at Jamestown, Ind., where he taught school. Then he became principle of the North Ward (later Jefferson) School in Columbus and was there when I was born. Then he went to medical school at Butler University in Indianapolis. It was a 2-year course of lectures. He took them all in one year, received his MD in 1884. He started to practice in Columbus but the west was beckoning, and he selected Princeton, Kansas as his next home, arriving about 1884 and leaving for Chicago in the fall of 1892, where he practiced medicine until his retirement in 1929. Realizing the inadequacy of his medical education, he entered Northwestern University Medical School on the south side in Chicago, and earned another MD degree."

Silas Richman practiced medicine on the south side of Chicago until his retirement in 1928. As a retiree he lived in Indianapolis and Columbus, Indiana.[2]

Margaret Richman Coons

Childhood Travels or I Didn't Travel Very Far!

The following anecdote[3] was written by my mother, Margaret Coons, to my wife, perhaps to warn her that I was "trouble incorporated." This was written about an incident when we lived in Indianapolis in the early 1950s.

Our two sons, Steve and Phil, rode the school bus to Nora Grade School. Steve was in the fifth grade and Phil was in the first when this particular incident occurred. At that time Steve wouldn't have considered sitting with Phil on the bus. They got off on the street next to ours, climbed the fence and went into the house from the garage. Steve led the way and punched the lock on the door after he got in. After a few minutes when Phil did not come in too, I asked Steve where he was. Steve said he didn't know and when I asked if he'd been on the bus, Steve hadn't seen him. I began to get upset and called two little boys in the neighborhood who were also in the first grade. They couldn't remember whether Phil was on the bus or not. I called the school and talked to the principal and also to his teacher. They went out and checked the parking lot and looked around the school and found no sign of Phil. They said they'd check with the school bus driver when he was through. By this time I was getting frantic and was wondering what to do next. Fortunately, before I did anything more, I heard a pounding on the door and, upon opening it, found Phil who was mad as a wet hen, saying, "Steve locked me out!" I asked him where he had been while I was making all those calls and becoming more worried by the minute and he said, "in Sandy's dog house." Now he says he was there two hours pouting, but I can't believe it was that long, or I'd have called the sheriff, state police and FBI.

My memory of the above incident differs somewhat from my mother's. Instead of going in the garage door, my brother and I always entered the back door after taking the shortcut from the next street over. Mother kept the back door unlocked for us since she was usually napping when we arrived home from school. Steve knew I was right behind him, but, for some reason, decided to lock me out that day. I banged loudly on the door, but no one heard me. I tried the back door to the garage, but it too also locked. Finally, in desperation, because it was a somewhat chilly spring day, I crawled into our dog Sandy's doghouse and commenced to pout. I don't know for how long I pouted. Eventually, the pangs of hunger got to me. I knocked on the door and was let in by my mother.

One might ask why I didn't just run away? Life was too good at our house. I never did run away from home. Once, when I was seven or eight, I did tell my mother that I was going to run way. I'm not sure now why I was peeved at her. Her measured response was, "Fine. I'll help you pack your bag." That certainly took the wind out of my sails. She was one smart mother!

Philip Coons

In the summer of 1962, between my junior and senior years in high school, I was awarded a scholarship from the National Science Foundation to attend the Indiana University Geologic Field Station in the Tobacco Root Mountains near Cardwell, Montana. I was one of eight high school students from across the nation to be awarded this privilege.

The Indiana University Geologic Field Station, now known as the Judson Mead Geologic Field Camp, was named in honor of Judson Mead, Ph.D., professor emeritus of geophysics at Indiana University and director of the field station from 1961 to 1981. The field station had its first course in 1949. Dr. Charles Deiss, the first director of the field station, had selected the South Boulder Valley in the heart of the Tobacco Root Mountains in Montana because "the region offers more extensive and varied geologic phenomena than any other area of equal size in the United States."[4]

When I attended in 1962, the field station consisted of a lodge, which served as a library, lecture room, and dining hall, and a number of steel buildings, which functioned as male and female bunkhouses, shower facilities, laundry room, and research facilities. The male high school students were housed in four-man platform tents. A beaver pond, now known as Lake Mead, was between the upper and lower campuses and often during the early evening beavers could be heard loudly slapping their tails on the water. Faculty trailers were added in 1966 to accommodate spouses and children of faculty members. The student dorms were not heated until 1996.

During my time at the field station the main course given to undergraduate college students was G429, an intense summer-long experience in field geology. At the time, a number of undergraduate and graduate students, who were working on various projects, were also in attendance. Students came from all over the United States and from several foreign countries. In 1962, in addition to students from Indiana University, G429 students came from 21 other universities around the United States. There were 51 G429 students, eight of them women. Of the high school students sponsored by the National Science Foundation, there were seven young men and one young woman.

Our experience actually began in Bloomington, Indiana where we boarded "carryalls," a crossover between our modern vans and SUV's. Our vehicles were painted dark green and emblazoned with the Indiana University Geologic Field Station logo. All were equipped with two-way radios[5] so that instructors could communicate with everyone in the convoy, thereby enhancing the teaching experience. Along the way we studied our guidebooks[6], which had been specially prepared for the trip. We must have been a funny sight crossing the prairies from Illinois to South Dakota. Thus, the course began with nearly a one-week trip from Bloomington, Indiana to the field station in Montana. Along the way we visited such impressive geologic sites as the Black Hills in South Dakota, Devils Tower, the Big Horn and Bear Tooth mountains, and Yellowstone and Grand Teton National Parks in Wyoming, and Hegbgen and Quake lakes in Montana. During the middle of our experience we made trips to Butte, Montana to visit the copper mines and Glacier National Park in northwest Montana.

The following letters were written to my parents back in Indiana. They are slightly edited for clarity.[7]

Indiana University Geologic Field Station Letters

June 13, 1962 (post card from Sheridan, Wyoming)

Tomorrow our caravan (11 carryalls and 3 cars) will start through the Bighorn Mountains. Yesterday and today we were in the Black Hills (Mt. Rushmore, Etta Mine, Homesteak Gold Mine) and Devils Tower. The trip through Ind., Ill., & Iowa wasn't too exciting, but now we're in the heart of "hard-rock country." It's been cool all the way (45-50 degrees tonight). It sure is beautiful country. I'll never forget my first glimpse of the snow-capped Rockies. I'm sure learning a lot of geology. We had our first field quiz today. It was just for experience though. Dr. Mead said that we should have the equivalent of 2 years of geology by the end of this summer....

The following letters were written from Indiana University Geologic Field Station in the heart of the Tobacco Root Mountains near Cardwell Montana

June 21, 1962

...For the last four days we've spent 9-10 hrs. in the field studying stratigraphy of this section and two hours in the classroom. On the way out we were up at five and we were lucky if we got to bed by eleven.

I really enjoyed the trip through the Black Hills & the Rocky Mountains. Yellowstone was quite a disappointment. The most beautiful section of the trip was the drive from Red Lodge, Montana to Yellowstone.

I've got a real good suntan already and my mustache and goatee are coming along fine. I've even gotten a cowboy hat. It's straw ($3.98) and it's perfect for keeping off the sun.

I live in a four-man tent. There are two other dorms, about 10 other tents, a lodge, and numerous other buildings (all aluminum), housing classrooms and equipment.

I did my laundry the other day. Aside from my blue jeans coming out stiff as a board, I did all right. My first effort at ironing was a success.

Up until now we've been following the G429 students around. Our first field problem is tomorrow. They will probably take us out in the middle of nowhere and have us figure out the formations around us. After tomorrow we will probably start work as graduate assistants.

The cute redhead is a G429 student...Pat Boyce [a senior high school student from Kokomo, Indiana] and I are real pals. He's a real nice guy. [An Iraqi graduate student] ...is a real character. The caravan is always leaving him behind. He wants to be sure not to miss anything. He's studying at I.U. on a scholarship.

...The food's good and I'm having a wonderful time.

Undated

Life is settling down to a dull roar now. We've equipped our tent with all the luxuries of life: bookshelves, shoe racks, a desk, and a tape recorder with Dixieland disks have been installed so far. Needless to say, we're living very comfortably.

I've served with two graduate students since I started my assistantship. The first was studying the Pony Series, that is Precambrian metamorphic rocks. The second was studying the contact between the batholith (look it up) and the metamorphics. The work is very interesting. I've seen quite a bit of the Tobacco Roots so far.

Each Sunday we have a day off. Last Sunday Pat Boyce and I climbed up to the summit of the Madison formation ridge (actually a small mountain). We were looking for caves but didn't find any. The view was spectacular from the top. It took us half a day. Next Sunday we're planning to climb Diamondhead Mountain, an all-day trip. On the Fourth of July everybody is planning to go to the rodeo at Ennis. Besides mountain climbing and rodeos, there spelunking and ghost towns and abandoned mines to explore. There's never a dull moment.

Tomorrow the whole group is going into Butte to see several mines (copper open pit and shaft). We have to get up at four thirty because Butte is on fast time. It ought to be a very interesting day.

There's a tremendous variety of wildlife out here. I've seen quite a few bears and deer so far. The bear was five feet away from me but out of a car window, of course. I had my first taste of elk at Red Lodge Montana. It has a real distinctive flavor.

The field camp is running at full capacity now. Besides the staff, graduate students, G429 students, and high school participants, there's the NSF Institute (high school teachers) who just arrived today. Later in the summer after the G429 students depart, the G200 students (geology minors) arrive. This is a very broad cross section. My work is to cover a very broad field. I'm to be given a taste of about every phase of geology there is. I won't name them here. I won't receive credit for this summer, but I will be able to take placement tests in college, if I decide upon geology as a career, and get credit.

I have no idea what the world affairs are now. I rarely see a current magazine or even a newspaper...

There's one boy at the table who is burning the candle at both ends, so to speak. He has two girlfriends and he put the wrong letter in the right envelope. His girlfriend seems to be pretty mad. It could be very embarrassing. The girl at the table where I'm writing is from Mt. Holyoke. She's pretty, plays the guitar, and is engaged!

My mustache and goatee go very well with my dark suntan. I doubt if you'd know me. I have a hard time getting into the movie in Whitehall for 40 [cents].

If I'm going to get up at 4:30 tomorrow, I'd better quit now.

June 27, 1962

I got Dad's letter today. I can't understand why you haven't received my last letter. The postal service must be terribly slow going out of Cardwell.

I have so little time to write. I just finished another ten hour field day and expect another two hour classroom session tonight. The rest of the time is taken up by keeping myself and my clothes clean...

You'd better send me some more money. I have about twelve dollars left. So far all of your money has been spent very wisely.

July 2, 1962

Last Thursday I went to Butte with the G429'ers to visit the Anaconda Company's Berkeley Pit and Steward Mine. Both were very interesting. We went down to the 4100 foot level in the Steward Mine in a tri-level elevator car at the rate of about 1200 feet per minute. Eight of us were packed in a space the size of a telephone booth. I asked the mine's geologist if the car was safe and he said that if it wasn't, I wouldn't have to worry about it. The temperature was over a hundred degrees at the 4100 foot level. Everything was safe, so don't worry. We were provided with mining helmets and lights.

So far I've been most interested with the mining and processing of ore, especially the processing. Mines barely break even but the processing phase holds a great future, especially in research. New processes for the extraction of minerals have to be developed and uses for waste materials have to be found. This is more chemistry than geology. A hobby of mining on the side would be fun. I may get to visit the Anaconda Company's smelter in Anaconda. This isn't usually done but since I'm interested Dr. Mead said maybe we would be able to work something out.

Last Sunday on my day off I visited the old abandoned Garnet Mine. It was very interesting. Don't worry either. I never take chances when I go through mines.

July 6, 1962

About those rocks you're expecting. Almost immediately after I started on the trip I learned that the rocks in the rock collections that you buy are pretty hard to come by. They come from all over the world, not just one locality, and are usually found deep in mines. They aren't found lying on the ground glittering in the sun. The mineralization and crystallization in this are isn't particularly good anyway; although I have found some good epidote crystals in a prospect pit. I also have a good ore specimen from the Steward Mine in Butte...

On the Fourth I went to the annual rodeo at Ennis. It was really a thrill. I also visited Virginia City and Nevada City, two restored western towns.

The weather has been wonderful. I really sleep good since it's so cool at night. Today I had to wear a coat in the mountains. I hear that for this time of the year it's unusually wet, everything's green. The snow is just finally starting to melt on the higher peaks. I walked through some today.

I never make my bed. I guess it's good training for Wabash [College]. I haven't started to smoke or drink yet, though, and I haven't gone to a "hore house." There is a whole row of them in just about every big city. I am learning plenty of dirty jokes and songs, however. Your Darling Baby! I hope I'm not worrying you. I'm just thankful your check arrived!

...Tell Grandma that I didn't get to see anything in Ottumwa. We got in about eight in the evening and then we had to eat dinner. We left at seven the next morning...

July 15, 1962

Last night I came back from the Glacier Park trip. The weather was miserable: it rained constantly during the afternoon and the next morning that I was there so I didn't get any good pictures, only about three.

That evening I duded myself up...after that I made up for the miserable weather. Just before the group sing a girl walked by, smiled and said, "Hi, Indiana." Of course I winked at her and said, "Hi." All during the group sing we were making eyes at each other and after it was over I walked up and introduced myself. Pretty soon we were down in the basement twisting way to the music of a three-piece combo. They have a dance every night except Sunday. She is a junior at the University of Minnesota and I was "freshman" at Wabash. If she knew the truth, she sure didn't let on. She was a wonderful conversationalist. We really had fun...

July 20, 1962

Since my wild idea about doing my project on the smelter in Anaconda, I have become very interested in the volcanoes of this region. Bill Hanna, the graduate student I'm working with now, is working on them. I talked to Dr. Mead about staying with him for the rest of the summer, except for some seismic work, and he said O.K. I'll probably be camping out in the Elkhorn Mts.

It poured down here all day Wednesday so I didn't have to go out in the field. I spent the day reading and sleeping.

Pat Boyce's parents arrived yesterday. He has been and will be showing them around today and tomorrow.

My mustache is growing luxuriantly but my goatee is doing very poorly. Dr. Mead was telling me that he shaved that much off in the morning.

July 28, 1962

...Lately I've been working with Joe Mengel. He teaches structure at the University of Wisconsin. For several years he was an oil well geologist. I think I've learned more about oil wells than geology.

Joe and I have been taking an average of 500 strike and dip readings of the Pony Series fractures every day. At night we have to plot them on two different sheets. Although the work is very wearing in the daytime, it's interesting to see how the fractures fall when we plot them up at night.

This afternoon was the first time I've had of my own for almost a week. After washing my clothes and shining my boots, I took a bath...Tonight I'm going into Whitehall to see "Sergeants Three." Although we have a very good geological library here, there's hardly enough time to use it. I do plan to read a book about geophysics though.

August 4, 1962

I got your letter today. We were rained out in the field today so I got in early and have time to write you before dinner.

We had a meeting last night during which a graduate student spoke about his project. It was the first of about nine or ten such meetings...

Our caravan will probably arrive late Tuesday night or early Wednesday. If it arrives on Tuesday night we'll sleep in the Geology Building and you can pick me up in the morning. In any case I'll send you a telegram when I become more sure of my time of arrival.

August 7, 1962

I just finished talking to you about an hour ago. It was sure good to hear from you.

This trip [Four of us male high school students hatched a plan to see the Seattle World's Fair at the end of our stay at the field station] will be a chance of a lifetime for me to see new places, meet people, and have a good time.

As for Pat and Bob, both boys are extremely intelligent, mature, clear-thinking, and cautious. Both have traveled long distances by themselves, so you needn't worry about them.

Please be prompt with your letter to Dr. Mead. I want to give it to him as soon as possible so he can plan the caravan accordingly. Our absence will make room for three more G-200 students...

As I told you over the phone, we're going on a camping trip tomorrow to sample the Elkhorn Mtn. volcanics. There are four of us and we expect to be gone three nights...

August 12, 1962

We came in yesterday after spending three nights in the Elkhorn Mts. The first two nights we stayed at Tiger Lakes. There were so many mosquitoes there that I could kill five with one slap. We had great fun poling an old raft around the lake.

We were up at five after the first night, off at eight, and back at seven. We hiked almost the whole day. The volcanics there are nothing but rubble and are very inaccessible.

It's hard to believe that a whole mountain could be nothing but rubble, but it's true. The walking was very tough and dangerous. It was also bitter cold.

Just 1000 ft. above Tiger lakes is Hidden Lake sunk into a crater-like structure open at one side. The crater walls tower another 1000 ft. above the lake. We were on top of all this. I sure wish I had my camera.

The third night we camped on the other side of the mountain at an abandoned mine just above the ghost town of Elkhorn. There were no mosquitoes there, nor was there any water. Since it was not cloudy, we slept under the stars. I awoke at about one thirty to see a meteor shower...

August 16, 1962

I've already talked to Dr. Mead. He seemed pleased to hear that we were going on to Seattle, but he said that we ought not to leave early because of our moral obligation to the NSF.

We've decided to stay at the YMCA. Matter of fact, we've already got the reservations.

This is an excellent opportunity to see more of the country, and what's more, to see a world's fair. I may never have a chance like this again.

The way things look now, I'll leave Whitehall on the 24th, spend the 25th-27th in Seattle, and be home by the 30th. I'll probably come home through Denver: the rates are the same.

I really appreciate your letting me do this. I tried to place myself in your shoes and I'm not at all sure I'd let my son do this.

I'm off to the Townsend Valley for 2 nights tomorrow.

August 22, 1962

I'll be leaving here Friday afternoon. It rained all day today so we didn't go out in the field. There was even some snow up in the mountains. I'm shivering right now. I'm not planning to spend any money on concessions, especially $5 to go up in the Needle.

August 27, 1962 (post card from Seattle, Washington)

I'm writing you between Acts I & II of "Mary, Mary." Saw "My Fair Lady" last night. The fair is tremendous, especially the U.S. science exhibit and the Touch Exhibit. I'll be home by Thursday evening, I hope. Am coming by bus.

Philip Coons

Letters from Wabash College

I attended Wabash College, a small private liberal arts college for men, in Crawfordsville, Indiana. Wabash is one of only three all male colleges left in the United States, the other two being Hampden-Sydney College in Hampden-Sydney, Virginia and Morehouse College in Atlanta, Georgia.

Wabash College was founded in 1832 by a group of Presbyterian ministers. However, the college is independent and non-sectarian. Its current president is Dr. Patrick White. Enrollment is currently 950, although in the 1960s, when I attended, it was just over 800. The college has a generous endowment and is ranked by *Forbes Magazine* as the tenth best liberal arts college in the United States.[8] Currently about 60% of the students live in one of nine fraternities. In the 1960s it was closer to 80%.

Wabash College and DePauw University in Greencastle, Indiana are known for their intense football rivalry, which began in 1890, and now played on a yearly basis. The victor of their yearly football game, known as the Monon Bell Classic, gets possession of the Monon Bell. This bell is a 300-pound bell from a locomotive that ran on the now defunct Monon Railroad in Indiana.

These letters from Wabash were written to my parents over the four years that I attended Wabash College.[9] Fortunately my mother saved all of my letters. I have included excerpts from these letters to illustrate certain highlights of my Wabash career, including pledgeship, dating, spring break, our panty raid at DePauw University, canoeing down Sugar Creek, the all-campus water fight of 1964, and the clean-up after the Palm Sunday tornado of April, 1965.

Pledgeship

Pledgeship is the period between pledging a fraternity and becoming initiated as a full-time member. In my days at Wabash, pledgeship was physically and mentally demanding. In addition to our house jobs, which mostly included keeping the house clean, there was much physical and mental hazing which culminated in "hell week," a three-day period during semester break in January, where pledges went without sleep for three days and underwent intense hazing practices.

My attitudes towards hazing and pledgeship changed markedly during my Wabash career and subsequently. Initially I looked on pledgeship with some fear and anticipation and even thought that some of it would be fun. By the end of "hell week" I was about ready to leave the fraternity. As a sophomore I did not participate in hazing and, as a junior, I became very disillusioned with the practice, as the house grade average fell to last place among fraternities, a fact I attributed mostly to pledgeship.

September 17, 1963

...So far fraternity life is fine, although pledgeship hasn't started yet. I like one pledge brother in particular. His name is Haines Lockhart...from Downers Grove, Illinois...

September 19, 1963

...We have a fill pledge class of twenty-two now, the best pledge class on campus...

September 25, 1963

...Last Monday night I was elected president of my pledge class. Last night pledgeship started in earnest. It was quite a shock to us all. I only hope that I can keep up enough courage and stamina to pull us all through. It's going to be very difficult...My roommates are Bob McCallum and Stu Mahler. They're really taking care of me. I just finished doing eight pushups for a slight offense. Many of the rules are asinine, and sometimes there is very little time to study, but I guess it's worth it in the long run...

October 11, 1963

Dear Mother and Dad,

So far this week has been uneventful except for a very tough line. I've been working my butt off. Sometimes I get the feeling that I ought to call it quits, but the feeling quickly passes...

October 18, 1963

Dear Mother and Dad,

This week has been a tough one...I barely have enough time to do my house job and complete my homework. Of course, I have time to associate with my pledge brothers, but I never have any time to sit down and think or go out for a walk and enjoy the fall colors.

This week my house job has been mail boy. I enjoy it because I ride a bicycle and Wooglin [the fraternity dog] follows alongside me. I dread to think of what it will be like in cold weather, though...

October 25, 1963

Dear Mother and Dad,

We had our second big line of the year last Thursday night. It was a "midnight snack" Of course we had to work up a good appetite, so we ran up and down the stairs about five times. The meal consisted of crackers – all they could stuff in our mouths – and butter –a bout ½ stick – vinegar to drink, and onions for dessert. Not a bad meal at all. I'm looking forward to our sixteen course dinner...

January 7, 1964

...I want to be home as long as possible before "hell week" begins (probably Wednesday of the next week...

Thus far everything has been pretty quiet and I expect it to remain so until "hell week." Down in the basement the sophomores have put up a chart – "Hell via Route 66." I expect that I'll build up quite a lot of mileage between now and "hell week."...

January 17, 1964

...Hell week doesn't worry me too much because all I have to do is exist. Actually I'm looking forward to my road trip. During semester break I'll have to do a lot of studying for our [fraternity] lore exam...

May 20, 1964

...Not much is happening except that I got thrown in the shower the other day by a junior and a sophomore. My pledge brothers wouldn't lift a finger to help me. They just stood aside and laughed. Pledge class unity – Ha!

Dating at Wabash

At Wabash dating is a time-honored tradition. Since Wabash is an all-male college, men have to travel for their dates and usually date women from nearby colleges and universities such as DePauw, Butler, Purdue, Indiana, Saint Mary of the Woods, Indiana State, and Ball State. During the week Wabash students knuckle down and study hard and on weekends they play hard.

The following excerpts describe my own dating experiences during my first two years at Wabash. As a more mature adult, I now look back and see how utterly naive I was. I was alternately high or low depending upon how well my dating life was progressing. When I didn't have a steady girlfriend, I engaged in much rationalization and felt sorry for the brothers who did have a steady dating relationship.

November 20, 1963

...I really enjoyed my date last weekend and was planning to have another date with her until I received her thank-you note. It says, "Though I hate to admit it to you, I certainly think that the DePauw men out-class yours. Can't put my finger on it exactly..." We (the other boys I showed the letter to and myself) all had a good laugh over it. How green can a girl get? If that's the typical DePauw girl, I don't want any part of it. I'm letting myself cool off before I write a reply or I might be tempted to make a few really caustic remarks. Even so, it's going to be a cold letter. Maybe she'll realize her mistake and apologize...

February 20, 1964

...The weekend after this is [Miami] Triad. Haines fixed me up with an Alpha Chi pledge from DPU [DePauw University]. I got a letter from her today. She sounds very clever. I wish you could read it...

April 9, 1964

...I'm going down to DPU this weekend for the Little 500. The girl from Evansville who I had up for the last house dance invited me. She even sent me a favor to her last dance even though we were there only thirty minutes. Playing the field really pays off, and I have no intentions of stopping. By the way, Haines Lockhart got pinned last night. The poor guy has to go down there every weekend and sometimes in the middle of the week...

April 15, 1964

...My date Friday night didn't turn out so well after all. [She] likes me but I don't like her. She can't talk. That's happened twice before. On the other hand, I liked [another young woman], but she didn't care for me. Maybe someday I'll meet a girl that I like, who likes me. Meanwhile I couldn't be less concerned...

Friday, October 9 [1964]

...I'm going to see Kathy [the daughter of my mother's best friend in high school] at DePauw Sunday. Perhaps I'll run into Nell [another daughter of one of my mother's college friends]. Anyway, I'm planning to see her sometime before long...

Friday, [December 13, 1964]

...[My date] is coming up for a dance this weekend. Don't worry. We plan to do a lot of studying...

Monday [January 4, 1964]

[A DePauw student] has asked me to the Gold-Diggers' Ball this Saturday.

April 17, 1965

...Changing the subject, I had a date with Nell last night. I've never met such a real lady. She has a tremendous sense of humor. I invited her to PanHel [Panhellanic] and she accepted enthusiastically even before she knew the date – which is – by the way, May 7 and 8. I hope you, Dad, weren't planning to stay Friday night after the bank meeting. – no offense of course, but...

Spring Break in Florida

Ever since the movie, *Where the Boys Are*, debuted in 1960, spring break for college students in the eastern United States has been a venerated springtime ritual. Initially many students went to Fort Lauderdale, Florida, but now students migrate to Florida, the Texas coast and many places in Mexico and the Caribbean. My first and only spring break experience was to accompany my childhood friend, Lee McDermond, to his uncle's motel in Vero Beach, Florida during my freshman year at Wabash.

February 12, 1964

Dear Mother and Dad,

I just know that you've been waiting for this particular letter since I've started my college education! Well, here it is. Lee has invited me to go to Vero Beach, Florida with him during spring vacation. How about it, Dad? I imagine that we could go down together sharing expenses, and I guess that we would be staying at his uncle's motel, free of charge. I don't think it will cost very much, and I'm willing to pay my own expenses. Of course, I would never refuse a little financial encouragement....

Love,

Phil

March 29, 1964 [post card]

Sorry I haven't written. I've been having such a good time. No sun yet, though, We're going deep sea fishing tomorrow. Lee and I have dates tomorrow night. I fixed him up, of all things. My date, Pat, is from Cleveland and is a freshman at Connecticut College. We spent the day together. No more room.

Love, Phil

Panty Raid at DePauw University

Panty raids are legend at coed colleges and universities. My parents had regaled me with stories about panty raids when they attended DePauw and Indiana Universities. Problem was that I attended an all male college. What to do? It didn't take me long to decide that I should stage a raid at DePauw University. I collected three other pledge brothers and we were off in one of their cars. We attacked Rector Hall, an all-female dorm of mostly freshman women. However, our loud shouts for panties failed to attract much attention and no panties were thrown from the windows. We decided to enter the dorm and raced upstairs. Still no reaction, so two of us raced back downstairs and then upstairs again. On the second run upstairs, some women had pushed a bed out into the hall so as to block us. I jumped on the bed and received a horrified look from one of the residents. Still no panties were thrown to reward us. We raced downstairs and out but not before our two other compatriots had created some mischief in the basement.

February 12, 1964
Dear Mother and Dad,

...I don't think that DePauw will ever be the same after last Sunday night. Three of us raced up to the fourth floor of Rector hall two times. After we came down the second time, we were privileged to meet the supervisor of Rector Hall. Two of my brothers turned on the fire hose in the basement, not very hard, mind you, but hard enough to slightly dampen the floor. The dean at DePauw called Dean Moore today, and, from what I hear, Dean Moore was slightly amused at the incident...

Canoeing Down Sugar Creek

Another time-honored tradition at Wabash is to canoe down Sugar Creek, which extends through Montgomery County and into Parke County, Indiana before it empties into the Wabash River. Sugar Creek flows through two Indiana State Parks, the Shades and Turkey Run. It is quite scenic and is the fastest flowing waterway in Indiana, so it is very popular with canoeists.

Although I hardly mentioned the trip to my parents, it was quite memorable. Another fraternity brother, Jim Rushton, and I borrowed my grandmother's car and drove down and left it at Turkey Run State Park, 30 miles distant from Crawfordsville. We hitchhiked back to Crawfordsville where we rented a canoe and started on our big adventure. It was warm and sunny that day. The creek was running fast due to recent rains. We packed a picnic lunch. All went well, until about two thirds of the way through our journey, we took the wrong fork around an island and got hung up on a rock. We finally dislodged ourselves, but the canoe filled with water. I lost my paddle. We finally were able to beach and drain the canoe and were on our way again, but with only one paddle. We were soaked and beginning to feel a little chilly, as it was late afternoon. Finally we arrived at the footbridge, which crosses over Sugar Creek at Turkey Run State Park. We loaded up our canoe and returned to Crawfordsville. We were exhausted but certainly had a thrilling day while experiencing the wilds of Indiana from our canoe on Sugar Creek.

April 22, 1964
Dear Mother and Dad,

A pledge brother and I are planning a canoe trip down Sugar Creek to Turkey Run State Park this weekend. It ought to be loads of fun...

All-Campus Water Fight

Water fights are another tradition at Wabash. They usually begin in the late spring just prior to final exams and are a good way to blow off excess steam. I believe that I was involved in two water fights while I was at Wabash. The first, described below, occurred in the spring of my freshman year.

A prior water fight had occurred six years earlier in May 1958. Although it began at Wabash College, it ended at DePauw University. After thoroughly dousing each other, about 125 Wabash students formed a caravan of 20 to 25 cars and drove a half hour to Greencastle and there attacked several fraternities and sororities. Before the water fight was over, 26 Wabash students, nine of them Betas, had been arrested and incarcerated in the Putnam County Jail. The Greencastle City Police, the Indiana State Police, and the Indiana National Guard had all been called out. The following day, newspapers in Crawfordsville, Greencastle, and Indianapolis all ran stories about the near riot.[10]

May 23, 1964
…We had an all-campus water fight in front of the Beta house last night. The Delts [Delta Tau Delta] and the Phi Delts [Phi Delta Theta] started it by attacking the Beta House. In due time the Sigs [Sigma Chi], Tekes [Tau Kappa Epsilon], and Phi Psis [Phi Kappa Psi] all joined in. At its height, there were two fire trucks, a squad car, and a riot truck parked out in the street. Naturally they were quite hesitant to use their fire hoses on us. They finally left, figuring, I guess, that we'd stand out in front of our houses as long as they remained. They were quite right. It would have ended by itself if they hadn't have come. Even Dean Moore was on the scene. He got a bit damp too, as did some of the policemen. He was bit perturbed that we picked such a late hour – 1:30 AM – to have our water fight. We sang "Old Wabash"; and, all in all, we had a jolly good time.

I think the fight was triggered by an article in yesterday's *Wabash Bachelor* commemorating an all-campus water fight and raid on DPU six years ago. Needless to say, Dean Moore was quite shaken up when someone in the crowd yelled out, "Let's go to DePauw!"

Love,
Phil

Clean-up After Palm Sunday Tornadoes

The Palm Sunday tornados of April 11, 1965 occurred during my second year at Wabash College. The tornado described below started on the southeast side of Crawfordsville and extended nearly 50 miles through Montgomery, Boone, and Hamilton counties. It caused 28 deaths, 100 injuries, and destroyed over 80 homes.

Overall the Palm Sunday tornado outbreak was the second biggest on record; it consisted of 78 tornadoes, killed 271 people, and injured 1500. This tornado outbreak was the third deadliest on record, trailing the Super Outbreak of 1974 (148 tornadoes in 13 states, which killed 315, and the Tri-State Tornado (Missouri, Illinois, and Indiana) of 1925, which killed 747.

April 17, 1965
Dear Mother and Dad,

Little did I know, I guess, when we talked on the phone last Sunday that the killer tornados would come so close to Crawfordsville. At the [Beta Theta Pi] house we could see that the clouds looked mighty suspicious. We knew that a "tornado warning" was out. What we didn't know is that a tornado warning meant that actual tornados had been sighted in the area. The fault of the weather bureau or the TV stations not to have explained this probably accounted for the majority of deaths.

The tornado hit just east of Shannondale and moved on a diagonal bringing it just east of Dover. The swath of destruction was at least ¼ to ½ mile wide. Entire farms were wiped out. All that was left were the foundations. Only splinters, one to two feet long and several inches wide, remained from the actual structures and littered the surrounding fields. Whole woods were blown down. Trees were snapped at their very middle. It looked as if a giant with a huge scythe had been at work. It was horrible.

I went out to help clean up on Wednesday with about 100 other Wabash men. We cleared several entire fields piling the remains in small piles about ten yards apart which were to be fired. We helped another farmer clean up around his house. We formed several gigantic piles. One was his house. He had lost everything.

There were a few gawking tourists, to be sure, on Ind. 32, but back on the dirt roads there weren't any. It was so horrible there was very little talking and joking among the students. The farmers had one goal in sight, to clean up and burn first. They were thinking very little beyond this.

It was just all too horrible for words....

Love,
Phil

Chapter 10

Expeditions

"There comes a time in every rightly constructed boy's life that he has a raging desire to go somewhere and dig for hidden treasure."

Mark Twain, *The Adventures of Tom Sawyer*, 1876

Frank Richman

My grandfather, Frank Richman, was a friend of Clessie Cummins (1888-1968), founder of the Cummins Engine Company in Columbus, Indiana. Mr. Cummins, an inventor and entrepreneur, was awarded many new patents for his improvements on the diesel engine. Cummins was also an adventurer and made numerous trips down the Ohio and Mississippi Rivers in boats that he designed and built. His life is documented in two books, one an autobiography[1], and the other[2], a biography written by his son Lyle Cummins. Both books chronicle Cummins' first trip down the Ohio and Mississippi Rivers.

Mr. Cummins' first trip down the Ohio and Mississippi Rivers to New Orleans in 1912 was a near disaster. Cummins had built his first boat and enlisted his wife's brother, Brainard McCoy, as the only crew. They set out from Jeffersonville, Indiana at dusk on November 9, 1912. As night fell, they crashed into the side of a barge. Although no one was hurt, they lost half of their provisions. Prevented by regulations from tying up for the night next to the barge, they proceeded through the ship canal and locks and headed towards the New Albany, Indiana side of the river, all the while, followed by a steamboat, which had been in the locks with them. On their second day out, un-calked seams began leaking in the wind-swept waters. After a number of days and nights of being drenched by rain, the two nearly met disaster again at the mouth of the Red River on the Mississippi. They hit a snag in the fog, started to sink, and only managed to salvage the boat by running aground. The next morning, after a rain-soaked night in the mud under a partially pitched tent, they managed to fix the hole in the bottom of the boat. They finally arrived in New Orleans on December 11, 1912 after five weeks of being on the river.

Evidently Cummins made several more trips down the Ohio and Mississippi Rivers before he enlisted my grandfather and another crony, Earl Butler, for another trip down the Ohio and Mississippi Rivers to New Orleans. Clessie's autobiography says nothing of this trip and it is described only briefly by son Lyle in his book. Cummins had built a new sailboat, the *Big Dipper*, from a kit that he had purchased from the Bay City Boat Works in Bay City, Michigan. Construction proceeded over several years from 1941 to 1944. It was fitted with a diesel engine produced by the Cummins Engine Company. The boat was built on Cummins' farm in Bartholomew County and then trucked to Madison, Indiana. Following their trip to New Orleans, Clessie crossed the Gulf of Mexico to Fort Myers Beach, Florida, where he and his wife Stella had a winter home.

What follows is my grandfather's unedited account, *Log of the Big Dipper*, of their trip from Madison, Indiana to New Orleans, Louisiana.[4] It's launching onto the Ohio River at Madison, Indiana was chronicled by the *Columbus Republican*.[5]

The boat had a beam of 13 feet and drew 4 ½ feet of water. The cabin had a drop-leaf table upon which the crew ate meals and the side seats would turn into bunks at night. There was a small bathroom and more bunks forward and in the engine room. The cabin was fitted with a stove, sink and refrigerator, all of the comforts of home.

Clessie Cummins' sailboat, the Big Dipper, 1944

Log of the Big Dipper: Madison, Indiana to Pensacola, Florida, 1944

September 6

Left Madison Wednesday Sept. 6 at 12 P.M. Aboard: Cap. Clessie L. Cummins steward [Earl Butler] roustabout Richman as crew. Passengers: Cap's wife, Lyle [Cummins], Mr. Feldmann, Elizabeth [Richman]. Arrived Louisville 5:30 P.M. Tied up at Municipal Yacht Club. All went up to town to Brown Hotel for dinner in Cap's Cadillac. Got back to dock at 9 P.M. after several retracings of route due to some one's ignorance of right road. Slept E in aft stateroom and others in main galley. Bed plenty hard. We probably will get used to it. Heard war news and called it a day.

September 7

Left Louisville 10:10 after checking with coast guard who were much interested in the boat. Over 40 ft. fall in the Louisville locks.

Ate lunch about 12:30 then entered Lock 43 and went through without delay. Drop was perhaps 10 feet. Took first picture below locks-rocky bank. Ind. Shore 1/50 - 16. In Short distance the rocky bluff shifted to Ky. side with flat ground across.

Second picture King's Landing pushing gravel barges 1/150 - 8. At Leavenworth talked to [daughter-in-law] Teddy [Richman] (charges reversed) and told her we would be at Evansville Sat. noon. (We won't make it.) Asked lock keeper about John Maker. He has moved to Alton. Mrs. is dead. They were separated in their later years. Tied up - anchor- below Leavenworth about 6. Put in some fishing lines. No luck. Had dinner of ham, potatoes, tomatoes, apple sauce, milk. The gravy was plentiful and thin. Got in bed, tuned in to [Tomas] Dewey. We agreed that he has something. With a higher pillow and two blankets slept fine until Clessie thinking it was 7 A.M., tuned in radio at 6 o'clock.

September 8

Breakfast at 6:30. My job is keeping boat clean, wiping dry all mahogany on deck. Dews are very heavy. Mop and sponge do the trick but better with chamois which we'll get in Evansville. Fog was so thick couldn't start before 8 o'clock. Took 3rd picture house high on Ky. Hill looking north on a beautiful stretch of river. 2nd picture at 9:30 of Vesta pushing Jones & Laughlin empty steel barge up river.

Red buoys are painted on top, black ones square. Going down river go to the right of red and left of black. Began to feel bad during the morning - slept for an hour in cabin. Ate lunch which shouldn't have done. Too much fried cooking. Called Teddy at Lock 45 and agreed to meet her at Hotel McCurdy 5 P.M. Saturday. Ate no dinner. Put out three fishing lines and caught one baby catfish which I left on hook over night taking rod down in the cabin. Listened again to Dewey - not so good a speech. Turned out lights at 9 P.M. and slept till 7.

September 9

Feeling better this morning but went slow on breakfast. Weather clear and warm. Not much fog. Got started by 8 took picture of the rock at Rockport and a little later, after going through Lock 46 a picture of 8 oil barges pushed by big stern wheeler. The channel below the locks was very narrow and it was our luck to meet the barges there. Passed about 20 ft apart. Arrived about 2:30 at Evansville, tied up at a float in front of the McCurdy Hotel. While Clessie and Earl went uptown for provisions stayed on the float and showed visitors the boat. I have more data on it now.

36 ft. 7 in. long, 12 ft. beam, displacement 15 tons, iron keel weighs 5600 lbs and lead in hold 2000 lbs. Six bunks, two in engine room, powered with 75 h.p. Cummins Diesel Model A. 4 cyl., main mast 42 ft. mizzen 36 ft., anchor on hand winch, chain drops into a box in forward cabin. Water

tank capacity 2 65 gal. (130 gal.). Fuel tanks 140 gal. So far we have averaged 7 miles per gallon, cruising speed 6 miles per hour in slack water. Mattresses on bunks are air foam rubber 5 in. thick covered with leather. Ice box 100 lbs. Put in 50 lbs. at Madison on Thursday evening still had about 25 lbs. when we re-iced at Evansville Saturday evening. Main stove burns coal briquettes or charcoal but is not in use on this trip. Alcohol two burner stove is bolted to top of other stove. Sink is stainless steel. Gravity feed to water faucets. Ship's head (toilet room) has lavatory and toilet with cupboard for linen and toilet accessories. Table with standard running lengthwise in center of main galley has two big leaves which lift up making places for 6 if necessary. In center standard is a little shelf with rims around to hold service dishes - salt etc. Now it has flashlight, spectacles, pencils, tobacco pouches, pipes and what not. All around the cabin are cupboards for bedding supplies, books, etc. There are two closets in which to hang clothing. My fishing rods stand up in one of them. On deck there is a midship cockpit, floor by 3 by 4 ½ feet, with seats on three sides, door leading forward into main galley. On forward wall is the wheel on starboard side. On aft wall are engine controls and gauges - reverse gear one lever, throttle, lubricating oil pressure gauge, water temperature gauge, and tachometer showing r.p.m. But we are driving about 1200 which gives best results with this hull.

Engine is in a well - or after cabin, behind the cockpit. It runs so cool that Clessie could put his cheek up against the exhaust pipe. There is a wooden helm for use when sailing. Lashed on the deck are the masts and yard arms. We have a 10 ft. dinghy, quite seaworthy, weighing about 90 lbs. which sits upside down on the deck on the starboard side. The U.S. flag flies from a standard at the stern. It is supposed to go up at 8 A.M. and come down at sunset.

Well. This is enough for present about the boat. Except its name is Big Dipper and its number 40C567.

At 5 o'clock met T and T and Mrs. Clark (Aunt Lulu) at the McCurdy, took them to the boat and then back to the hotel for dinner. Clessie came in late and ate with us.

There was too much traffic along the river front to feel comfortable so about dark pulled across the channel beyond the marking buoys and anchored in about 8 ft. of water - boat draws 4 ½ feet. Sat on deck a little while watching the lights and then to bed at 9 P.M.

Sunday, Sept. 10.

Up at 6:20. Saw a new L.C.T. being towed down river and decided it might interfere with our getting through the locks. So got under way before breakfast. There was no dew last night, therefore not necessary to wipe down mahogany. About 9 o'clock decided to mop the deck and sponge out cockpit. So we are clean upstairs. Mailed two cards, one to Cooney [Harold Coons] and other to Elizabeth [Richman] at Lock 47.

Most of the locks have two gates that hinge at either side and open out from. the center. #47 has one gate at each end that is pulled back and forth into a tunnel in the bank.

River is prettier here than around Evansville, some hills. Are nearing Mt. Vernon whose spires, courthouse dome, and smokestacks show up several miles up river. The next day marker, a target with black center is almost on a line with the courthouse, but near the shore line

Went through lock #49 without delay. Locks are numbered down river from Pittsburgh.

At junction of Wabash River took last look at Indiana. Took picture of Light 847.9 - miles from Pittsburgh. Last picture on first film. Weather warmer. Took off shirt but am sitting in the shade to avoid sunburn. We are only about 8 miles from Shawneetown where we expected to tie up tonight. But at 2:30 we still have 2 ½ hours of running time.

With the smoke of Shawneetown in sight, spotted an army camp on Ky. shore and a lot of solders crossing from the Ill. side on pontoons, life rafts, and old boats. Picture 9 was of 3 pontoons tied together. Picture 10 of one pontoon load with a couple of boys swimming behind. We got a good cheer from them. The river is lousy with boats showing off. Evidently gasoline is plentiful in Shawneetown.

After we passed Shawneetown the river ran almost straight a little east of south for 7 or 8 miles with a strong south wind that made white caps. The bow as I am writing sprayed water over the cockpit.

We went through lock 50 just before 6 o'clock and anchored a mile below. While the cook was busy I caught 5 fiddler cats which we later threw back, no one wanting fish. We listened to radio until 9:30. But were too sleepy to wait for 10 o'clock news.

Made 86 miles today.

Monday, Sept. 11

Up at 6:30, breakfast of grapefruit juice, soft boiled eggs, butter, jelly, and coffee. Under way at 7:30. Took 11th picture of rock bluff sheer to the water on Ill. side a little above the town of Cave-in-Rock where there is a picnic ground, well kept, reached by concrete road on Ill. side and ferry from Ky.

Soon after I wrote above it started to rain and kept it up fitfully all day. Every time we reached a lock it rained harder. I put on my duckbax trousers, woolen socks, raincoat and kept warm though damp.

The last lock on the Ohio is No. 53. About 2 miles below it we anchored for the night. Our wet clothes went into the engine room and were dry in the morning. We settled down after a steak dinner to the Monday evening good programs. After the Carnation Hour [orchestral music] we turned, off the lights.

Sept 12.

Up about 7 and on our way soon. Our breakfast was eggless. While I was scrubbing the toilets and cabin floors we sailed almost to Cairo. Cap decided not to stop because there is no place to tie up. I decided that if Elizabeth was worse I would get news through some of the government boats as I told [my wife] Edith [Richman] I could be reached through the Coast Guard.

Cairo isn't much of a town but there is a lot of barge traffic coming both up and down the Mississippi and Ohio. I took a picture of a light on the point that separates the two rivers. A bridge across the Miss. shows up in the background. We have a higher stage of water in the Miss and are traveling. Clessie thinks we will be in Memphis tomorrow night which is a day earlier than he expected and two days earlier than I wrote to Edith. We are wasting no time on this part of the river which is somewhat difficult to navigate and not very interesting. Ahead of us is a big tow of barges pushed by a screw propelled steamer which doesn't throw as much waves as a paddle wheel. If it is going as fast as we today we shall follow it down.

I took the wheel for a while so that the others might shift the dinghy to the port side with its bow forward to give more vision to the pilot.

We came up behind a big tow - a Miss. Valley Barge Co. Steamer pushing 12 or 13 barges. It had to slow down for a sharp bend in the river with a narrow channel close to a chalk cliff where at some stages of the river there is a violent river pool that has been known to suck under a barge. We steered alongside at a distance of about 100 ft. to avoid her backwash and stayed there until the channel widened. Now we are letting her forge ahead and will follow. Our boat is capable of a little more speed but we know that where the tow goes we can follow as she draws more water that the Dipper.

The day is cloudy with sun shining between rifts. The boat is clean and we are very comfortable.

4:30 P.M.

We have revised our calculations as to arrival in Memphis. When we stop tonight we'll be about 140 miles from Memphis, which means a day plus run, as we are making about 100 miles per day. Took a picture of a crazy looking tug boat pushing barges up stream. It was painted several colors and looked like a crazy quilt. The day has remained clear. We have run all directions today, east, west, north and south. The river twists and twists. All sorts of schemes are in use to prevent it from cutting across low places to make new channels. Long stretches of piles sticking far out in the stream. On the banks concrete slabs in rows. Sometimes long stretches of concrete.

I am interested in the whirling, swirling waters wherever the current is swift. There are pockets of' sand beneath the water, holes dug out by the whirlpools and constantly shifting bottom. The whirlpools catch the boat making it a constant necessity to shift its helm from side to side, not much but enough to swing the other direction.

We anchored about 6 o'clock after a run of 102 miles. Our fuel consumption has averaged 7 ½ miles to the gallon.

Sept. 13.

Up at 7. We have been following a tow until she slowed down. Ahead of her was an engineering steamer changing buoys. We have just passed her while she was sounding. She stopped and floated with the current while a man on either side used the lead to find the depth. Beyond her toward the west shore was a bar on which the waves broke. Shoals can be detected by the way the waves of a passing vessel break. If they get larger near the shore the water is shoal. An experienced eye can detect where the bar begins although there may be water a mile wide between the bar and the shore.

About 11 A.M. took a picture of a dredge boat with long line of barges and pipe on top of pumping sane. At the end of the pipe was a spout of dirty water. 1/150 - 11.

At 1:30 a big naval vessel passed us going about 18 miles per hour. She surely made waves. We swayed through them until we got directly behind her and then were in the clear. We should have counted the tows of barges. Oil going up. Chemicals and what not down. A hundred or more already.

The 16th picture was of a typical day marker with light alongside to which we had headed from the opposite side of the river 1 ½ to 2 miles distant. I used a filter to get the clouds. 1/150 -16.

#17 sandstone bluffs on Tenn. Shore 147 miles from Cairo. These bluffs forced the river to turn east in a sharp bend with narrow channel.

We stopped about 6 o'clock having a little trouble getting anchorage near the foot of a bar. The current was strong. When we got out of it in stiller water and dropped the anchor into shoal water and we just touched the bar. I lifted and dropped the anchor three times before we felt safe. Did I sweat? The winch with a full sweep of the hand raises the anchor only about six inches. It took many sweeps.

Sept. 14.

On our way at 7:10 about 42 miles from Memphis. I've cleaned the boat, shaved, taken sponge bath, got the ropes ready for tying up at Memphis which is in sight. Took one picture this morning, a log pile, truck unloading, barge loading on the Arkansas side.

Arrived Memphis at 11:30. The channel used to run along the water front a block from the business district. Many fine homes were built on the heights north of the business district overlooking the river. Now there is a long wooded island east of the channel and between the island and the former shore line a narrow dirty canal into which sewage and greasy water runs. The opening cannot be seen from upriver. We went up this canal about 2 blocks and tied to the Tri State Boat Co. barge, Mr. Ainslee proprietor. We could not have chosen a better or safer place. He had a derrick with which on a wide "belly (sling) band" he lifted the stern of the Big Dipper about 2 feet so that Clessie could repack and tighten the stuffing box around the propeller shaft which has been giving us some concern all the way down. There has been a leak making it necessary to run the electric pump about 4 or 5 minutes every hour. But this morning (15th) the leak is of minor consequence.

There was fresh water and a 50 lb. hose on the barge and we filled our water tanks. Standard Oil brought fuel oil to us. It took 75 gal. to fill our tanks which means that we have averaged 6 7/9 miles to the gallon.

We are able to get 100 lbs. of ice in the box, which will last at least to Baton Rouge where we have to go in to check with the Coast Guard. We also laid in a supply of food, milk, butter, eggs, steak etc. to last until New Orleans, a run of about 6 days.

Had lunch at a hotel the name of which I do not remember and dinner at the Peabody. Clessie and I each talked to our homes. Elizabeth has recovered and is going to school. Harold is probably headed overseas. [Daughter] Marge [Coons] arrived safely and is now at the Mills Hotel in Ozark. Mrs. Johnson [mother of Bruce Johnson, one of Frank Richman's sons-in-law] is worse and probably will not live beyond January. My older girls are having their troubles.

In bed at nine except Earl who went to a movie and came in at ten.

September 15.

Up at 6:40, breakfast a little café about 1 ½ blocks from the boat, mailed letters home and got some road maps to orient ourselves with the river. On our way at 8:15, a beautiful day, cool while running but we need no sweaters. Below Memphis there is a power line crossing the river, with a tall steel tower on either side. On the east side the tower was originally on the shore but the river has washed out behind and now the tower stands out on the river on four tall caissons that look like smoke stacks. I took a picture # 19 but the light was not good and it may not show up - 1/150 - 8.

#20 a "snagboat," a part of U.S. E.D. equipment for pulling out snags. They also set buoys. We passed it in shoal water. It bounced us up and down until the water sprayed back in the cockpit.

#21 is the Tenn. Shore line at the end of long stretch of concrete blocks. A marker at the shore is at the break of the old and new construction and should show what the river does to the most sturdy kind of embankments.

At 1:20 passed a raft of logs pulled by a little houseboat. A darky standing on the raft to nail saplings to the logs to hold them in the raft v section. Took two pictures # 22 and # 23 of it. Each 1/150 16.

24 landing quarters of Engineering Dep't on cargos moored to the shore just above place where a large crew was working swinging concrete blocks to shore and lining them up in a long revetment.

About a mile beyond this work is a cut oft of about ½ mile that saves about 20 miles of river travel.

Wherever the river is narrow and shallow passing a big tow bobs our boat up and down. Several of the waves broke over the bow and splattered water over Earl's pajamas hanging in the forward cabin.

His name is now the Earl of Buttermilk. When he opened a milk bottle for lunch he discovered that he had bought six quarts of buttermilk, in lieu of milk, at Memphis. Well, they say buttermilk is good for you.

At 3 o'clock passed Helena, Ark.; about the same distance from Memphis by road as by river.

#25 work on revetments down river from Helena. Anchored at 5:30 100 miles from Memphis. Steak dinner. Until sundown lay on deck. No shirt on, but it wasn't long until had shirt and jacket. Then some mosquitoes arrived sending us below with closed hatch. Slept with one blanket.

Sept. 16.

Up at 6:30. Undertook to make pancakes of Aunt Jemima's flour and measurably succeeded. At least got Cap out of the cabin and on deck.

No dew last night. On our way at 7:30. Have been through 2 cuts this morning. Below these cuts a few miles two dredges were in operation, one on each side of river, sucking out some of the sand washed out of the cuts. We sailed between them and I took # 26 and # 27. 1/150 4-5. We are headed due east now, after having gone west earlier this morning for 6 or 7 miles.

After one has watched the pattern of the markers it is not difficult to guess at where the next one will show up. Ordinarily you can not see it until after the last one has been passed.

There will be several lights on the higher bank which mark the outside of the curve, under which the river continuously undermines causing great hunks of shore line including large trees to fall into the water. Where a point, or apparent point, on the shoreline is reached there will be a marker (light at night) and the next one will be a mile and a half or two miles away on the opposite shore. This will be followed awhile until the channel shifts across. So one travels back and cross, back and cross, never with a right angle turn. Sometimes indeed the line is almost straight down stream, first close to the left and then to the right bank.

The river today is monotonous, little traffic, hazy light, quite warm. The engine purrs along and is conducive to sleep. I've been on deck most of the day, occasionally at the wheel for a few minutes. Earl has been reading a detective story lying in the cabin. Clessie sits in his revolving chair, at the wheel, whistling, singing, picking up the glasses - very fine Zeiss lens 7-50 (7 power 50 mil. opening) to pick up the number of miles painted on the marker and check up with his charts on the location of the channel. The miles are numbered from the Delta. New Orleans is 95, or in round numbers, 100, Memphis 730. The Ohio, on the contrary, is numbered down river from Pittsburgh. We stopped last night at 6:30. Today we are averaging 10.6 miles per hour and should be close to # 520 when we anchor.

29 is an engineering quarters barge moored to the Mississippi state shore north of Greenville. Both Arkansas City and Greenville used to be on the river but it is now miles away.

Anchored about 5:30 just above Greenville bridge, a highway bridge that crosses the river several miles below the town. Just before we reached our anchorage we passed a big naval ship 101 - don't know the type - which evidently had propellor trouble and was tied up to the shore, with barges between, and had its stern lifted with floating dry dock, but apparently not high enough. So it looks like he may get a tow down to New Orleans.

Just after we anchored a landing ship tanks came down shoving the water aside and giving us several rolls. We anchored at light 524.5.

Steak is cooking. We have just heard the baseball and football scores, the news from all the war fronts and will have music for dinner entertainment. The river is about 3/4 mile wide here and we are within 1/8 of the east shore in 12 ft. anchorage along a bar. From now on we let the world go by.

Sunday, Sept. 17.

After we anchored last night several more big naval ships went down the river including 101, which was being pushed by a tow boat. We turned off the lights at 9 o'clock and were up at 6:40. I had a chance to swab the decks before breakfast and afterwards cleaned the cabin and rearranged the baggage so we can get at things more easily. I had missed my Sat. night bath so took it this morning, put on all clean clothes and feel like a new man.

The river is very wide and the channel close to the center, with wide long crossings. A haze obscures the markers on the east shore, where the shadows of the trees make it difficult, even with the glasses, to pick out the markers. Not much traffic this morning.

30 is the McDermott, a pile driver, 1/150 11.

At marker 466 plus we saw the first live cypress covered with Spanish moss. We have seen stumps of cypress for many miles and uncovered in recent years by shifting currents.

Passing Vicksburg at 4:10 P.M. - marker 431. Took # 31 1/150   16 with yellow filter. The town is a disappointment. No signs of war activity on the waterfront. Bridge just below has seven spans 6 over water.

Anchored at 5:45 at 414 having traveled 110 miles in 10 hours. We swung out of the channel alongside a bar in rather swift water, Dinner of steak, green beans, asparagus tips with french dressing.

Sept. 18.

Our brilliant cook at the request of the crew last night stewed prunes for breakfast and this morning gave us V8.

During the night a tree, or some portion thereof, caught in our anchor chain, aroused the captain and the steward but left the deck hand sleeping until the other two created such a disturbance that he poked his head through the hatch to find out what it was all about. Yells for the pike pole, which the others couldn't find because it was carefully stowed where the deck hand couldn't stumble over it, took me out on deck. Trouble soon subsided and so far as I was concerned sleep was resumed.

After dinner last night we watched two towboats about two miles apart struggle upstream about two miles per hour. We decided the current must be plenty swift. This morning it is proved for in the first 45 minutes we have gone 12 miles.

At marker # 383 from a distance it seems as if dredge pipes completely cross the river. Then red and black buoys show up marking a passage toward the center of the pipe line where a barge is located close to two little houses on the pontoons carrying the pipe lines. Clessie has now reduced the engine speed to 500 r.p.m. We can see a place where they evidently will cut the pipe line. I'll get a picture as we go through.

The construction company in charge of' the dredging operation held us up a half hour. They first signaled us to go through a 50 ft. passage between the dredge barge and the shore where the water was boiling with a 10 to 12 mile current. Clessie refused and they finally opened the line in the center where we expected it to be opened. I took 2 pictures 31 and 32, the latter facing the opening in the dredge pipe.

Passed Natchez at 12:15 P.M. Took two pictures, # 33 headed over the bow at the town, # 34 of some of the houses on the bluff overlooking the river. There is a new bridge just below the town but government regulations forbid pictures of bridges or naval vessels, so forbore getting a good picture with the light just right. # 33 may show up because I used yellow filter but I have my doubts. # 35 is the car ferry at the La. Shore. The engine has just pushed a flat car almost to the box car on the ferry. At 1:15 we passed the Sprague, the biggest tow boat on the river, stern paddle wheel 48' in diameter. Has been known to have 90 barges at one time. Engines have 3000 h.p. I got a picture and Clessie was taking movies just as we passed. Earl was eating lunch and was called up to take the wheel so we could get our pictures. Then Earl yelled to me, "Get the wheel," and he dived below to put his long arms around the table to keep the dished from sliding off. About that time we hit the swell and poured the water into the open forward porthole, bounced the boat up and down like an egg shell in a mill race. The channel was narrow. We were between the Sprague and the shore and while he slowed down his paddle before he reached us to take a little of the edge off the bouncing, we had plenty. Everybody laughed except Earl who couldn't see what was coming. He sleeps in the forward cabin. Will let him discover a wet bed.

From 330 to 320 there is a beautiful stretch of river, wide, deep, long bends, with trees growing in even rows along the outer shore or the bend. At 320 I took # 37, showing a beautiful oak tree on top of the bank and some typical shanty boats at the water's edge, with one lifted high and dry about half way up the bank.

Since the Sprague, and a little later, another large stern paddle wheel bounced us throwing water over the deck and into the forward port hole, we have monotonously chugged down the river, most of the times with Earl at the wheel. As we go further down navigation is simpler, the bends are longer, the river is deeper, there are few whirlpools, and "Old Man Ribber just goes rollin' along." I stayed on deck in a shady place, shirtless, shoeless, too lazy to go below to read a book. It's a very restful vacation.

The going is so easy that we have decided to go into New Orleans Wednesday evening. Arrival after 4 o'clock is too late for it takes several hours to get through the traffic and the canal to West End on Lake Pontchartrain.

So we roll until 6:45 P.M. to marker 290.6, a total of 125 miles.

We are out of steak, buttermilk (thanks), running low on ice, but are not starving.

Tuesday, Sept. 19.

Up at 6:30 on our way at 7:00 of a beautiful morning. One of the reasons for running late last night was to take advantage of a long east bend while the sun was at our backs, rather than in the morning.

About 10:15 last night I heard water begin to lap against the hull and climbed up to investigate. A wind from the S.E., the prevailing direction, had stirred up wavelets. We were anchored with bow to the west of north so the waves hit broadside. Clessie came up also. We saw searchlights coming from around the bend and decided to watch the ship go by. We thought at first she was the Sprague but, while of the same type, she was not big enough to even wake the sleeping Earl of Buttermilk.

At 11:30 checked the mileage. We are averaging today only 10 miles per hour. There is a little current to aid us - possibly 2 miles per hour. This is the hottest day. Clessie has changed to shorts and is barefooted. It helps. No traffic has shown up so far. Baton Rouge is 10 milers away. Ocean lines can navigate that far up the stream.

38, 39, and 40 of Baton Rouge, Hewey Long's temple, the state capitol which stands out in two. The third # 40 was attempted behind the dinghy to avoid taking the coast guard station or letting anyone there see me taking pictures. It was supposed to catch the old capitol building.

I was cooking pancakes when we passed B.R. and popped up and down to get the pictures and still watch the pancakes. But we are all fed and good for another five hours.

4:00 P.M. The sun has burned me today. I have kept out of the direct rays but reflected light from the water has done the work. The monotony of a 10 mile per hour speed has been broken by a tow of which I got a good picture 1/150 6 with yellow filter.

42 the Baton Rouge pushing a barge filled with sulphur and some large green barges.

Behind us is a large naval vessel just wishing to pass as we hit the back wash from the tow. He has signaled to pass us to starboard and we are making toward the shore. Immediately behind her water is reasonably smooth so we quartered through the bow wash to travel her. I have made a picture of her stern. There were no identification marks on her.

Not because we wished to run so late but because of no place to anchor appeared we ran until 7 o'clock and anchored near the upper end of a none too wide bar at # 173 a run of 117.6 miles. Before finding this place we tried another but the deep water was so close to shore that to get even twenty feet depth for anchor an off shore wind would blow the stern against the bank. That's the kind of wind we had keeping the mosquitoes and flies away, cooling the cabin. About 10 o'clock after we had been "lights out" for an hour, C and I went on deck to argue our position, he insisting that we were farther off shore than when we anchored, but I half convinced him and he was satisfied in the morning.

Wednesday, Sept.20.

We started at 6:30, not at full speed because of fog, which after an hour is not entirely gone. But we'll be in N.O. by 2:30 P.M. which will give us plenty of time to get through the locks at the canal and over to West End. We'll have dinner at one of the places. No ice, no bread, it's time.

9 A.M. It's a lovely day, an east wind, and we are traveling east and southeast. The sun is in our eyes making it difficult to see the markers, but the channel is wide and deep (no eddies) and we have no navigation difficulties. The river is prettier here than in the stretch from Cairo to Natchez. 11:30 we passed a navy tanker Tule Canyon. # 43

United States Navy tanker Tule Canyon, 1944

We ate lunch at 12 so that we would all be on deck to see N.O. from the waterfront. About 1:30 passed under the Huey Long bridge, a massive structure with long approaches. From then on until we tied up to Higgins experimental dock at the Yacht Club we were too busy looking to write and I took no pictures. The river goes around N.O. - it's called the Crescent City.

When we got to West End we were not more than 4 or 5 miles from the river north of N.O. but in the meanwhile we had traveled 5 hours going through one lock, under numerous bridges several of which had to be lifted to let us through.

Everywhere we looked we saw Higgins name. Clessie called him to get permission to tie up to his dock. He said, "Sure, I want to see you anyway." (He drove over next morning but Clessie missed him by about 5 minutes.) The dock had uniformed police protection and we didn't lock up. The chief engineer let us use his telephones, the policeman got ice for us, and we had most satisfactory moorings.

As we passed N.O. in the river and canal we must have seen at least 500 sea going gray and camouflaged ships either ready to leave or about ready and many more in process of construction. When this war ends and its contracts are terminated there surely will be an exodus of shipyard workers.

We wasted no time getting dressed. The chief engineer drove us to the Roosevelt Hotel where Earl vainly tried to get a room. He checked his bag and we made for Antoine's. Including the liquid refreshments it cost us about $10 but now we can say we've been there. The food was good but we could duplicate the meal for $5 or $6 at other good places in N.O.

C and I took the streetcar back to the boat, about 30 minute ride. On deck it was cool but the sun from the west had beaten in and the boat was lower than the dock so we were not too cool without covers.

September 21.

In the morning we went down on the car and met Earl at the post office. He and I spent most of the day together, some window shopping, a little actual shopping, a haircut, a shampoo and shave, and we were back on the boat by 4 o'clock.

In the meanwhile C had a man out for a couple of hours on the lake (mildly salt) checking the two compasses. After laying in some provision we headed for a restaurant about (walking) where we had an excellent meal. We got back after dark and did our telephoning arranging for my reservation to Louisville leaving Pensacola Sunday night.

About 10 o'clock in bed. During the night a violent thundershower. I didn't shut the port hole tight enough and when I went back to bed found a puddle on the rubber cushion. So there was some shifting of bedclothes, etc.

Sept. 22.

On our way at 6:45. I have marked our course on a highway map. We are on salt water steering sometimes by compass but assisted at the uncertain places by buoys. It's a beautiful north wind, fresh air, just enough waves to swing in gently. We couldn't ask for better crossing weather. We expect to tie up in Pascagoula tonight but it will probably take us until dark.

Speed is about 9 miles per hour. We ran until about 8 P.M. getting into Pascagoula harbor and anchoring on the opposite side of the channel, just above the ship yards. It was a big hard day, part of the time rolling in the wash between the waves as we went crosswise with the wind. When the course changed so that we headed against the wind, the big waves broke against the mast lashed to the deck and sprayed salt water over the helmsman and passengers. This isn't anything but a sheltered inland water way. Sometimes little waves have a sweep of 25 or 30 miles from the north or northeast. Our course usually was nearer the islands that make it a so-called inland water way, so we were sheltered from south winds but they were not coming from that direction.

I've lost track of the pictures taken, but they will be recognized when developed.

Sept. 23.

On our way at 8:00 A.M. after refueling at a Standard Oil station just across the channel. We retraced our track for miles down the line of buoys that leads from: the Gulf to Pascagoula. Then we turned to the east and really hit the waves. Closed all portholes, anchored all movables below, got my raincoat on and stood in the cockpit, while the spray blinded my glasses and salted up my face. We had probably thirty miles of this until we got into shoal water between Mississippi Sound and Mobile Bay and were anticipating a rough time crossing the bay. But the wind had died down and we're now chugging along in comparatively smooth water. It was cool this morning but now we're shedding garments. I thought I got a pretty naked picture of C steering from the rear cockpit but now he's completely nude. I don't want to break the camera.

I wrote too soon about the lack of inland waterways. For 8 or 9 miles we have been traveling down the center of a 150 canal cut and dredged through the land, in some places rock. It's slow going when you have the comparison of an auto speeding along a road that parallels the canal.

The prettiest stretch of landscape of the trip from N.O. to Pascagoula began soon after we left the canal. Little lakes - brackish water - have been connected by dredged channels, and on some there are cottages. The pine trees are larger and the shores are not so barren.

After estimating the distance to Pensacola and checking the charts which showed a lot of crooked channels with markers that would be confusing at night, at 6 o'clock we anchored in a little lake with sandy beaches, put the dinghy in the water for the first time since leaving Madison and had a swim in Nature's bathing suits. We were still 25 or 30 miles from Pensacola. Not worried about our anchorage we slept fine.

Sept. 24.

At 8 o'clock weighed anchor and against a brisk east wind got into deeper water and ultimately into Pensacola Bay where the waves were quite choppy but did not break over the deck. For miles and miles along the shore are the permanently built structures of the Naval Air Station. Sea planes were taking off and landing, Coast Guard launches and crash boats stationed on both sides of the bay in anticipation of accidents. The bay is a fine harbor for sea going ships, really the only one that is convenient between N.O. and the west coast of Fla. peninsula.

A light house on the shore with light visible for 20 miles lead directly from the Gulf to the bay through a wide deep channel. Mobile and Pascagoula, as well as Gulfport have long narrow dredged channels leading to the anchorage. Clessie says that lack of railroad facilities at Pensacola and perhaps lack of wealth in the town have been responsible for backwardness in developing its natural advantages.

About 11:30 we tied up at a dock of Warren Fish Co. and our journey was at an end, without a scratch on the boat or any of it's cargo, with one exception.

Earl had concave round shaving mirror, which he prized very highly. He was in the habit of setting it on the drain board of the sink where he stood to shave and carelessly left it there the morning we were coming out of Pascagoula . When we hit the rough water and rolled in the trough of the waves it fell and was broken. I made secure all secure all the other breakables that morning but didn't see his mirror.

Only once did we ground and that was also coming out of Pascagoula. In dredging the channel the sand is deposited along the edges and C, while trying to 1ine up our course with the markers behind up on one of the sandy banks. He slowed the engine immediately, reversed and backed off.

The day before Earl and I were navigators while C was taking a nap, we got confused by a couple of markers - buoys - one of which guarded a shoal shown on the chart as 4 ft. and must have gone directly over it, but without grounding.

Some of the range finders are quite interesting. They are towers, pyramidal in shape with light at the top, one in front of the other in the line of the channel. To get the course, either day or night, after one marker is left behind, it is necessary to get the two ahead directly in line with the one behind and keep them so, which is often quite difficult against winds or tide. Usually a white marker is in front and a black one behind. At night there are two green lights on the markers which must be kept in line.

After we tied to the wharf we cleaned up and started for the hotel - the same one Edith, Elizabeth and I had stayed in when we were in Pensacola in January 1938. On our way Jack Higgins who manages several of the principal industries - a fleet of fishing schooners, a ship yards where crash boats are under construction, marine supply store which sells Cummins engines, drove up as we were walking about a block from the boat hailed Clessie as "Hello Boss", took us to the L and N station where he had reserved pullman space for me to Louisville. I got my tickets and then he took us to the hotel. After dinner, like most sailors ashore, we made for the water front, watched a sailboat race from the porch of the Yacht Club, and then walked back to the boat. Earl left us, got a room in the hotel, came back with a taxi at 6 o'clock, took my luggage to the railroad. station, and then to the hotel for supper. We walked Clessie back to the boat where he will spend his days and nights for perhaps a week until the sails are rigged. The boat will be pulled out of the water so that the stuffing box, which gave us more or less trouble all the way down, may be repacked an the hull painted. In Memphis it got quite discolored by the black oil that was in the canal. Benzene, soap and elbow grease will take it off before the repainting. From now on the boat will be in the clear salt water of the Gulf. The salt does the paint no good but does not discolor.

My pen went dry and I'm finishing this recital of a very interesting voyage of about 1500 miles on an L & N train Monday Sept. 25 as we leave Decatur, Ala. Home tonight at 9:15 and back at work tomorrow.

Chapter 11

Travel Diaries

"What is a diary as a rule? A document useful to the person who keeps it, dull to the contemporary who reads it, invaluable to the student, centuries afterwards, who treasures it!"

Ellen Terry, *The Story of My Life*, 1908

Elizabeth S. Bowman

My wife, Elizabeth Bowman often keeps diaries of our travels. Her main reason for writing these diaries is so she can label the pictures she has taken once she has returned. For me these diaries provide a wonderful review of our trips taken together.

The first diary, printed below in its entirety, is her diary of our vacation to France in 2003. The next series of excerpts from her travel diaries contains highlights from our travels to Canada, Europe, and Central and South America.[1]

Paris, Normandy, and Human Nature: A 2003 Hoosier Perspective

Phil and I arrived in France on September 11, 2002 and returned on Friday, September 20, arriving back in Indianapolis around 8 PM. The trip was magically wonderful. Except for two gray days and a little rain in Paris, we had fabulous weather: clear skies and mild temperatures during the entire time we were out in the countryside of Normandy. Our guide kept gushing over how good the weather was, and how many years it had been since that part of France had gone for a week without rain. We took her word for it and goggled at the incredibly picturesque villages, farms, chateaux, rivers, vineyards, gardens, and the roads lined by rows of trees extending toward the horizon. There is really no way to verbally convey the charm of Normandy. Small wonder so many artists painted it.

We began with two nights in Paris. The afternoon of our arrival, Phil and I strolled around the Tuilleries garden (a block from our hotel) and watched the children sailing their boats in the fountain. We explored the two islands in the Seine that make up the very heart of the oldest part of the city. We took the advice of a friend and made sure we kissed on quite a few of the bridges over the river. The French are far more demonstrative in public than either of us (especially Phil), so we figured we would just blend in. That evening, we took a river cruise on the Bateaux Mouches (sightseeing boats). The weather had cleared and the sunset and cool air were lovely. As we sailed by Notre Dame Cathedral, we could hear the organ playing. It was magical. The next day we took the obligatory "overview" bus tour and saw the Mona Lisa, the Eiffel Tower, and various quarters of the city. We next took the funicular up to Mont Martre topped by the majestic, gleaming white domes of the Sacre Coeur church. The rest of Mont Martre is very charming – little shops and artists everywhere. It is where the film Amelie was shot. We found lunch beside a square jammed with artists displaying paintings. We were told that this hill (Mont Martre) was composed of rock rich in gypsum that was mined for centuries to make plaster (thus the term Plaster of Paris). To build Sacre Coeur, they had to blast out the caves from the mines to get to bedrock. I learned something new every day.

Our hotel was to have been the Intercontinental, but we were out-booked to the Lotti, a half block away, because a Mid-Eastern royal family decided to extend their two-month stay at the last minute. Money talks.....theirs did anyway! The Lotti, though smaller, was also gorgeous. Our room had a large marble bathroom and its own little balcony. The hotel was in a very upscale district, half a block from the Ritz on Vendôme Square. We were on the "jewelry" street, with the "crystal" street just a block over. Nice window shopping! Cartier was a block away. Resisting the urge to shop was sheer torture, but I held up. (Sigh…) The Godiva Chocolate store was only 1 block away. I am so proud that I didn't even go in it! Yes, I was sorely tempted. The huge, ornately carved, column-lined, gold-statue-topped old opera building was about 7 minutes walk away and was utterly impressive. Paris is just so elegant. Fortunately, there were also plenty of small cafes in the area, so we were able to eat "normal food" (Italian, etc) when we weren't being stuffed with elegant French cuisine in the hotel. We each gained 1 pound or less, thanks to a lot of walking every day.

The next day we left for the Loire Valley by way of Versailles. The weather was gorgeous, so the photos of the Versailles palace grounds should be wonderful. The gardens and fountains continue to amaze me. No wonder the French had a bloody revolution. That kind of excess in the face of an impoverished peasantry was a time-bomb – something of which we should take note. I thought about the eventual outcome of our ever-growing gap between the rich and poor in the USA. Phil and I skipped the palace tour. We'd been there and done that one. Besides, we can't replicate the interior design (or structure) at home! To this gardener, the gardens were far more interesting. We stopped next at Chartres to see the famous cathedral with two different spires. It is equally impressive inside. Fortunately, they buried the stained glass windows during WWII, so they survived the bombings. These were generations of poor ordinary people who worked for centuries on this massive cathedral with their own hands. It is an astounding mute testimony to the power of faith. The carvings inside (behind the choir area) were incredible. The place is so huge it is overpowering. It's a good analogy for the presence of God.

We then headed into the lush Loire Valley. The land was extremely green, dotted with charming old stone farmhouses and small villages of equally quaint buildings. The vineyards of the Loire valley were just at harvest time, so some were still laden with grapes. The chateaux were incredibly impressive, ranging from the "small" one in which we stayed two nights (17th century Chateau Marçay with 35 hotel rooms) to some huge castle-like ones on hillsides presiding over the valleys and villages below. Most were Renaissance and Enlightenment era, but some dated to the Middle Ages. The towns that were not bombed to smithereens in WWII were adorable. The streets are narrow, lined with stone buildings with tiny, neat, flower gardens. The churches were mostly from the 17-18th century and often had more classical Gothic style, except for their steeples. Many of the steeples were modern and clearly didn't fit the rest of the church architecture. WWII German snipers often nested in church steeples, so the Allies blew up a lot of them. They also bombed several villages to complete rubble, like Caen, so they were nearly completely modern in style, much more ugly than the old villages.

After two nights in Paris, we spent the next two at the Chateau Marçay, beside the tiny village of Marçay, near the village of Chinon southwest of Tours. Chinon has good local wine, but they drink it all in the Loire valley, so it isn't something we'll ever taste again. The 17th century Chateau Marçay was built atop a 12th or 13th century cellar, but had lovely walled outdoor courtyards and gardens, and was surrounded by its own vineyard. We weren't roughing it. Despite the ancient wood beams crossing the ceiling, the interior of the room was quite modern, right down to the padded fabric wall covering and the very modern marble bathroom with hair dryer. Our British guide was in a tower room and told us she thought it was haunted. In the middle of the night, she saw lights coming from beneath a door off of her room and when she opened it, there was nothing but an abandoned stairway full of cobwebs there. She said she spent the rest of the night with the light on! Fortunately, our room was less "exciting": the only lights were coming from the garden below and from the floodlights on the village steeple about a quarter of a mile away.

The chef at the chateau was very impressive. The five to six course dinners at Chateau Marçay were beyond description, but I'll try to put some dishes into words. We had quail eggs flavored three ways as part of our appetizer, served as part of what looked more like a work of art than a platter of food. One night our appetizer was foie gras de canard with slivers of very tender beef tongue through it. Melted in my mouth. We also had local fish (from that part of the local river) and meats, and the local wines (of course). I couldn't begin to tell you the name of some of the things I ate, but they were superb. The French don't know how to drive (Parisian drivers are a nightmare and a public health risk) but they are incredible in the kitchen. The only saving grace is that Phil and I got so tired by the end of the third course (which came about 9:30 or 10 PM) that we often skipped dessert. Often, but not always! I am taking chemotherapy for a malignant brain tumor. It saps my energy, but not my spirit! We each gained one pound – not bad, considering the food we were offered. How the French escape coronary artery disease is beyond me. Maybe it's all that wine, or maybe just the genetic endowment of those whose ancestors survived that rich food long enough to pass on their DNA.

The Chateau Marçay was delightful. In the walkway between the exquisitely decorated lobby and the bar, the exposed stone wall still had the weapon slits visible. There were more plastered-in weapons slits on the outside of the two towers. These really were fortresses. No wonder there might have been a restless spirit there – I imagine a few people died in battle there. We visited several large chateaux with historical significance (and drove by a lot more). One, the huge Chateau Chenonçeau, is built across a river, serving as a home and a bridge. It was built by a French Noble or King for his mistress (Diane de Poitiers). When he died, his wife, the strong-minded Katherine of Medici, threw Diane out and took over the chateau. Of course she completely re-decorated it to obliterate the memory of her rival. She even had her own garden designed, so as not to have to share a garden with the former mistress. Human nature is remarkably stable, isn't it? This chateau was a hospital in WWI and still had a fresh flower memorial to the wounded in the large corridor that likely served as the major ward. We had an exquisite lunch at the restaurant on the grounds.

We also visited the Clos Lucé, a chateau where Leonardo DaVinci spent the last 3 years of his life and died. It was charming and had miniature models of more than 30 of Da Vinci's inventions in a museum there (the parachute, water cannon, hang gliders and other things he sketched). When he died, Italy claimed his heart, but the rest of his anatomy was interred in France. I don't want to think of the condition of that heart by the time it reached Italy again…. I hope it was transported in the winter! We passed the ancient castle where Joan of Arc came to beg the King of France for an army, and later in Normandy, the town of Caen where she was burned. Society (especially the church) still can't tolerate strong women. *Plus ça change*…oh, I already wrote that!

We went next to Mont St. Michel, the quasi island village on the Atlantic, topped by the St. Michel Abbey and church. The causeway no longer floods at high tide and we were there at mid-phase of the moon when the extremely high tides (more than 30 feet) do not occur. We stayed dry, visited the abbey's many levels perched atop the hill and marveled at the sanctuary where the back two-thirds is Romanesque and the choir and altar areas are Gothic. The church and abbey are perched on the top of the very steep rocky island, so they only could put the very center of the nave on bedrock. Consequently, over the centuries, three of the four arms of the cross-shaped church collapsed and had to be rebuilt. The last one to collapse was the very front, so it was re-built in the current style (Gothic). The lower levels of the monastery go back to the 11th century. It's a maze. Wouldn't have wanted to try to find my way though it without our guide, Anne-Marie. The rest of the island is a single street steeply winding ever upward around the island, below the towering church above. The street is lined by contiguous 15th to 17th century buildings and tons of shops and restaurants. We ate lunch there overlooking the sand flats that surround the island. We were told they contain deadly quicksand and can only be traversed safely with an experienced guide. The guides carry ropes and long sticks when taking groups out there. In the Middle Ages when the only way to get to Mt. St. Michel was over the sand, there were true guides who provided safe passage and false guides who took pilgrims out there and intentionally got them into quicksand to rob them and leave them to die. I presume that's why they had confession in the church! Encore, *plus ça change*…. We stayed in a little modern hotel that was at the junction of the mainland and the causeway out to Mt. St. Michel. That meant spending dinner (great seafood) watching the floodlights come up over the monastery and the island slowly light up in the dark. Our room faced the island, so we feasted our eyes on it all evening. Clouds came in so we didn't get to see a fabulous sunset. Still, it was charming beyond words.

We spent the next day touring the WWII landing beach area of the Normandy coast. We saw the Point d'Hoc (American soil now) where the first Rangers came up cliffs by rope to take the gun emplacements (which had been abandoned by the Germans). It has been left 'as it was' on 6-6-44, complete with huge bomb craters everywhere. We walked on the now peaceful flat sands of Omaha Beach in good sunny weather, staring in awe at the dunes once topped by German machine guns and bunkers. We visited the more than 9000 white grave markers in the American military cemetery nearby, on Sept 15. It's gorgeous, but quite sobering. There is a garden for unknowns, missing, and unidentified remains. It contained the names of 1500 soldiers carved into the semicircular stone walls around it. The memorial had numerous floral tributes placed there during the Sept 11 terrorist attack ceremonies just days earlier. Now we are at the brink of war with Iraq. We don't seem to learn, do we? *Plus ça change...*

We stayed the next two nights in Deauville. More on that later. The next day we visited Caen where the peace memorial was built. It's even more sobering. The architecture includes an entrance that looks like a jagged gash in the side of the building. It's a symbol of the destruction of war. Caen is an inland port and was bombed to smithereens by the Allies. It, like a few other Normandy towns, is very modern. The peace memorial detailed the economic and political events between WWI and WWII. We saw a film of D-Day (called Jour J in French), another showing the destruction of Normandy in the war, and a third looking at our incessant clashes of war since then, and the hope for reconciliation. It was quite moving – including original footage of WWI, WWII, Vietnam, Vietnam War Protests, the Civil rights movement, the destruction of the Berlin Wall, and even chilling footage of starving children in Africa, the Balkan's wars, and Desert Storm. There were tons of European school children there, from several countries. The Europeans understandably want the next generation to know enough about war that they will try hard to avoid another one. There was a large contingent of Swedish teenagers there during one of the films. We also saw the Enigma machines and other WWII memorabilia. Fascinating. The collaboration of some French with the Nazis is still a sore subject. Revisionist memories exist, of course. Our guide said that after the war , everyone claimed to have been in the resistance! *Plus ça change...*

We also visited Bayeux, A charming town of Renaissance era half-timbered buildings and the famous Bayeux Tapestry. We saw the "Tapestry" which is actually a 230-foot by 20-inch embroidery piece displayed in a museum. It is from the 11th century and tells the story of the events preceding William the Conqueror's (Duke of Normandy) invasion of Britain, the Battle of Hastings, and his subsequent crowning as King of England. It was amazing in its detail, and its political propaganda. It was probably commissioned to tell the story to an illiterate population (and win their political support). I can't imagine how many people and how many years it took to complete it. Fascinating, especially for me, with decades of embroidery experience. We also heard the French version of the invasion, which is quite different than the Anglicized sanitized version we got in school. William had been promised the English crown in a duly signed treaty, and Harold reneged on the treaty after the English king died, so William enforced the treaty by force. The older I get, the less I think I was taught any accurate history in school. Talk about political propaganda…*Plus ça change*…

While seeing all of these Normandy sights, we spent two nights in Deauville, an incredibly unique town just east of the Normandy landing beaches. It is a resort town, filled with extremely ornate late 19th century mansions of gingerbread, brick, and other architectural details that defy description. The modern buildings were the casinos. Phil and I walked around gaping at the houses. It is where rich Parisians go for the weekends. They have a horse race track. Our room looked out over the very nice beach. Some of our tour saw race horses exercising on the beaches, but we missed that. The American Film Festival is there yearly and had just ended before we arrived. We stayed in another very upscale hotel (Barriere Royal) in the lap of luxury, eating scandalously good food in an unforgivably ornate dining room. I exposed an equally scandalous amount of film on the yacht anchorages and on the neighboring town of Trouville just across the bridge that divides it from Deauville. Trouville is full of half-timbered houses, and more gingerbread. Words fail me; there is really no describing it. Many of the coastal towns of Normandy are like this, old half-timbered farm buildings that look like they are straight out of the middle ages, contrasted with brick and stone 19th century mansions.

We also visited Honfleur, another incredibly picturesque Normandy village nearby. It is full of half-timbered old buildings, a little enclosed boat harbor off the river, and a commercial fishing harbor on the river. We saw live shrimp and eels coming off the boats, and strolled around the old square. After pizza outdoors in the square beside the boat anchorage, I found a lovely blue-gray pottery mug with silver spots there. Another mug for my collection on the kitchen walls! We strayed into the local church, which has a double nave of wooden ceilings that look like the insides of the hulls of two fishing boats. It was all wood beams – no gorgeous marble or soaring stone gothic as in Chartres. These were humble and probably poor fishing people who reproduced their livelihoods in their church architecture several centuries ago.

We visited Claude Monet's home and gardens in Giverny on the way back into Paris. The famous lily pond and Japanese Bridge were lovely, but were nothing compared to the huge flower gardens around his house. The lily pads weren't in bloom in September. The flower gardens are about the size of our entire property (1/3-1/2 acre) and are row after row of riotous color. The dahlias (more kinds than I knew existed) were in full bloom, some 7 feet high and some the size of salad plates. Cosmos, marigolds, roses, nasturtiums, and annuals presented an almost overwhelming barrage of color. It was sensational (I exposed a lot more film there) and exquisitely tended by quite a few gardeners. I thought of my heat and drought blighted Indiana flower garden and figured I should just quietly slink back home and cut it all down. There's no substitute for a damp cool environment and a corps of full time gardeners!

The village of Giverny is tiny, one street. It's charming. Phil and I strolled down it and found a little lunch (used more of my primitive French skills to get a sandwich. We visited the tiny humble parish church, itself quite smaller than Monet's home (which contained 8 children).

Then it was back to Paris where we figured out how to use the Metro and found the Salpetriere Hospital where modern psychiatry and modern neurology were born. There were about 70 buildings on the map of it. It's a huge modern medical center under the huge dome of the towering "chapel" that was really a huge old stone church. That was a thrill for us. We found the neurology hospital (yes, they have one just for neurology) named for the famous 19th century neurologist, Joseph Babinksi. We saw other buildings named for other neurologists, and even saw Sigmund Freud Street on the map of the complex. The Salpetriere is so huge, it makes Indiana U. Med Center look small by comparison.

Phil and I also found the Latin Quarter (still full of universities and students) and found the Pantheon where we made a pilgrimage to the crypt to see the grave of one of my idols – Marie Curie. Voltaire and Henri Rousseau are also buried down there. Marie appears to be the only woman in that crypt. The Pantheon is modeled after the one in Rome, and is a massive building of incredible grandeur. It was a church until the French Revolution when lots of churches were closed or destroyed by a populace that was fed up with all kind of institutional excesses. Our modern business executives should take note, huh? *Plus ça change…*

I wandered alone into the gorgeous Luxembourg Gardens that border the French Senate building. By this time, security in Paris had become very, very tight. There were gendarmes at every corner of the building. France had released Maurice Papon, a WWII Vichy government Nazi collaborator from prison the day before and we saw riot police strolling about the city. There had been an outcry and protests. Papon sent 1500 people to concentration camps and served only 3 years in prison. *Plus ça change…*

That evening, we met for a drink in the hotel bar with Phil's cousin, Tom Richman, who had come in from Amsterdam on the train, and Phil's brother who had come in from Luxembourg. That was fun. Then it was on to the farewell dinner in the Intercontinental Hotel – with agneau (lamb) and other goodies. It was lovely. Then to Charles DeGaulle the next morning to fly home. It was restful and inoubliable (unforgettable) – a real vacation!

Travel Diary Excerpts

New Zealand

2-21-90

…On return, went with [four] other passengers up in a 6-seater Cessna. Took off from a proper paved runway, went out over Milford Sound a ways, turned around, then flew up steeply glaciated canyons with glaciers on top, lakes & rivers at the bottom, and the famed Milford track below. Came out over the north end of lake Te Anau (which means rushing water) and flew down this huge lake. Landed quite smoothly on a grass runway of tiny Te Anau airport…

Tuesday, Feb. 22, 1990

…After lunch, went to the airport & flew in a 1939 Tiger Moth biplane. It was built for an aeroclub in England & was pressed into service to train RAF pilots for WWII. I was put in a huge canvas & sheep-skin lined flightsuit (I could have gone swimming in it), a leather aviators cap, goggles & gloves. I was strapped into the cockpit and off we went. What a thrill! We went to Mt. Tarawera, a mountain that was split apart by a volcanic blast in 1886. Over Lake Tarawera we did a loop & then a roll. What a thrill. The world spins and it was very disorienting, then all of a sudden you're right side up again. Flew over the geo-thermal area, Rotorura, & Lake Rotorura. I'd do it again in a minute. Landed at very low speed in a headwind on a grass strip…

Iceland

Wednesday, July 24, 1991

...We drove to Strikkishalmur for a wonderful lunch at the hotel, then boarded the ferry Eyjaferdir for an unforgettable 2 ½ hour experience. We headed east northeast & stopped at island of basalt columns running vertical, slanted and even horizontal with their ends sticking out at us. We saw puffins and kittiwakes, the latter with furry young gray birds in their nests. We got close and could see them clearly, the sea being calm. We went on to another island & got to within 3 meters of nesting black cormorants. Saw their young 2-3 weeks old. Was truly stunning being that close. They seemed relatively unbothered by it. We went and entered a bay used by Erik the Red (on his way to discover Greenland). It was magnificent with basalt columns, some with birds nesting on them in the cliffs. We passed through the roaring 80-knots/hr tide, an amazing sight as it came in, to see more puffins and the great black-backed gull, the latter with large ungainly brown-grey young. Was truly amazing. We were close. Even the cold wind & intermittent rain mattered little amid the wonder of the experience. It was awesome. On the way back we let down a net & gathered shellfish. The haul was scattered on a long table in the stern area. Everyone gathered around and pried open the scallops. I ate a raw very fresh scallop and found it delicious. There were several live crabs (thrown back into the sea), a red starfish and sea urchins. The Japanese family cut open the sea urchin & ate the orange eggs! They are considered an aphrodisiac in Japan! Returned to Reykkolt via Bargannes.

Argentina & Chile

Tuesday, February 27, 1992

We arose very early, quite sleepy. After breakfast we left at 7:30 for the port to get the hydrofoil to Uruguay. It takes all of 10 seconds (if you're slow) to get a taxi here. The hydrofoil left at 8:30. We sat in the lower front area. The river (Rio de la Plata) is 50 km wide here & it takes about an hour to cross. The hydrofoil goes like a bat out of hell and the river looked like a brown ocean, very rough waves in a strong wind. A lot of people asked for seasick bags. We were met in Colonia, Uruguay by our guide and driver...

Monday, March 2, 1992

Awoke to 10 degree C temperatures & broken high clouds. Were driven by bus to the port of Llao Llao where we boarded a large hydrofoil "El Condor." It holds 300 people but there were only 14 of us, about half speaking English...went down the main part of Lago Nahuel Huapi & turned into

Puerto Blest area. The boat sounded 3 times as were passed the island where Perito Francisco Mareno is buried. This arm is very similar to the Norwegian fiords. The walls are steep with forests of pine on the lower parts. The upper walls are granite. The fiord arm narrows to closure at the end. It has become cloudy and we no longer have the sun. We cannot see Mt. Tronador. Arrived at Puerto Blest and had lunch at the hotel...We boarded a bus for a 3 km drive down the road through the thick forest of Alceres & bamboo, stopping at a 580 yr old tree. We arrived at Puerto Alegre where the road ended. Puerto Alegre consists of a wooden dock and a small ferry. The lake is a murky light green, lots of glacial silt. We boarded the tiny ferry for a 20-minute ride down Lago Frias amid towering cliffs with trees where South American condors live. Because of the rain they weren't flying around. Mt. Tronador was obscured by clouds. A pity. Puerto Fria was a bit larger - two small buildings. We were processed through immigration & boarded a bus to drive across the border to Chile. We wound up the dirt road amid cane and came to the crest at 3000 ft where an arch of wood marks the border. We descended steeply in hairpin turns through incredibly lush bamboo, fern, tree, moss & tangled rain forest. The sun began to shine and it was beautiful. We stopped at the border guard area & looked back over the flat valley of the Peulla River to see Mt. Tronodor gleaming in the sun amid wisps of storm clouds. It was simply stunning with snow and two glaciers winding their way down the mountain in the late afternoon sun. The river flows through a rocky bed & is like the braided rivers of New Zealand. We went through baggage check at Peulla & went to the hotel, a charming white building made of wood, looking out over the even flat valley. The hills around us are very steep & covered with woods. On the way down we were privileged to see a condor in flight high above us on the hills. It was magnificent. The entire time we watched, it soared and never once flapped its wings. It caught updrafts and just soared. I never thought I'd see one fly in the wild.

Tuesday, 3 March 1992

   Awoke to high clouds which began to clear by late morning...We sat in the sun in the garden awaiting our 3 PM departure for the port...We boarded the bus and went to the port to board the ferry Don Walter for a 2 hour ride across Lago Todos Santos, a large glacial green lake with several arms. Initially there were green steep hills with a few fields, then the craggy steep peak of Mt. Puntiagudo came into view to the north. It slopes up and ends in a very sharp upswing to a crag. It had some snow and a very small glacier. We traveled on as the perfectly conically shaped volcano Osorno came into view ahead of us to the northwest. It's spectacular. The top has 1/3 snow and ice.

The whole trip was beautiful. We arrived at the port of Petrohue at the west end of the lake, at the southern foot of Osorno. From there we drove by bus ...into Puerto Mott, a port city on the huge bay that cuts deeply into Chile. It is 120,000 people and very picturesque. Our hotel is right on the bay.

Ecuador

Wednesday, March 10, 1993

...we came down to Alausi, a charming little town in a steep valley. Jorge was driving like a bat out of hell. We thought he was worried about making the 9 AM train, but when we got there we took a coffee break.

We waited 2 ½ hours for the train. The track had just been fixed, so the train had to wait in places between Riobamba and Alausi. It was two hours late. It isn't exactly a train. It's a bus set on rails. We walked around town while waiting. After the train arrived, all the passengers got off and went through the town and up the hill to get coffee. The station bathroom was a real pit. We got on top of the train & sat on cushions set on slats of wood. It was comfortable. We finally left at 11:30 AM for an exhilarating one-hour ride to Chunchi.

The descent to the valley was steep. We then wound around the valley floor beside the river before ascending the precipitously steep hillside (cliff is more what is was). There were gorgeous brilliant red flowers on little stems above a plant with leaves like a begonia. We came to the Nariz del Diable and stopped for pictures before descending the unique switchbacks. It is so steep that the train goes down by reversing directions at the switchbacks. Below is the tiny station and town of Sibambe where we stopped. The tiny church atop a hillside appeared abandoned, at least as the steps up there indicated. From Sibambe we began a long climb up the green hills. The tropical vegetation at Sibambe rapidly disappeared and fields appeared. The scenery was spectacular, wildly plunging green hills, fields, houses, people, dogs, donkeys, cows, pigs, cats, & chickens, etc. We ascended into the clouds & finally emerged above them. Above the clouds we arrived at Chunchi, a village where we ducked power lines as we turned around before disembarking at the station. It was a ride of a lifetime, exhilarating, beautiful, with wind in the hair. I'd do it again in a minute. Jorge had driven the van to Chunchi & picked us up. We proceeded by van to Ingapirca, 2 hours away. The road was definitely more rough. We were above the lowest layer of clouds & could see them crawling up valleys between plunging mountain ridges.

Costa Rica

Monday, March 14, 1994

Arose for a delightful buffet breakfast & watched incredibly colorful birds feeding on fruit they put in the tree near the corner of the restaurant. Left for Los Chiles, a town about 8 km from the Nicaraguan border. The Rio Frio flows by it on its way to Lago Nicaragua...We boarded a riverboat to go up the Rio Frio towards Cano Negro (a wilderness preserve). A small remnant of rain forest lines the banks. We saw a host of wildlife: howler monkeys in the trees and bright green lizards that are the color of leaves. They call one type the Jesus Christ lizard because it escapes predators by skittering across the top of the water. We saw a beautiful large bird like a cormorant, called a hinga. They spread their wings to dry in the sun after fishing. We saw a host of smaller birds, including kingfishers. We came upon a reptile that is the size and shape of a crocodile. They are called caymans. We saw a lot of them. We had lunch on a bank on a small bluff over the river, beneath a huge kapok tree...Across from us a herd of Brahman cows looked at us. Reboarding down the steep grassy slope we continued on to a place where we were very fortunate to spot a troop of three spider monkeys high in a tree above the river. They are very difficult to see in the wild. No one even knows how long they live in the wild. On the way back we saw 10 bats clinging to the bottom of the root of a tree above the river. They looked like dead leaves and were as ugly as sin.

British Columbia

August 2006

...We took the noon floatplane of Whistler Air on an incredible 30-min tour of the area. We flew over the side of Blackcomb Mtn, the ski runs & summit of Whistler Mtn, past the up-jutting black core of Black Tusk Mtn, and over the huge brilliant dark blue Garibaldi Lake, held in by a now eroding lava flow of long ago. It was breathtaking. We circled around the Black Tusk, as Phil and I furiously clicked photos, and then back to town. We flew over several small glaciers, looking at snow-topped peaks in all directions from the valley & river where Whistler Village lies like a medieval doll village. After a steep bank we came down quite smoothly on Green Lake. It was utterly grand and memorable...

Chapter 12

Recreation

Thomas Nelson Richman - *The Ride to Fargo: A Journey of Imagination*

My first cousin, Thomas Nelson Richman, or Tom as he was called, was born on August 29, 1942 in Boonville, Indiana and died on January 27, 2003 near Baltimore, Maryland. He was the grandson of Frank Nelson Richman (1881-1956) who was judge in one of the post-World War II Nuremberg. For many years Tom worked and wrote for *Inc. Magazine*[1] in Boston, Massachusetts. He was a graduate of the United States Naval Academy and served two tours of duty in Vietnam. He was an avid bicyclist. He wrote *The Ride to Fargo: A Journey of Imagination*[2] and a number of other travel articles.[3]

In *The Ride to Fargo*, an unpublished book written in the few years before his untimely death, Tom recounts various bicycling trips that he made around the United States. His most ambitious ride was to roughly retrace the expedition of Lewis and Clark from Fort Clatsop, Oregon, the expedition's winter headquarters, to Fort Mandan, North Dakota and on to Fargo. Tom never completed the ride. Although he crossed the Cascades and northern Rocky Mountains, he ended his ride in western Montana. Tom made a number of other rides in the nation's South, Southeast, Northeast, and Midwest. "Hey, Tom," chronicles his 1999 ride in Indiana with a number of other bicycling enthusiasts. The latter ride was called TRIRI, or Touring Ride In Rural Indiana.

Hey, Tom

Indiana, the smallest state but for Hawaii west of the Appalachians, has produced its share of celebrity Americans. Notable natives include Jimmy Hoffa, Ernie Pyle, and the Jackson Five. However, perusing a list of famous Hoosiers, one might spot a pattern. There are those celebrities who left Indiana and achieved fame, like Eugene V. Debs, James Dean, Bill Blass, Theodore Dreiser, Joe Ann Worley, Sydney Pollack, Gary Burton, Red Skelton, or Kurt Vonnegut, Jr. And there are those whose fame was homegrown: Dan Quayle comes to mind, of course, and James Whitcomb Riley.

[Indiana] is lacking the drama of a seacoast or mountains and absent a center of significant urban culture, [but] Hoosiers take pride in what is at hand: their poets, of course, and their highways, for instance, and their high-school basketball teams. More than one book I read about and published in Indiana pointed out that more interstate highways cross the state than cross any other. People there attend high school basketball games – and root and cheer – when they don't even have kids. It's a place of simple, straightforward pleasures.

I drove from Boston with the bike – no trailer – on the roof of the car, taking my time through scenic northern Pennsylvania and arriving at the home of my cousin Vernon and his wife Lou in Plainfield, on the western side of Indianapolis, late in the afternoon of the third Saturday of June.

Vernon is my cousin, my mother's youngest brother's son. He and Lou are nice, church-going folks, which terrified me, certain as I was that the irreligious gay cousin raised back East would give offense the first time I opened my mouth. Standing at their door, I felt like Daniel about to enter the lambs' den or like Elton John applying to the Boy Scouts. Moreover, I so wanted them to like me. We were, after all, kin, even if strangers. I hadn't seen Vernon in more than thirty years. Lou I had never met. Although Vernon and I were practically littermates, having played together as pre-schoolers in Indianapolis, genes and life had given us different shapes.

Not only was I back home again in Indiana, I was going to spend the next seven days and six nights in the company of three-hundred-and-some other cyclists on an organized group ride. TRIRI, it was called, <u>T</u>ouring <u>R</u>ide <u>I</u>n <u>R</u>ural <u>I</u>ndiana. It might as well have been the TDF, <u>T</u>our <u>d</u>e <u>F</u>rance; I was that nervous about it.

Back during the late winter, when I was thinking about different kinds of rides I might make during the coming season, at least one organized group ride had been part of the mix. Not because I wanted to ride with a bunch of strangers, but because I thought I should. Maybe I would like it. There were scores of sponsored rides to choose from, listed in the calendar sections of bicycling magazines and touted in ads. I sent away for brochures and entry forms, which began arriving in a stream of mail. Of all of them, TRIRI appealed most to me because it was far from the largest, its daily ride lengths seemed the most reasonable, and because of the nostalgia factor: on both my paternal and maternal sides, Indiana was home.

Saturday evening, Vernon grilled man-sized steaks of amazing tenderness and Lou supplied as accompaniment enough tasty carbohydrates to power me through the first several days of riding. Sunday's breakfast seemed superfluous, but that didn't stop me from eating it before driving the few miles to the Mooresville High School parking lot, the TRIRI starting point.

When I arrived at eight o'clock, some riders had already taken to the road. More drove in after me in cars and pickups with bikes clamped to roof racks, hanging from trunk racks, wedged into back seats, lying in truck beds, or in one case towed in a special trailer. People wearing jerseys with bright slashes of color, some displaying club logos, were topping off tires and adjusting brake cables. They re-packed bags, hailed friends, and clustered in noisy chattering groups, none of which included me. Riding solo, one at least has one's self for company, but in this crowd of strangers, I was utterly alone. Among these hundreds of cyclists, I knew no one, and no one knew me. Furthermore, I assumed that every bike in the crowd was fancier than mine and every rider more accomplished faster than I was. In short, at that moment, I would have happily traded three more days of Georgia's cold rain and fried food not to be there. I find groups quite frightening, and it seems to me that I don't do well among lots of strangers. But, having chosen to try, here I was.

I stuffed a rain jacket, cell phone, camera, and notebook into their, by now, usual places in the rear rack-pack, mounted up, and rode off, taking a while to find my pace, as usually happens at the start of a trip. The TRIRI organizers had provided one especially nice touch: the bright orange fanny flag they'd given everyone. Printed in black on the flag were the rider's name and town of residence. The fanny flag was also your food ticket, with a spot for each meal to be blacked out by monitors as you entered the breakfast or dinner line. While riding, you were to wear it on the back of your jersey or anyplace easily seen from behind, because it was not only a safety device – bright, as I said, orange – it was also your name tag.

"Hey, Tom!" said the man on the gold-colored carbon-fiber Trek racing bike with just five spokes per wheel as he pulled up even with me. He wasn't the first stranger to hail me by name. Already I had had short rolling conversations with the president of Dartmouth Printing Company in Lyme,

New Hampshire and with a man from Minnesota. The Minnesotan wanted to tell me that he and his wife had loved visiting Boston and the Isabella Stewart Gardner Museum and that he had just finished (as I, coincidentally, had) reading Douglas Shand-Tucci's biography of the *outré* Mrs. G. "I guess my problem," the man said, "is that I just don't know enough homosexuals." Isabella knew plenty of them; she seemed to collect them along with her art. But why was he mentioning this to *me*? (A little touchy, Tom?) He dropped back eventually to rejoin his wife.

Nevertheless, even when John Smith [not his real name] hailed me a short time later, I was still surprised for a second that someone I didn't know and who hadn't even seen my face yet could call me by name and know where I was from. Of course, it was the fanny flag pinned to the back of the rack-pack, but you forget that it's there.

John's grown sons had given him the fancy bike to replace a lower-tech model, and he was still learning the gears. They chattered when he shifted, and they were intended for racing, not touring. On the large bumps that pass for hills in south-central Indiana, my pedals spun and my bike crept slowly but easily up the grade while John was standing and pushing hard through each stroke. At the top, he would catch his breath, we would go on talking, and in what seemed to me like only minutes, we had covered thirty of the day's fifty-five miles. That couldn't be right. My cyclometer must be off. "Hey, John. How far have we gone?" His gadget's reading confirmed my own.

Wow, I thought, the miles really roll by fast when you're distracted by conversation. Now I had a friend; I was no longer alone on this crowded trip; and I had learned quite a lot about John. But if something had been gained, something had also been lost: it came as a small shock to realize that I had absolutely no recollection of the landscape we had ridden through. Had there been trees, houses, birds, and views? I suppose, but I hadn't noticed them. When riding with someone, I was too busy talking or listening, mostly the latter, to pay much attention to the scene I was riding through. And when riding alone in the group, I was still too much concerned with the other riders: Should I pass that bunch? Fall in behind? Should I speak? And say what? Sometimes I envy people like my partner Bob's father, Dick, who buys only a couple of dollars worth of gas at a time for his big V-8 car; the more often he has to stop, the more gas-station conversations he can have. I've seen him talk to total strangers on the subway when he and Bob's mother visit Boston from their home in Terre Haute – and the strangers talk back. I don't have Dick's gift of gab, but of painful self-consciousness, I've more than enough.

The first-day ride passed through Brooklyn, Martinsville, Mahalasville, Helmsburg, and Beanblossom; and while we rode through those towns, my new friend told me his story – of a soured business partnership; of booze, cigarettes, and withdrawal at the Mayo Clinic; of once-errant children and a wife who has crippled herself with obesity; and of the travails of a new business venture. It was a privileged confession, the kind people only make to strangers at a bar or, as in this case, to one on the road. Moreover, it had the effect of reminding me that no bicycle-ride, however steep the hills, cold the wind, or hot the sun, is as trying as ordinary life.

Sunday's ride and John's story wrapped up in Nashville at Brown County State Park. In my parent's younger days, I've been told, Nashville and Brown County were special places, accommodating and conducive to artists and artisans whose work displayed local distinction. My folks lived in a Brown County cottage right after they were married in the 'thirties. Just the other day I came across a small notebook in which my dad had recorded expenses then. Electricity bill: $3.15.

The artists and artisans may still work in Brown County, but generic art – the same banal T-shirts, coffee mugs, and schlock paintings that are peddled in every tourist town in America – has overwhelmed their influence on Nashville's retail character. I grabbed lunch, a pizza, and went back to the park.

By mid-afternoon the large field set aside for TRIRI was splotched with color, thickest at the perimeters, where people apparently felt the choicest tent sites to be. No Microsoft of tent-makers yet dictates standard design, so the tents people brought were elongated, square, round, tall, squat, pitched, domed, angled, and peaked according to the owner's taste. Some tents were wire-sprung, and erected themselves when pulled from their bags. (It was the re-stowing of this kind that became the chore.) Some tents had multiple rooms and vestibules, and others were no more than a sleeping bag with a roof. Laundry, as colorful as the tents, hung from lines stretched between trees and decorated branches and shrubs.

One factor to consider in siting a tent, whether camping alone or in groups of hundreds, is exposure to the sun. A place in the afternoon shade makes for more comfortable post-ride napping, but laundry and gear – tents and sleeping bags, for instance, still wet from an overnight rain or dew – dry better in the open. Another factor, peculiar to group camping, didn't occur to me until about four-thirty the next morning when the earliest risers decided to rise – and to share their banter and laughter with the rest of us, who up to then had been sleeping. Another siting issue peculiar to group outings arose several days later. I had erected my tent at the edge of the field, near the trees, but with plenty of company; my gear was unpacked for its daily airing; and I was about to shower the road dirt off myself when a man approached and warned me and others that we might not want to camp just here. He pointed to a tent several removed from mine. "He snores," he said. Indeed, for much of the night, choking sounds, as if someone were being violently strangled, passed easily through the thin fabric of the indicated tent. In the morning, the victim emerged, apparently unharmed and well rested.

This was a whole lot more togetherness than I was accustomed to. I'll confess that I didn't – and still don't – understand exactly what it is that attracts people to group rides, but it must have more to do with socializing than riding. One man boasted that the only time of the year he mounted a bike was TRIRI. "That's amazing," a woman said when I told her that most of my touring so far had been solo. "I can't imagine," she added, and others said the same. But I can't imagine biking exclusively in company, as they do.

Opportunities for solitude for most of us, especially those of us who live in the city or its suburbs, are too few. We are frequently alone, but nearly always in a crowd: on the street, in the subway, in the store or the market, even in the office. Alone in the car, we're usually caught in traffic. The world – other pedestrians, riders, shoppers, workers, drivers; the screech of metal wheels on metal tracks, announcements, television screens with MTV or CNN that seem increasingly to fill any formerly quiet space – intrudes and leaves us no peace. How do we know what we think when there's no place left for thought? How do we know how we feel when we've no time to take stock of feelings? How do we know who we are when we see ourselves only with others?

After dark on Sunday, a few million fireflies blinked in the trees limning our field. The air was warm, soft, and humid, and it lacked only heat lightning to be the kind of Indiana night I remember as a four and five-year-old child sitting with his grandmother on her front-porch swing.

Monday we rode south, then west – a backwards "L" – for seventy-nine miles to Spring Hill State Park, passing through Stone Head, Story, Spurgeons Corner, Brownstown, Vallonia, Medora, Sparksville, Fort Ritner, and Bhudda. (Here they say "Boody.") Most of the land was given over to compact farms with neat barnyards and houses wedged between corn fields small enough to be seen whole in a glance. Wild roses and blooming trumpet vines lined the roads between towns, which began and ended cleanly at the signs marking their corporate limits. Steep but low ridges ran across the otherwise flat land, and I thought I had lost my way after lunch when I apparently rode over without noticing them the two "hills" we had been warned about during the post-dinner group gathering the night before. At the mention of hills, people had moaned and booed. The definition of hill, I suppose, depends on what one has become accustomed to.

Just short of the lunch stop, I suffered my first – and on this trip, only – flat tire.

If a flat tire on a bike is no one's fault – you ride over the tiniest sharp object at just the right angle, and, phssh, your rim is on the road – fixing a flat is nonetheless an embarrassment. It's like having to take a crap while on the road: everyone knows why you're slinking off into the woods or behind the large rock, because they've done it themselves. Still....

To fix a flat, you must squat in the dirt with your bike upended, gear strewn about, and fingers black from chain grease. If you do it in plain view beside the road, other bikers will blow by, coasting for a second. "Everything okay?" they'll ask, or "Need any help?" They would help if you asked, of course, but they would really rather not have to watch your self-conscious mortification. It's a reminder of their own vulnerability. We share with strangers – as John Smith did with me – details of our most intimate joys and sorrows, our triumphs and defeats, because those events seem to set our lives off from all others. What embarrasses us in front of others is to admit to the most commonplace, to our basic human functions – like shitting, menstruation, and fixing flats.

I was able to slink off the highway behind a scrim of low brush onto a dusty trail that bordered a cornfield to make my repair in private. When the coast was clear, I returned to the road and rolled cheerily up to Hudson's store, where people had gathered to buy food and drink, as if the flat had never happened. "Hey, John," I greeted my friend, who had just arrived himself.

Despite the healthy length of today's ride, I got to Spring Mill State Park, our next overnight stop, by quarter past one. It was those chatty early risers again, who had me up before five a.m. and on the road before seven. On the other hand, I noticed last night that by nine o'clock, the campground was dead quiet; only a few tents glowed green, orange, or red from the lights of readers inside. I wondered if the readers and the early risers were the same folks. The snide Lady Narborough, a character in Wilde's *The Picture of Dorian Gray*, says of people who live in the country that "They get up early because they have so much to do, and go to bed early because they have so little to think about."

Thomas Richman camping at Spring Mill State Park, 1999

Daily, before TRIRI riders arrived, state park crews erected large mess tents, arranged dozens of picnic tables underneath them, and set up a portable stage for the night's entertainment. A comedian worked the crowd one night; on another, two singer-song writers performed. On a third night came the inevitable talent show. The best part of every evening, though, was listening to Joe Anderson, who with his wife, Barbara, organizes the TRIRI rides. Joe would tell stories about the day's ride just finished and describe the ride to come tomorrow with a kind of humor characteristic of Indiana, a benign irony that doesn't aspire to sarcasm. Hoosier Herb Shriner, whom I remember from black and white TV in the early 'fifties, had it; so does David Letterman and my, now, late Uncle Harold, my cousin Steve's dad. Joe even looked a bit like Letterman, sitting with his legs dangling over the edge of the portable stage. "It is very hard to catch up to someone who is behind you," he advised us one night, adding after a just-right pause, "It is also difficult to wait for someone who has ridden on ahead." Tomorrow's main attraction, he announced Monday night, would be Mabel, a woman who maintains remarkable collections of unusual items at her place in Punkin Center.

Indiana has two towns called Punkin Center, three called Needmore, five called Mt. Pleasant, but only one called Gnaw Bone. Tuesday's rides – three loop options of 30, 70, or about one hundred miles – passed through one of the Punkin Centers. Let the heroes boast – as of course they did that evening – about riding a century in Tuesday's heat; I intended to pedal the short loop – out to Mabel's and back. We were staying a second night at Spring Mill.

By seven-thirty Tuesday when I finally pushed back from the breakfast table, it already felt like the 85-degree day it was going to become. The distance riders had left early, the late risers weren't up, and I found myself gliding nearly alone between fields that alternated in corn and soybeans as the empty road ambled south. At a dusty corner, I paused for water and a map-check. Clop-clop, clop-clop: a single horse pulled an Amish father and his daughter in a two-wheeled cart across the intersection ahead of me, then passed out of sight to my left behind some corn.

Punkin Center consisted of a frame house on one side of the road and on the other, a building that had burst its seams. Inside the building, Mabel Gray held court. I will repeat the story that she must have told ten thousand times or more. Her husband died in 1988. He started his store in 1922, built this building in 1933, and married her in 1934. During the Depression, he augmented their income by hauling Amish brides and their goods to Indiana from Iowa and Ohio in his truck. "We had a good business," Mabel said to a small group of us gathered around her inside the cluttered but surprisingly neat former store. One day, she continued, when her husband was still living, someone came by the store with a tool that he couldn't identify. It was a cherry pitter, something he didn't need, so he left it. Then people brought other things, which began to accumulate. "We didn't go to sales much," she said. They closed the store business in 1970. I don't know how old Mabel is; I'm sure she would have told me. She's old. Her mother died at the age of one hundred and six. "Her mind," Mabel said, "stayed pretty good." What Mabel has inside of and spilling out from the old store, which is also where she now makes her home, is too much to tell. She has a 1922 Gray automobile, for instance, which she says would run with a little fixing up. She has a bridge – "Old Stampers Creek Bridge, Built 1880," says the sign – in the back yard. She has a bottle-cap collection and several balls-and-chains of diverse design. She has quite a few left-handed pencils, on which the imprinted words read from the eraser end. There's a doggy restroom (with a stump for country dogs and a hydrant for city dogs) and a spring-driven barber pole mechanism. The inventory goes on. Mabel – well coiffed, nicely dressed, and not the least eccentric to the eye – tells her story to the curious; she sells Coca-Colas in green bottles out of an old vending machine, post cards, penny candy, and the pencils.

Mabel is a local hero. The state has more. Returning to Spring Mill Park, I noticed in Orleans a well-maintained sign set beside the road. "Future Farmers of America," it said at the top; and under that: "Orleans, Home of 1993 Soil Judging Champions." At an intersection near the junior high school in Heltonville, which we would ride through on Wednesday, the town has erected a ten-foot stone monument. Carved into one side is Indiana's familiar outline with Heltonville's location marked and the following message inscribed:

> "Damon Bailey
> From your hometown fans in
> recognition of all you have
> achieved. With great pride
> and much love."

On the other side, in bas-relief, stands Damon Bailey (1994 First Team All Big-10, etc.) with a basketball in his raised right hand.

It was pre-dawn Wednesday and still completely dark inside my tent when I heard *zip-zip, zip-zip*. Then *plink, plink, plink*. I identified the second sound: aluminum tent pegs being dropped into their bag. *Flip-flop, flip-flop, flip-flop*. Jim next door, wearing his rubber sandals, was breaking camp. *Wrinkle, wrinkle, wrinkle, wrinkle*. Now he was stuffing his tent into its sack. *Snap, snap – snap, snap, snap*: tent poles being taken apart. I found my glasses and checked my watch; it was four-fifty a.m., and when I unzipped and peeled back my own tent flap, Jim had already cleared out. Congratulations, Jim. You'll be first in line for breakfast, way before they start serving.

By six-thirty, I was on the road myself, bumping up and down little hills that wrinkle the flat landscape like accordion pleats. The hollows between pleats overflowed with a viscous ground fog. At mile nine, the ride passed through Boody again and by the sign in front of the "White River Baptist Church."

Wednesday's ride ended at McCormick's Creek State Park, where we pitched our tents around a swimming pool brimming over with shrieking children. The water in the showers seemed to have been piped in straight from Canada, but the lodge dispensed free hot coffee. Some time after midnight, sharp cracks of thunder were drowned by the drumming of rain on the tent, which leaked in just one place – a spot directly over my head. I end-for-ended myself, lay the Gore-Tex® jacket over my feet, and slept dryly through the rest of the night.

TRIRI was more than half over.

Welcome Bikers to Brazil

Thursday we crossed a series of steep but short hills and passed through Coal City, a town whose future seems to have passed. From there to Clay City, the road lay flat, and at the Clay City Pottery factory, the day's featured stop, I bought Bob a present: a Clay City ceramic toothbrush holder. Okay, maybe it was less gift than he deserved for the concession he seemed to have made.

There had been nothing complicated about the issue confronting us: his desire to have his partner at home conflicted with my current interest in bicycle touring. If the issue was simple, it also defied easy compromise. To travel is not to stay home; to stay home is not to travel.

The best we could do was to adjust at the margins   I promised to keep the trips as short and as infrequent as I reasonably could. He promised, not to stop disliking my being away; that he couldn't do. But he promised that he would stop complaining about it.

Besides, I knew Bob would appreciate the kitschy quality of an Indiana-made ceramic toothbrush holder, which just happened to match the color of the tile in our bathroom at home.

By this, the fifth day of TRIRI, I was beginning to get an inkling of why people might like these group rides: they're easy, in that you only have to follow directions. You don't have to search for food or shelter, only to decide where along the pre-planned route you'll stop for a break and where on the designated field to site your tent. Someone makes your meals, cleans your mess, transports your gear, and furnishes the entertainment. During the day, you can talk: no need to confront yourself when conversation is always at hand. Most people, I noticed, usually rode with someone else or in a group. Furthermore, with the maps you're given and the arrows (called Dan Henries by those who had been on earlier TRIRI rides and knew the inside joke) that have been spray-painted on the pavement, it is hard to get lost.

It can be done, though. I managed to turn Thursday's planned fifty-one miles into seventy by following the wrong arrows out of Clay City, which put me on Friday's route. I rode for almost ten miles through the emptiest stretch of Indiana I had yet seen – empty even of other riders, which is what finally tipped me off to my mistake. There was nothing to do but turn around and ride back to Clay City to pick up the trail again. The accidental detour threatened to make me late for my lunch date with Bob's folks.

Dick and Barb had already arrived at Shakamak (Indian for "eel") State Park when I rolled in. Here was another major breakthrough. Bob wasn't actually gay, his parents had at first persuaded themselves and assured him in a nasty letter written years ago, soon after he had told them about himself and his relationship with me. His recent divorce, they claimed, had only made him vulnerable to my predatory attentions. In the years since they sent that unfortunate letter, the four of us had spent time together just twice. Today, however, Dick and Barb had driven nearly an hour from Terre Haute with fried chicken, turkey sandwiches, potato chips, and cookies they had bought at the Kroger to meet me for lunch. It wasn't only a picnic; it was progress. On our best behavior, we snacked and chatted at a table under one of the mess tents while the hot sun dried the camping gear that they had helped me spread on the field. My sleeping pad, I couldn't help but notice, had acquired a foul musty odor and badly needed light.

It is not antiquated anti-sodomy laws or social disapprobation that keep most closeted gay people I know in the closet. It is the dread of parental disapproval. Men and women who can fearlessly flaunt their queerness in, say, gay pride parades will still shudder at the prospect of coming out at home. The public homophobes, the priests and preachers and politicians, whose bigotry is impersonal and institutional, can only rant, and their hatefulness is easily ignored. Mom and Dad, however, really know how to hurt a kid. They withdraw their love, and it's a brave child who even as an adult will run the risk of that loss, even for the sake of living a life that is otherwise fulfilled. Many, therefore, don't. Bob, however, did, and Dick and Barb are, if not happy about it, nonetheless coming around.

Ignorance used to be another effective device for keeping a homosexual child from realizing him or herself, though it is far less useful today I grew up in the 1950s and '60s knowing full well that, when it came to sexual desire and emotional attachment, my preference was for boys. What I didn't know, because no one – parents, teachers, pastor, adult friends, or TV sitcom writers – responsible for my education ever informed me, was that I wasn't the only male to feel that way. Gay role models? None. In my suburban universe, you necked with girls, got married, had kids – or you didn't, but no one ever mentioned an alternative. Therefore, I necked, got married, and had kids (for whom I am, of course, grateful), without realizing how frustrated and angry I was that something – What? – was being kept from me.

In the late 1970s, when I was long out of the navy and already married with kids, I got out of New Hampshire long enough to notice that in places like New York and Washington, D.C., male couples were openly making a loving life together. I already knew by then, of course, that I wasn't the only homosexual in America, but this was the first credible evidence I had that people could be gay and still lead normal lives. It was an astonishing revelation.

If by then I had paid a price for my ignorance, years of self-denial, frustration, and unfocused discontent, so, too had my blameless wife and kids. As a husband, I was unaffectionate. As a father, I was distant. Had I known as a child what I (and most kids today, I hope) know now, I would never have tried to be what I am not, nor would I have entangled others in my error.

"How many people today," Joe Anderson asked the crowd after dinner that night, "saw the mailbox that looked like a John Deere tractor? How many saw the one that looked like a corn stalk?" The Indiana landscape does tend to start looking much the same from day to day, and it takes a sharp eye to notice the high points.

Friday, east, west, north, and south were mere abstractions in morning's fog, which also leached the color from the scene. The vivid green of the maturing cornstalks turned black; the yellow-brown of the soil, soft gray. So different was the coloring that I was hardly aware of riding again on roads I had already ridden twice the day before. By eight o'clock, however, the sun had dispatched the fog and restored the rural palette.

A couple of us, ahead of the pack, stopped at the Kroger in Brazil looking for bananas. The manager on duty pointed to the produce bins at the far side of the store and learned that we were part of a larger group still to come. Before we could find our fruit and return to the check-out, this agile young merchant, alert to a selling opportunity, had set a table opposite the front door, filled it with bananas and Gator-Ade, and hung a sign: "Welcome Bikers to Brazil."

The road beyond town makes a large S-curve through the fields. Ahead of me, I could see what looked like a long line of bicycle helmets floating just above the top of the corn – gliding first to the left, then to the right, then merging into one as the road straightened and the line of cyclists wearing them became a column again, moving in precisely the direction it had before entering the curve.

The ride to Turkey Run State Park took us through Parke County, which, with thirty-two covered bridges, has more than any place else in the world. J.J. Daniels built most of them. At Bridgeton we passed the best-known Daniels bridge, 245-feet long; "1868/J.J. Daniels, Builder" is painted over the entry arch. Five miles on, we passed another, the last bridge Daniels built, the Neet

Bridge, 1904. In between, we crossed the "Ten O'clock Line," marking the boundary of a large tract of land sold by Indians to the United States in 1809 – three million acres at about a third of a cent per acre. The line runs from its starting point in the direction of a shadow cast at ten o'clock – a boundary as ephemeral as the integrity of the white men who conceived it.

A plaque on the lawn surrounding the county courthouse at the center of the square in Rockville notes that the town was named for "the ancient boulders found here" in 1824. The courthouse itself, a two-story limestone cruciform, is immaculately kept. Polished black-and-white floor tiles inside reflect light admitted through tall windows more than twice a person's height; dark-stained door moldings rise toward ceilings that must be fifteen or more feet high. A double staircase dominates the center hall.

On the last night of a ride – tonight – no one has to do laundry.

I looked for John to say goodbye and found him camped, as on other nights, far out on the perimeter of the little fabric town. He was sitting in the folding chair he'd brought, not reading, just watching. He had turned his life around – put the business in its place, licked the booze and cigarettes – on his own volition; I admired that and wanted to tell him so.

Zip, zip. Zip, zip. Wrinkle, wrinkle, wrinkle.

This morning, the few started way before four, and by four-thirty the many had risen and joined in. By ten past five, I was in the breakfast line, and in the saddle by six.

In the saddle...on the saddle. Through all the trips thus far, from the ferry landing in Anacortes last summer to Turkey Run State Park where we'd just spent the night, the saddle on my bike – or more precisely, the points at which I connected with it – had been the weak link in this man-machine combination. As each trip wore on, the surface of the skin on either side of my perineum grew rough and raw, and the agony of connecting with the saddle grew more exquisite and debilitating with each day of riding and with each hour within the day. Late in every trip thus far, the pain had become a serious enervation, and spending a large sum of money on a custom-made bike seemed not to have alleviated the condition. Something would have to be done.

"It will be a straight shot to Mooresville," Joe Anderson had promised us last night, and from Marshall's triumphal arch – a peculiar structure far too grand for the dumpy little town it stands in – to North Salem, a distance of thirty miles, I could have locked the handlebars to point dead ahead. I passed up the suggested snack stop, a Phillips 66 mini-mart in Roachdale (*Roachdale?!*) and pushed on to Danville and – Omigod, what have we here, under this blazing late morning sun, but a Dairy Queen.

The low wall around the DQ, a perfect height for sitting, was the last place that this week's crew of riders would gather, and I found myself talking to a man I hadn't yet met but had certainly noticed. He called himself "The Sergeant" and was the very picture of a marine. "Oh, yeah," he said, "I know Ollie North and Chuck Krulak. I took 'em through Quantico." But he didn't seem to know any of the marine officers I knew who had gone through training at Quantico at about the same time as North and Krulak, and somehow he had never heard of the book – Robert Timberg's *The Nightingale's Song* – that paints the defining portrait of that generation of navy and marine officers. We ate our sundaes – mine was caramel and hot fudge, medium, not small, as this was no time to count calories – and filled the time with talk.

During much of the ride's final twenty-mile leg, a single biker kept pace with me, but about a quarter mile ahead. I would lose sight of him at turns and sometimes in the traffic, which thickened as we skirted the Indianapolis suburbs, but he would eventually reappear to remind me that I wasn't alone. Two riders I didn't know passed me, and in a few minutes, they must have slowed, because I caught up to and re-passed them. "Go for it, Tom," one of them said, reading my fanny flag, and I thought how much more I had enjoyed the company of strangers during the last week than I had thought I would.

Vernon and Lou seemed pleased to see me back – another relief – and on Sunday, we three drove to Evansville to visit his dad, my mother's younger brother, whom I hadn't seen in twenty-five years. Uncle George had run a filling station in Indianapolis when I was not yet in first grade. To me, he still looked the same – a small, sweet, gentle man. Now he's dead – he died less than a year after our visit – and only three of his generation on either side of my family remain.

On Monday, I started for Boston, driving the interstates I had avoided on the way out, and by Tuesday noon, I was unpacking my cycling gear at the house that Bob and I soon would no longer call home.

Chapter 13

Genealogy Trips

○ ○

"We've uncovered some embarrassing ancestors in the not-too-distant past. Some horse thieves, and some people killed on Saturday nights. One of my relatives, unfortunately, was even in the newspaper business."

Jimmy Carter, as quoted in the Free Lance Star, Fredericksburg, Virginia, June 4, 1977

One of my favorite genealogy pastimes is learning all I can about a particular ancestor. In order to do so, I often take "genealogy trips" to places where he or she lived. Seeking out records in courthouses, county libraries, and county historical societies and seeing where they lived and where they were buried makes that person and my family genealogy come alive.

The following letter from James Bean, a nephew of my great grandmother, Nancy Alice Wilson Rogers describes one such trip that he took in search of his Wilson ancestors.[1] I made the same trip about five years ago. I found Alexander Wilson's tombstone with its autobiographical record, and the graves of two of his deceased wives. Unfortunately I was not able to find the "old stone house" described by James Bean in his letter.

James Bean's Trip

James Wilson Bean (1882-1964) was a nephew of Alice Wilson Rogers. His father was a physician. He was a Presbyterian minister who was born in Fairfield, Iowa. He was a minister in Hastings Nebraska, Winfield Iowa, Emporia Kansas, Canton, Ohio, and St. Paul, Minnesota.[2] He wrote his aunt,

Alice Wilson, about his trip with his wife Harriet in search of his Wilson roots to Clarion County, Pennsylvania.

[Note by Francis R. Johnson 1982 (Letter to my grandmother. Alice W. Rogers, from her nephew James W. Bean, son of Elizabeth W. Bean)]

October 23, 1934
Dear Ones and All:

I want to tell you about a little expedition that Harriet and I enjoyed two weeks ago. I had been going pretty steadily for thirteen and fourteen hours a day for six weeks, and felt that I just must quit for a couple of day. So, we got into our "little Chevy" and drove over into Pennsylvania.

Our objective was the Cook Forest Park. A reserve partly of virgin timber and partly of second growth which has been converted into a park by the state of Pennsylvania. I think there are something like seven thousand acres.

We enjoyed very much our drive over there and not less our stay. We were Monday night and up to the earlier part of Tuesday afternoon. The colors were lovely. It is beyond the power of one so prosaic as I to describe it, but the changing panorama of glory was to say the least, marvelous. The hard maples were scarlet and vermillion against a dark green background of hemlock and pine. Scattered allover the side of the hills were also birch with their trembling yellow, and oak with their russet and brown. It was the red maples, however, which most greatly thrilled us.

That Tuesday morning, after having had a night in an Indian cabin, (There is a semicircle of cabins in a clearing ten or twelve rods from the hotel where we spent the night. The other cabins were unoccupied, so thankful it was as lovely and still a night as could have been hoped for.) we spent doing one or two of the trails through the big trees. The air was exhilarating and we went from one scene of beauty and grandeur to another.

That noon after having had dinner, the old gentleman whose father owned much of this timber and whose name it bears, asked us if we wouldn't like to go for a drive, so he gave us a personally conducted tour over some of the roads through the forest; leading eventually up to his family mausoleum. The mausoleum stands in the center of a clearing on a hill and afforded us a marvelous view.

Then nothing would do but we must go to his home and meet Mrs. Cook. We found in her a most delightful lady, several years her husband's junior. Harriet was doubly delighted because, in Mrs. Cook, she discovered a former Regent-General (or is it president-General) of the D. A. R. She was a most gracious hostess and showed Harriet and me some of her riches in the way of heirlooms and old dishes and other furniture of which she had come into possession. The house was beautiful; the various rooms having been finished in native woods. The library in cherry and the music room in bird's eye maple were especially lovely, but so too was the dining room which was in walnut. It might be said in passing that the marks of the times are on that fine old residence now. Mrs. Cook spoke of the fact that she was getting along without much help.

The greatest thrill of the trip, however, was in our visit to old Callensburg, the old-time center of the Wilson tribe. Callensburg, you may remember, is in Clarion County and is about thirty miles this side of the Cook Forest.

At Callensburg, we first stopped at the post office and made our inquiries as to whether any Wilsons were to be found still remaining in the vicinity. We learned that there was one remaining in the vicinity. One commonly known as "Tiny" Wilson. "Tiny" being his nickname; a shortened form of Constantine. His full name being Andrew Constantine Wilson. We learned that this second cousin of mother's, for such he proved was on his old place about three miles from town, so we drove out there. We found the man eighty-two, blind because of cataracts but vigorous and most interesting in his conversation.

We were finally received both by him and Mrs. Wilson, who I judge is about ten years his junior. This cousin of ours told me that he was a grandson of Lewis, who was an older brother of the Alexander who was our great grandfather. He told us about the going west of great uncle Sam Wilson and how Wilson Murray, then a young man went along. That "uncle Sam" required of Wilson Murray that if he went along he get an extra team of horses. This the latter did and when they were encamped near Chicago, a man living in that vicinity was so greatly taken with Wilson Murray's team that he offered him eighty acres of land for them. This eighty, "Tiny" says, has long since become real estate in Chicago.

Tiny told us also about the location of the stone house that great grandfather built and that it was still standing. He told us also of other items of interest. Our stay with him was entirely too short but I had to get back home by Wednesday noon because of a wedding. He urged us to come back and finish our visit. This we hope to do.

Mrs. Wilson has proved herself the same kind of woman that Wilsons have a habit of marrying. She was interested in all her husband was interested in and gave us a most cordial welcome. She is carrying on in the church just as you would expect. She is president of their little missionary society and a member of the board of directors that looks after the cemetery.

In the finding of "Tiny" Wilson, we found the only person remaining of the tribe in the vicinity of Callensburg, at least so far as we know. In this we really made a new discovery, because I had asked Mother twice about the possibility of my going back to Callensburg and she said quite emphatically that there were none of the name or connection living there any more.

Harriet and I stopped at the cemetery and we found a great many stones bearing the names Wilson, Elliot, Murray and other names that I had heard mother speak of. The greatest thrill, however, in this connection was finding the really fine monument to our great grandfather, Alexander Wilson and his wife, Jane McCombs. I am enclosing a kodak print of the monument. It reads on one side:

> "Alexander Wilson
> Died September 10, 1878
> Aged, 100 years, 3 months, 6 days"

On the opposite side is this:

> "Jane, wife of Alexander
> Wilson, Died July 19, 1836
> Aged 57 years."

On the third side is the inscription:

"Father Wilson was born in Westmoreland County in 1801, and settled on Licking Creek near Curlsville; lived three months among the Indians without seeing a white man; was friendly with Turkey John the giant Indian, and great hunter of that day. Removed to Clarion River; built the first grist mill near Callensburg. He blazed a road from Callensburg through the woods to Curlsville, and conveyed Robert McYarrach back to the Concord church, who preached the first sermon there. In 1857, he moved to the west; remained six or seven years; returned to Clarion County where he died in 1878."

This stone was made of monumental bronze but treated in such a way as to make it look like granite. It is dated 1884.

Near the cemetery is the school and beyond the school and nearer still to town, is the church, which stands in quite a lovely grove. I remember mother speaking about this grove. The present church was erected about 1890 but I am told practically upon the same site on which the old church stood; the frame building which was attended by our grandparents and where our great grandparents worshiped even before the first church was built. I am also enclosing a kodak print of the church as it is today.

I talked briefly with the present pastor, who lives at Sligo, a town a little larger than Callensburg about four miles away. The minister told me that there are now just about forty in the membership of the church, practically no young people, but that these forty are just "the salt of the earth" and fine folks to preach to. Mrs. Lottie Pollock Craig, the wife of the clerk of Session told me that not a single farm, so far as she could think was owned by Wilsons, Murrays, Elliots or Doughertys, is now owned by people who are interested in the church. Her eyes got shiny as she told me this.

When we visited great grandfather's farm it had gotten so very dark that we could not take a kodak of it. The place is owned now by Henry Tipperay, whose father purchased it, I think, from a Mr. Dougherty. We did not find the Tipperays at home but we did find Timmons, "the man." He was much interested in our visit and indeed interested in the old house. Forty years ago, the elder Tipperay built a frame house for himself and his family. Since then, the old stone house has been used as a building in which to store things. At that, everything in it is kept neat and clean so that it was a pleasure to look in. Although there was electric light in the springhouse, there was none in the stone house and we did not have a flashlight with us, so all our illumination was by matches. However, it was a great joy to see the great stone over the main door, carved undoubtedly by his own hand and chisel.

"A. Wilson – 1838"

The stone has a border of decoration. We were so interested to see it. The old Dutch oven is still there in which our great grandmother baked the bread, the pies and the cookies for the family. It was still in use a few years ago. Mrs. Tipperay told Timmons that it held heat so well that she was able to bake, with one firing, enough bread to fill it twice and then have heat enough left to bake cookies and pies. Some great grandfather we had! He certainly knew how to build things right. The spring, which was the chief reason for locating the house, is still furnishing good, clear, cold water which the Tipperays use, not only for drinking but as furnishing "their refrigerator."

The farm comprises 240 acres and is located in a bend of the Clarion River, by the way, which is still called Wilson's Bend. The farm is so situated that although it has only 240 acres, it has two miles of riverfront. About one hundred acres is under cultivation and the balance equally divided between timber and pasture.

I would have been so glad to have met Mr. Tipperay and talked with him as well as talking at greater length with cousin "Tiny." I want, when I can, to go back and to locate some of the other farms, especially the place where grandfather Allen Wilson lived. "Tiny" gave me to understand that there is still a grist mill at Callensburg, but whether it is the same one that used to be operated by grandfather or its successor I do not know; "Tiny" gave me the impression that it was the same.

I do wish I might have made this visit while our mother was still with us. When would have so greatly enjoyed learning about it and I am sure with her clear memory, she could have placed a good many things, even though the family left Pennsylvania so early in her girlhood.

I am glad to share this with you, Aunt Alice, and am so happy that you are still with us enjoy this word from the home of your childhood. I trust also that some of your brothers, sisters and cousins, will get at least a portion of the joy in reading this account that we had in the visit.

With much love to one and all,

James Wilson Bean

Chapter 14

Family Scandals

o o o o o o o o o o o o o o o o o o o o o o o o o o o o o o o o o o o o o o o o o o

"After you record your genealogy as historical fact, you can impress your neighbors and friends by creatively translating your findings into a second file by substituting: sanitarium for penitentiary, died suddenly for suicide, martyred for hanged, adopted for illegitimate, hospital for insane asylum, and when your creative juices dry up, there's always the reliable 'unknown'"

Legacy News, July 24, 2001

What family tree does not involve at least one scandal? Our family is no exception. What follows are snippets of correspondence between my grandmother, Clara Van Cleave Coons, and her brother, William Edgar Van Cleave. The back and forth letters concern the paternity of their grandfather, Jesse Van Cleave.

My grandmother, Clara Van Cleave Coons, was born on September 28, 1889 in Montgomery County, Indiana and died on July 22, 1967 in Crawfordsville. She married my grandfather, Merle Coons, on June 7, 1910 just after his graduation from Wabash College. Both Merle and Clara were schoolteachers in Montgomery County. In 1914 Merle was principal at Wingate High School when the school won the Boys Indiana State High School Basketball Tourney.[1] Merle ultimately became Superintendent of Schools in Montgomery County (1922-1930) and represented the county in the Indiana House of Representatives from 1935 until his untimely death in 1940.[2,3] After he died, my grandmother served out his term and then ran for election and served terms in the Indiana House in 1941, 1943, 1945, 1947, and 1957.[1,4] Both of my grandparents were representatives for the Webster

Publishing Company in Webster Grove, Missouri, and, as such, traveled extensively throughout the state. When the legislature was in session, my grandmother often stayed at the Lincoln Hotel in Indianapolis.

Clara Van Cleave Coons

William Edgar Van Cleave has been previously described in Chapter Eight. At the time these letters [5,6] were written, William Edgar van Cleave, had retired from the Indian Health Service and was living in McAlester, Oklahoma with his wife Kate.

Jesse Van Cleave (1813-1895), grandfather of Clara and William Edgar, was born on March 27, 1813 in what is now part of Shelby County, Kentucky. His mother, Mary Van Cleave (1793 to about 1870) married Thomas G. Van Cleave (abt. 1792-1856) on January 1, 1815 in Shelby County, nearly two years after Jesse was born. Jesse outlived his first two wives[7] and ultimately married my great-great-grandmother, Charity Brewer (1815-1890) on January 11, 1839 in Putnam County, Indiana.[8]

Letters

Hotel Lincoln
Indianapolis, Ind.
March 3, 1945
Dear Ed,

...I have heard the old "Allen" story – it was first thrown in my face when I was a little girl and going to school at No. 1. Anne Brown [not her real name] got spunky with me one day and informed me about my grand-daddy. I never asked father anything about it and never remember of him saying anything. But anyway his name had to be Van Cleave because his mother was a Van Cleave and she married a Van Cleave. They were said to be second cousins...

3715 N. Meridian St.
Indianapolis, Ind.
March 18, 1945
Dear Ed,

...I had a talk with Frank Coons and he immediately began the "Allen story." He even went so far as to say that grandfather told him the story and said it was true and he couldn't help it. I interrupted him and said, "Well our father never told us anything like that." And he said, "Well Uncle Dan [Daniel Van Cleave, father of Clara and Ed] wouldn't." I never heard him tell a story in my life! He doesn't know what great grandmother Van Cleave's name was, so I suppose we are safe in saying that he was the son of Thomas and Mary because we knew he wasn't the son of Samuel...

...When grandfather [Jesse] Van cleave was thirteen years old he came out here and lived with Uncle Jonathan Van Cleave...

Wm. E. Van Cleave, M.D.
36 West Seminole Ave.
McAlester, Oklahoma
March 29, 1945
Dear Clara,

...It is just like I told you in a former letter, the only ones who ever told or referred to the "Allen story," was Uncle Joe or Frank Coons. Of course I never had any evidence or reason to doubt that the story they told might be true, however in the absence of any confirmatory evidence from father or other [relatives], it was just allowed to go at that. For even if a fact, it was no fault of grandfather's if it was a precocious event. During my lifetime I have seen many a child who was born out of wedlock, and many, many more who were evidently conceived before wedlock. Such a label faded with the years, and by the time of the next generation was entirely forgotten. So I for one, expect to give the story little credence.

So far as the significance of the "Allen" in Uncle Joe's name, I recall a visitor at grandfather's one fall, whom we know as Uncle Allen ___ somebody. I am quite sure that Allen was his first name rather than his last. The reason for me remembering it, is that we had been gathering and hulling dried beans. I think they were the white navies, we raised in the corn field. One of us boys while in play pushed a bean up into the nose so far we couldn't get it out. We lived then back on the old place near grandfather's. Well mother hustled us off to grandfather's, and it was this uncle Allen who brought the bean out of the nose. He mashed up a tobacco leaf into powder or rather like snuff in his hand. He then held his hand under the boy's nose and commanded him to draw some of the dust up into his nose. This started the boy to sneezing, and out flew the bean. I remember this all quite well. This Uncle Allen as they called him, was about the same age as grandfather, but I feel sure his name was Allen. So Uncle Joe could have been given that part of his name in honor of this gentleman. I think this man spent two or three months at grandfathers. His last name could have been McMullen, Brewer, Jones, or what not. Frank C[oons] might remember who he was.

...he [Jesse Van Cleave] left home when but 13 and went to live with a distant 42nd cousin because of friction or malcontent in his home. And since he never discussed family affairs with us, his family was a blank to us.

March 31st

...No, if grandfather did not see fit to broadcast how he was born, or that there were any unusual circumstances connected with it, I am not going to dig up his bones and smear him now...

I feel that genealogy is hooking up so well, that I may let the "A" scandal stay just where it stands now. Am quite sure I could put it up as a little side story started way back in the past, by a member of the family who was always finding and peddling scandal, and since my father seemed to know nothing about it, gave it no value. The story was that prior to the marriage of Thomas and Mary Van Cleave, Mary had a little lamb, by another buck named Allen. He was therefore looked upon by the legitimate children of Thomas and Mary as an ugly duckling and was kicked about and abused so, that he ran away at age 13 and separated himself entirely from his family by going from Kentucky up into Indiana to live with a distant cousin by the name of Jonathan Van Cleave. How does that sound?

Well must close and get this into the mail as it is closing time.

Sincerely,

Ed

Postscript comment by Philip Coons

Therefore, it appears from the correspondence of my grandmother Coons and her brother Ed that Jesse Van Cleave was born out of wedlock. His natural father's first name was Allen but his last name was in dispute, although it may have been Van Cleave. Jesse ran away from home at age 13 because he may have been abused or teased. I would guess that there might have been friction in the home because of his uncertain paternity.

Chapter 15

Pilgrimage

o o o o o o o o o o o o o o o o o o o o o o o o o o o o o o o o o o o o o o

"As I make my slow pilgrimage through the world, a certain sense of beautiful mystery seems to gather and grow."

Arthur C. Benson, College Window, 1906

I can think of no better way to end this book than to include this submission by my niece, Caroline Coons. In a way, all of the submissions in this book have been pilgrimages whether these persons were to move to a different locale, fight for a cause, obtain education, secure a better job, find a life mate, seek recreation, or wander in search of ancestors.

In an internet search, I found the following quotation about pilgrimages:

"Because all men and women are travelers, though they be often wanderers, all are bound to find out in time that life *is* a pilgrimage; that the human soul is bound for a holy place, and to reach it in proper fashion one must take the right road and walk that road in the right manner."[1]

I really believe this. As human beings we are always seeking. Whether we want to admit it or not, we all have a spiritual side, although we may not be a member of an organized religion. We are all on a search for life's ultimate meaning.

In her submission, Caroline and her friend Wes are trekking "El Camino de Santiago de Compostela," or "The Way of St. James." This famous Christian pilgrimage route in northern Spain has existed for over a thousand years. According to Catholic legend contained in the *Historia Compostelana*, the apostle James, brother of the apostle John, preached in both northern Spain and the Holy Land. After his martyrdom by Herod Agrippa I, James's earthly remains were sent by boat to northern Spain and buried in the city of Santiago de Compostela.

For modern pilgrims, the pilgrimage starts at St Jean Pied de Port, France. This city is at the foot of Roncevaux Pass, which crosses the Pyrenee Mountains into northern Spain. The pilgrimage traditionally ends at the city of Santiago de Compostela, where St. James is believed to be buried. This trek extends over 780 kilometers or 484 miles. Some travelers continue past Santiago de Compostela to Cape Finisterre, the westernmost point of Spain on the Atlantic Ocean. Most pilgrims purchase a credencial or pilgrim's passport, which enables them to stay overnight in a refugio or hostel for a nominal sum. At the end of their journey, pilgrims are given a compostela, or a certificate of completion.

Swimming in Europe

Starting Off

Thursday, April 30, 2009

We arrived to Pamplona this morning from Barcelona, walked the avenue for the running of the bulls, and hit the Info office to locate some requisites for our walk, ie shoe repair services. Next stop is a ride east via Roncevalles then down the mountain to St Jean Pied de Port where we can collect our pilgrim's passport and begin!

We hope to start the trek from St Jean Pied de Port on 1 May.

Today in Pamplona back trekking, ie hitchhiking northeast to the town St Jean Pied de Port, where we plan to begin the Camino de Santiago, or the Way of St James, and the trek across northern Spain. St Jean Pied de Port, St James at the foot of the mountains, is just outside the Spanish border in France. It's a traditional pilgrimage starting off point.

Starting Days

Sunday, May 3, 2009

We arrived in St Jean Pied de Port on the night before May Day to begin the Camino as hoped on 1 May. We discovered right away that it's a European holiday, and their Labor Day, so there were more pilgrims on the path!

Fortunately, we got a very good introduction from an enthusiastic Spanish woman on the taxi ride across the border from Spain to France. She shared about staying in the pilgrim's hostels provided by the town municipalities, and she let us know the proper thing to say to each other on the path, and that is Buon Camino, it means Good Way. This is the auspicious way to greet one another and wish each other well! It is an international path, and one of the most interesting parts of the journey is assuredly meeting people from all over the world and sharing together why we're each walking, and what we do, how we think. As we traverse this most amazing landscape of the Navarra country in Spain and the Pyrenees mountains the way has been cold, windy, rainy, muddy, sunny, up and down ... It's quite a lot to experience and we all reach the end of the day's journey then to share bunks in a common room in the town municipalities or something akin to such. It's really a joy to walk this path with so many others! ... And it's really interesting to meet the people who run the hostels who provide for the pilgrims. Of course, we pay, but it's little compared to normal prices for accommodations. Some of the people are volunteers who are giving a service at the hostel, so there is a very meritorious feeling of the good deed that is being given as the pilgrims are doing the deed of doing the walk. Nice.

Our first day we walked 27 km to Roncevalles through the Pyrenees and up a 1300-meter pass. On Day 2 we traversed from Roncevalles 22 km to Larrasouna. Day 3 took us near the river and through the valley to Pomplona and just above the town on the west side to a town called Cizur Menor. It is lovely here. We are in an old villa and the gardens are full of irises, roses, calendula, and daisies. Even there are 9 turtles that live in the pond here!

We are well and happy, and each time we look out at the landscape we are in awe of the beauty. The people are friendly, and we are practicing to speak French, Italian and Spanish! We are also appreciating so much the architecture, and finding good vittles along the way, too!

We'll update when we can!

Across Navarra and into La Rioja

Friday, May 8, 2009

The countryside is spectacular. Day 4 greeted us with waving fields of green wheat as we passed over a 500-meter pass and down the other side across the Navarra terrain. There are yellow mustard flowers, deep red poppy flowers, daisies, chamomile, nettles and more along the roadside and path. The path is long and feet are hurting for most of the pilgrims. We are traversing olive country and now here in La Rioja we are more in wine country and the fields are that of grapes just starting out their season with only short green arms beginning to grow across the lines that are set for their long reach of the season. The days are long. The sun rises by 7 am, but it is not dark until well after 9 pm. We have traveled just more than 200 kilometers now, and one sees the effects of such a walk on the body. Many of the pilgrims feel the distance in the body as one becomes more aware of one's constitution. Many of the towns established hospitals for the pilgrims, and now I see why. I imagine a lot of foot and knee doctoring happened along the route.

We traverse through the countryside for most of the day and every 5 to 15 kilometers we are walking through an old town. The modern town is built out along the fringes of the old town centers, and the camino, the way, takes us to the heart of each city and through to the other side and then back out into the country. We enter into old stone city gate, pass by and sometimes enter the very ornate gold gilded churches, follow the yellow arrows through the narrow stone streets to pass out of the town gate on the other side. Many of the town centers and churches were built around the 11th century.

Today we wake up to clouds and cold. We are in a town built by the Moors called Azofra. It is very small and there are two storks that have an enormous nest on the top of the church tower!! Imagine! And the church bells ring every hour, and the constant din of Mass bells ring two or more times a day as well!

Today we hope to travel to Santo Domingo and perhaps beyond. We hope to meditate more today and to take a small break on this full Moon day! We are thinking of all our family and friends with the deepest love and concern. Please share any insights and inspirations, and information. We know little about Saint James. Perhaps Uncle Phil and Aunt Liz can share some history!!

Mid-Stream and Swimming

Friday, May 15, 2009

Sometimes it seems though we're swimming through a sea of green since the wheat fields blowing in the wind looks like green waves in an ocean, especially here now where we're walking. We're traversing a meseta across Palencia and Junta Castille y Leon towards the town of Leon now. The land is vast and one feels part of that expanse. Today we walked a straight dirt and rock road without variation for 10 straight miles with no town in sight and no sound of road. It was like a desert and one's feet really felt like wheels just step by step turning towards our destination, the next town, which never appeared but at the last since it sat just a hundred feet or so below the meseta on which we walked. The wheat fields surrounded us and sometimes the way was lined by a row of poplar trees. The feeling now on Day 15 of continuous walking, day after day, is profound in the sense that one is really absorbed by the feeling of the air on one's skin, the sight of the red earth beneath one's feet, the sight of the sky and clouds, the play of the little birds darting in the wind, the steady repetition of step by step going by some internal momentum that seems only to have a destination now that is a volition to reach the end of this land mass. Indeed, this will be the Atlantic Ocean! The terrain of Palencia, a province the Romans inhabited in 900's and before, is mostly flatlands, wind and sky. The air has been cold here these three days that we've been walking, and the town architecture has been Romanesque, though the towns have been much littler than the ones we found earlier on the path, and without the traditional town center as we're formerly used to walking through. It's so interesting how it changes and we don't know what to expect, yet there is so much in common day to day. We walk through the morning and into the afternoon, then we find a place to take rest, we shop in the local store in the evening for fresh food to cook, we cook in the communal kitchen of the places we stay, and we share conversation and sometimes food with the others we meet on the path. Last night we were sharing a table with North Americans only! This was the first time we had such company alone since mostly we are meeting Italian, French, and Spanish travelers. The company of pilgrims last night was a couple from Canada, a couple from Atlanta, Georgia, a man from Mississippi.

The accommodation has mostly been in the municipal albergues where we share a dormitory style room with others, but this changes and from time to time we have a double room, and/or we stay in the parroquial albergues (which are donation only, and so a very different feeling since the persons there are there to serve the pilgrims as volunteers and there's no need for the pilgrim to give any money remuneration, but most do) ... The parroquial albergue at Granon in the province of La Riojia was very special. We stayed in the quarters just attached to the church an even there was a doorway and small hall entry way into the back of the church, San Juan de Batista! We even were able to walk up the tower into the bell room, but it was shockingly loud!! We stayed in a loft room on sleeping mats with about 16 others. There was a skylight just above my mat and we could see the stork's nest on top of the small bell tower! The sunlight streamed in at that spot, and that's why I chose it. The hospitalaria who led us up to the loft asked which place we'd like and we went straight for the window. We got there and landed means we unpacked and lay down on the mat to rest, stretch, listen to the conversations of others coming in, talking too ...

One person says, "One thing about this camino (this walk), it's not boring. It's different every time."

Truly! Every day, though walking, is quite different, even when the landscape is scarcely changing as it has been recently!

Another woman comments to us right as we settle into our spaces in the loft, "It was like a gateway opening when I came into this albergue here in the church and the hospitalar (the volunteer) offered me a cup of water. I was so tired and it seemed as if he saw, and just gave it and let me sit quietly." She was profoundly moved, and it's like that sometimes ... some surrender is there and there is some opening that is moving and freeing the heart towards greater lightness. She was so cheered by the effort of that volunteer, and he was so happy to selflessly give. He also walks the camino and knows the strength it takes, and so he can see and give what's needed, and we are not always so open, but then to receive this open heartedness just opens our own heart ... The parroquial albergues have more of this sincere true pilgrim spirit ... as it's a place where nothing is expected, but what is needed is given. The two men serving for two weeks at this one prepared a meal for 44 of us from the donation monies that had been given the night before. We all set up and cleaned up, and we all really appreciated the small confines, the piano, the guitar, the good spirits of one another ... That evening some of us went into the back of the church and had some prayers up in the very old choir stalls ...

People are coming for many reasons on this camino. It's usually a mix, but it is also either religious, cultural, spiritual, or for physical fitness ... One young woman told me when I asked her what brought her ... "A lot of things, some good and some bad." Someone last night said that the walk will change you ... no matter what. Indeed it is interesting to everyday make this concerted effort to walk, and towards a destination that is so far away ... We do this in life all the time as we set goals and reach them. Perhaps here only is that it's confined in a limited space of time and the camino is one's sole occupation ... sort of like a 10-day meditation course in ways ... only different.

Perhaps in about 6 days time we will be ascending another mountain up to 1,500 meters, and then we'll be well on our way towards the ocean and to Santiago. We'll write as often as we can.

All friends, family and loved ones are in our thoughts.

Day 18, the Lion City, Leon

Monday, May 18, 2009

We made it to Leon and have crossed much of the meseta. Still going and on our way to the base of the mountain where we will ascend to the 1,500 meter plus pass. Day 18. 464 kilometers trekked, and 300 more to go!

Tonight we're accommodating at the albergue, the shelter, at the Monastery with 150 other pilgrims! We hope to hear the monks chanting tonight, then plan to start off early on our way to Orbigo tomorrow.

Recently we have discovered the pastries!

Much love to all! Best wishes for continued good health to one and all. We love you!

We've Arrived

Saturday, May 30, 2009

It's Day 30 and we've arrived at Santiago!!

We continued across the meseta in Castilla y Leon until we reached the Bierzo and then we climbed another mountain. The conditions changed as we finally got some rain and colder temperatures. But wow!! All so beautiful ... and once at the top of the mountain we reached the province of Galicia which is so very green. We've been climbing up and down green hills passing rose gardens through our way across Galicia. The path has narrowed as we came into this Celtic land (yes, Galicia has Celtic roots) ... and we passed instead of poplar forests through majestic oak forests ... and some pine ... and now even eucalyptus. But everything seemed to come narrower and closer, and Galicia itself is so very small and the towns are quaint and small too.

Today we walked the last 20 km into Santiago, but passed so unseen it seemed as the path traversed the forests and away from the towns. It's the climax of the journey and yet it seems like just another day ... YET TRULY how fantastic to see this very old cathedral! It's stunning! And the old town of Santiago is charming with its narrow stone streets and big plazas.

We've continued to meet very nice people, and today it has been fun to see those we've gotten to know on the path at different stages ... some who strode ahead, some who fell behind but arrived here safely anyway by other means than one's feet ...

Yesterday we met another Vipassana mediator from US who spent the past 3 months serving at Dharma Neru outside of Barcelona ... so ... we caught glimpses of what's ahead as we plan to serve starting in mid June. We plan to continue to walk to Finisterre, to the westernmost point of Europe and to the Atlantic, then perhaps walk some in Portugal before returning to Barcelona and the Center.

One nice thing we got to read today was that this (Santiago) is the end and the beginning ... and the journey continues ... that journey ... the journey of the pilgrim ... is to continue to know oneself, to know others, to get closer to God ... that is the way of the Christian pilgrim.

Tomorrow is Pentecost Sunday in Santiago. I think there will be a lot of festivities as it's the day 50 days after Easter when though everyone spoke different languages ... there was mutual understanding among all. Certainly we've gotten to know people from all over ... perhaps we'll all easily converse tomorrow, May 31, Sunday!

Best to all!

Finisterre, the end of the world

Tuesday, June 9, 2009

We've reached Finisterre and the end of the world according to Camino legend and the beliefs of the Celts who used to send their deceased out to sea from this place, the westernmost point of Europe. We've been here for 5 days now as we've found a very agreeable place to spend our time at the "pilgrim home" of Miguel and Julianna and their one year old son, Julios. We've found a home with a meditation room, art room, living room and kitchen where others who have been walking on the Camino are also coming to take rest after the long walk. In the evenings those who wish to share a meal make something to share and others who like do the same, then we're sitting down together in a circle to eat and give thanks. It's quite an international mix, and really one sees how the Camino joins together the world community as *everyone* (old and young and from every country) comes to make these walks. We've discovered that the paths are many as one can start from just about anywhere in Europe. The tradition is to walk from one's own home and then to walk back. Even you can go from your own doorstep if you live as far north as Russia, as far south as southern Italy. There are actual routes across Europe to Santiago and then to Finisterre. However, some of the routes are better marked by the yellow arrow and scallop shell than others. The tradition is at the end of the walk to collect a scallop shell from the ocean and then this becomes one's credential so that others know one is a pilgrim and then is offered pilgrim's menu and pilgrim's rates for accommodation. The scallop shell is a good choice because this type of shell is plentiful on the beaches here, they're strong, and they have the symbolism of the many lines of the shell coming to one point. ...Certainly this has been part of the way as well since everyone is not only coming from his or her own physical destination and starting point, but one's own philosophical and mental understanding. There are many interesting conversations among the pilgrims about one's beliefs ... and about "the way", which is another way to translate the word "camino". What I've heard most are statements like this: "*It's about helping others, doing good like that; Life is about giving and sharing with others and doing for others and like that one helps oneself.*" There seems to be a lot of shared community sentiment that is this very notion. We hear stories now, too, from pilgrims telling about their experience on the camino ... telling how hard it had been, and what were some of the "tests" that each one was presented ... such as a lot of anger coming up. Or some we are meeting deliberately walked the path very slowly as a walking meditation, or just so not to have the goal in mind so much as to experience the way each and every day as one was going, or the musician who carried his guitar and so could only go short distances. Each one has something to say, and many are in life in a transitional place changing from one profession to another, and all are very happy to reach the end and to feel the accomplishment of having come so many kilometers on foot. One Frenchman was so moved he couldn't express, but just he said he felt "sentimental" and said he didn't know, but all it was is that he could feel this feeling in his heart and it was so strong for him. He walked from Le Puy in France and came about 8 weeks of walking.

For us we are grateful to be here, and we are enjoying our time at the Casa de Miguel and Julianna. Since 5 days it has been more rain and wind than sun and so we are making best use of time spent inside! We have been resting, sharing with others, meditating, doing yoga (and teaching it to others), cooking, reading, making origami with the children and other pilgrims (Wes has been teaching all of us), walking at the beach some. We've even had an offer to stay for the summer if I want to teach yoga to the pilgrims (and then we could make some concerted efforts to learn Spanish, too!)

As of now ... our plan is to return to Barcelona before June 17 as we've signed up to serve a ten day Vipassana meditation course at the Vipassana Center, Dhamma Neru, that is near Barcelona. Perhaps there we will get more clearly about our next "camino" so to see what arises in our own minds about our next plan. Currently we are gathering a lot of information about walking in the Sierra Nevada Mountains in Andalucia; I'm thinking about getting the credential to teach English, and then to teach English and yoga. Of course, we would both like to learn Spanish! ... We've realized that this takes time and that spending time in places is the way to achieve this very goal (a tutor and text book are a good idea too).

With love to all, and our best wishes, too!

Chapter Notes and References

Introduction

1. http://bartholomewco.com/archives/searcharchives.php

Chapter 1

1. Bartholomew County Historical Society. *History of Bartholomew County, Indiana - 1888.* Columbus, Indiana: Bartholomew County Historical Society, 1976, p. 239.
2. *Biographical Record of Bartholomew and Jackson Counties, Indiana.* Logansport, Indiana: B.F. Bowen, 1904, p. 256.
3. *History of Bartholomew County, Indiana.* Chicago: Brant & Fuller, 1888, p. 664.
4. Frank N. Richman. Biographical sketches, undated.
5. Mary A. Arbuckle. *History of Sandcreek Township, Bartholomew County, Indiana,* pp. 7, 116.
6. James Raney. Unsourced web document at http://www.rootsweb.ancestry.com/~kymercer/LowDutch/migrate.html.
7. Vince Akers. Henry County's Low Dutch Company. Henry County, Kentucky: Henry County Historical Society, 1979, pp. 1-9.
8. The Low Dutch Company: A history of the Holland Dutch settlements of the Kentucky frontier. New York: *de Halve Maen,* Vol. LV, No. 2, Summer, 1980, pp. 1-21.
9. The Low Dutch Company II: New York: *de Halve Maen,* Vol. LV, No. 3, Fall 1980, pp. 12-15.
10. The Low Dutch Company III: New York: *de Halve Maen,* Vol. LV, No. 4, Winter 1981, pp. 9-17.
11. The Low Dutch Company New York: *de Halve Maen,* Vol. LVI, No. 1, Spring-Summer, 19810, pp. 6-19.
12. Grandchildren of James. Busenbark. Data taken from old family Bibles of John Busenbark and his son James. Unpublished manuscript.

13. Pat Cline (Ed.). *Montgomery County legend and lore*. Crawfordsville, Indiana: R.R. Donnelley & Sons, 1988, p. 68-69.

14. Ted Gronert (Ed.). *Sugar Creek Saga: A history and development of Montgomery County*. Crawfordsville, Indiana: Wabash College, 1958, p. 8.

15. Virginia Banta Sharpe. *A history of Waveland Indiana*, 1958, p. 1.

16. *Portrait and biographical record of Montgomery, Parke and Fountain Counties, Indiana: containing biographical sketches of prominent and representative citizens, together with biographies and portraits of all the presidents of the United States*. Chicago: Chapman Brothers, 1893, pp. 314-315.

17. *Montgomery County Magazine*, March 1996, p. 9

18. H.W. Beckwith. *History of Montgomery County*. Chicago: H.H. Hill, 1881, p. 205.

19. Bessie Armstrong. Reynolds migrated to area in 1830. *Montgomery County Magazine*, February 1979, pp. 19-20.

20. Silas T. Richman. Letter, December 8, 1928.

21. Asahel A. Shumway. *Genealogy of the Shumway family in the United States of America*. York, Pennsylvania: Maple Press, 1972.

22. Mary F. Urbahns. Taxpayers list of Bartholomew County, Indiana for the years 1842, 1843, and 1845. Columbus, Indiana: Joseph Hart Chapter DAR, p. 218.

23. Obituary of Aurilla L. Bland. *Columbus Ledger*, February 14, 1918.

24. Wenzel, Allan R. *The pioneers, the Van Cleave family, Vol. II*. Seattle, Washington: Allan R. Wenzel, 1987, pp. 495-496.

25. Lester H. Binne. *Early Brethren Families in the Eel River Congregation in Kosciusko & Wabash Counties Indiana*. Warsaw, Indiana: Kosciusko County Historical Society, 1999.

26. Justin Replogle. *Ancestors on the frontier*. Cedarburg, Wisconsin: Justin Replogle, 1998, pp. 185-188.

27. William Dolllarhide. *Map guide to American migration routes, 1735-1815*. Bountiful, Utah: Heritage Quest, 1997.

28. Marcus Winfield Lewis. *Early emigrant trails in the United States east of the Mississippi River*. 1933.

Chapter 2

1. Nancy Alice Wilson Rogers. *Memories*. Columbus, Indiana: November, 1934

2. Grandchildren of James. *Data taken from old family Bibles of John Busenbark and his son James*. Undated and unpublished manuscript.

3. William Allen. Letter to his brother. Ureka, Siskiyou County, California: November 16, 1853.

Chapter 3

1. Frank N. Richman. Notes and biographical sketches of Bakers, Richmans, and Shumways, 1952.
2. B.F. Bowen (Ed.). Charles S. Baker. *Biographical Record of Bartholomew and Jackson Counties, Indiana.* B.F. Bowen, 1954, p. 456-459.
3. Major Thomas N. Baker. *History of Bartholomew County, Indiana.* Chicago: Brant & Fuller, 1888, pp. 664-666.
4. Thomas N. Baker. Civil War letters, 1863-1865.
5. Thomas N. Baker. Love letters, 1852-1854.
6. Adjutant General's Office, Executive Department Indiana, September 16, 1891.
7. Civil War records of Thomas N. Baker, Company F, 8th Indiana Cavalry, National Archives.
8. *Report of the Adjutant General's Office Indiana*, Indianapolis, Indiana: W. R. Holloway, Volume 2, pp. 390-391.
9. Bartholomew County, Indiana Circuit court records. David Vanskike vs. Jincy Vanskike (Divorce). Box 78, 1859.
10. Bartholomew County, Indiana court records. Thomas Baker. Jincy Baker GDN Reports, File B, 1851.
11. Civil War records of William I. Baker, Company F, 8th Indiana Cavalry, National Archives.
12. Interments, Sandcreek Friends Cemetery. http://ingenweb.org/ inbartholomew/cemeteries/Sandcreek.htm
13. Jacqueline S. Nelson. *Indiana Quakers confront the Civil War.* Indianapolis, Indiana: Indiana Historical Society, 1991.
14. Harold Coons. World War II letters, 1944-1946.
15. Siinto Wessman, Boris Muccia, George Swistak. *The Black Panther 66th Division.* Baton Rouge, Louisiana: Army and Navy Publishing Company, undated.
16. Panther Veterans' Organization. *40,000 Black Panthers of the 66th Division.* Panther Veterans' Organization, undated.
17. Black Panther, picture tabloid, date and publisher unknown.
18. Alan Andrade. *S.S. Leopoldville Disaster: December 24, 1944.* Tern Book Company, 1997.
19. Jocqui Sanders. *A Night before Christmas.* Cutchogue, New York: Buccaneer Books, 1963.

20. Stars and Stripes. 66th: The Story of the 66th Infantry Division (pamphlet, 32 pages), 1945.

Chapter 4

1. Thomas N. Baker. Civil War letters, 1863-1865.
2. Harold Coons. World War II letters, 1945.

Chapter 5

1. Asahel A. Shumway. *Genealogy of the Shumway family in the United States of America*. New York, New York: Tobias A Wright, 1909 (reprinted by the Maple Press, York, Pennsylvania, 1972).
2. Letter from Love Aurilla Shumway, 1862.
3. Letter from Margaret Baker Seward, 1863.
4. Lester V. Horwitz. *The longest raid of the Civil War*. Cincinnati, Ohio: Farmcourt, 1999.
5. Letters from Margaret Coons, 1944-1945.
6. 765 U.S. men lost in transport sinking. *New York Times*, January 26, 1945.

Chapter 6

1. Elizabeth Lapp Bowman. Our Trip from Oregon to California, 1898.
2. Harold Coons. World War II letters, 1946.

Chapter 7

1. Thomas N. Baker. Love letters, 1852-1854.

Chapter 8

1. Letter to Mr. Harley J. Van Cleave dated March 1, 1945
2. Statement of Dr. William E. Van Cleave regarding his service as the early administrator of the Choctaw-Chickasaw Indiana Hospital at Talahina
3. William Edgar Van Cleave document, undated
4. William Edgar Van Cleave. Indian Medicine. *Tobuckey News*, Vol 15(3), September, 1988, pp. 6-9.
5. William Edgar Van Cleave. Indian Medicine. *Tobuckey News*, Vol 17(3), September, 2000, pp. 26-29.
6. Edith Rogers Richman. *Nurnberg Diary*. 1947.
7. Truman names jurists. *New York Times*, June 1, 1947, p. 53.

8. Frank N. Richman. Draft of a speech given to an unknown audience, undated.

9. *Trials of war criminals before the Nuernberg Military Tribunals under Control Council Law No. 10*. Nuernberg, October 1946-April 1949, Vol VI. Washington DC: United States Government Printing Office, 1952.

10. Suzanne S. Bellamy. Hoosier Justice at Nuremberg: Judge Curtis Shake. *Traces of Indiana and Midwestern History*, Fall 2008, pp. 20-29.

11. Suzanne S. Bellamy. Hoosier Justice at Nuremberg: Judge Frank Richman. *Traces of Indiana and Midwestern History*, in press.

12. Frank N. Richman. The Nurnberg Trials...as seen by an Alumnus. *Alumni Bulletin* [Lake Forest College]. February, 1950, pp 3,7.

13. Michael W. Hoskins. Nuremberg Justice: Hoosiers who played a role in Nazi war crimes trials. *Indiana Lawyer*, March 19-April 1, 2008.

14. Joseph E. Persico. Nuremberg: Infamy on trial. New York: Viking Press, 1994.

15. Wayne Van Cleave. Letters to his parents, 1924-1925.

Chapter 9

1. Dr. Richman is taken by death: Retired physician, father of attorney, dies here, funeral Wednesday. *Columbus Republican*, January 4, 1938.

2. Frank N. Richman. Biographical sketches, undated.

3. Margaret Coons. Personal reminiscence, undated.

4. History of the Judson Mead Geologic Field Station: http://www.indiana.edu/~iugfs/facilities/history.php

5. Charles J. Vitaliano. Indiana University Geologic Field Station: Early days. In, *Guidebook: The Tobacco Root Geological Society 1976 Field Conference*. Butte, Montana: Montana College of Mineral Science and Technology, 1976.

6. Thomas E. Hendrix. *Guide book: Bloomington, Indiana, to Indiana University Geologic Field Station, Cardwell, Montana*. [Prepared for the course Geology G429 Field Geology in the Rocky Mountains] Bloomington, Indiana: Department of Geology, Indiana University, 1962.

7. Philip M. Coons. Letters to my parents from the Indiana University Geologic Field Station in Montana, 1962.

8. Richard Vedder. How to Choose a College. *Forbes Magazine*, May 19, 2008.

9. Philip M. Coons, Letters to my parents from Wabash College, Crawfordsville, Indiana, 1963-1965.

10. Philip M. Coons. The Great Wabash-DePauw Water Fight of 1958. The Collected Stories of Wabash Men at http://www.wabashstories.com/

Chapter 10

1. Clessie L. Cummins. *My days with the diesel.* Philadelphia: Chilton Books, 1967, pp. 64-74.
2. Lyle Cummins. *The diesel odyssey of Clessie Cummins.* Wilsonville, Oregon: Carnot Press, 1998, pp. 44-51.
3. Lyle Cummins. *The diesel odyssey of Clessie Cummins.* Wilsonville, Oregon: Carnot Press, 1998, pp. 281-282 and 306-307.
4. Frank N. Richman. *Log of the Big Dipper,* 1944.
5. "*Big Dipper,*" Cummins sailboat, is launched. *Columbus Republican,* August 29, 1944, pp. 1-2.

Chapter 11

1. Elizabeth Bowman. Travel diaries, 1992-2006.

Chapter 12

1. *Inc. Magazine.* Boston and New York.
2. Thomas N. Richman. *The Ride to Fargo: A Journey of Imagination.* Unpublished manuscript.
3. Thomas N. Richman. Out of Control (at Last): A perilous vacation teaches the healthy difference between control and influence. Inc. Magazine, Aug 2002.

Chapter 13

1. James W. Bean letter, 1934.
2. James W. Bean. *Who Was Who in America.* Chicago, Illinois: Marquis Who's Who, 1981, p39.

Chapter 14

1. Clara Coons dies; served in Legislature. *Indianapolis Star,* July 23, 1967.
2. Funeral of state assembyman to be Tuesday at Crawfordsville. *Indianapolis Star,* September 29, 1944.
3. Justin E. Walsh (General Editor). *Biographical Directory of the Indiana General Assembly, Vol. 2, 1900-1984.* Indianapolis, Indiana: Indiana Historical Bureau, 1984, p. 86.

4. Justin E. Walsh (General Editor). *Biographical Directory of the Indiana General Assembly, Vol. 2, 1900-1984.* Indianapolis, Indiana: Indiana Historical Bureau, 1984, p. 85
5. Clara Van Cleave Coons, letters
6. William Edgar Van Cleave, letters.
7. Anne McMullen (1815-1835), Ellen Sullenger (birth and death dates unknown)
8. Wenzel, Allan R. *The pioneers, the Van Cleave family, Vol. II.* Seattle, Washington: Allan R. Wenzel, 1987, p. 525.

Chapter 15

1. *The Theosophical Movement.* Vol. 72 (9), July, 2002. http://www.teosofia.com/Mumbai/7209pilgrimage.html
2. Anonymous. *Historia Compostelana*, about 1100 to 1140.

Genealogical Charts

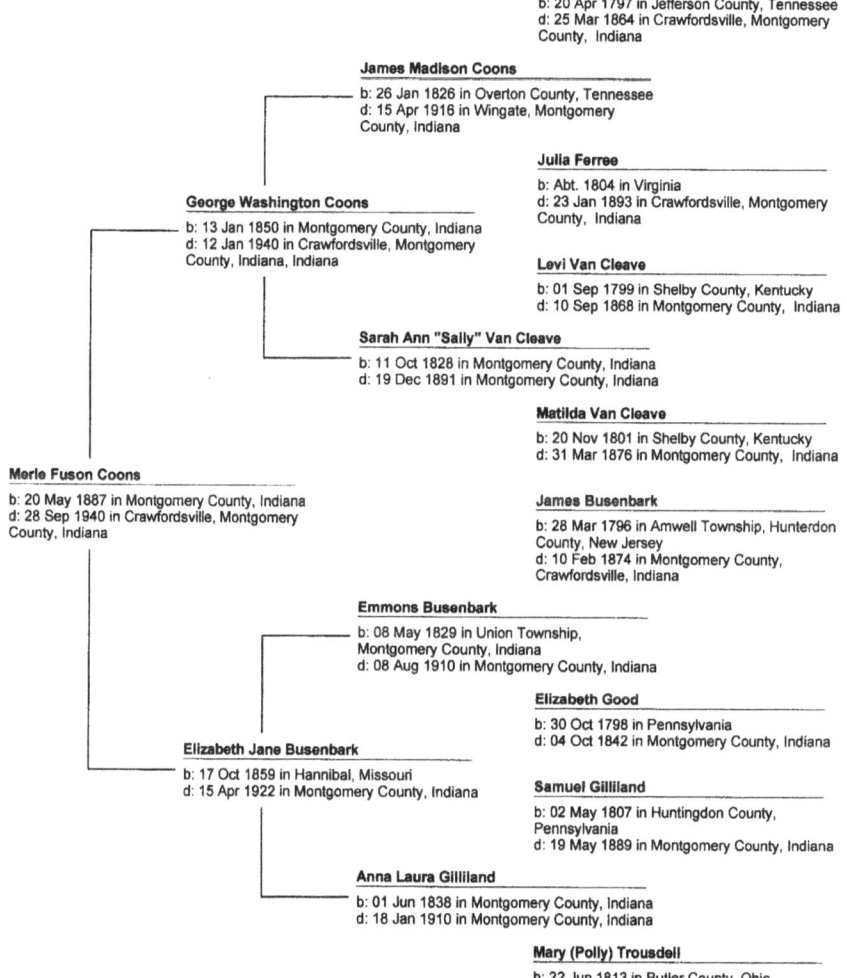

George Washington Coons

b: 20 Apr 1797 in Jefferson County, Tennessee
d: 25 Mar 1864 in Crawfordsville, Montgomery
County, Indiana

James Madison Coons

b: 26 Jan 1826 in Overton County, Tennessee
d: 15 Apr 1916 in Wingate, Montgomery
County, Indiana

Julia Ferree

b: Abt. 1804 in Virginia
d: 23 Jan 1893 in Crawfordsville, Montgomery
County, Indiana

George Washington Coons

b: 13 Jan 1850 in Montgomery County, Indiana
d: 12 Jan 1940 in Crawfordsville, Montgomery
County, Indiana, Indiana

Levi Van Cleave

b: 01 Sep 1799 in Shelby County, Kentucky
d: 10 Sep 1868 in Montgomery County, Indiana

Sarah Ann "Sally" Van Cleave

b: 11 Oct 1828 in Montgomery County, Indiana
d: 19 Dec 1891 in Montgomery County, Indiana

Matilda Van Cleave

b: 20 Nov 1801 in Shelby County, Kentucky
d: 31 Mar 1876 in Montgomery County, Indiana

Merle Fuson Coons

b: 20 May 1887 in Montgomery County, Indiana
d: 28 Sep 1940 in Crawfordsville, Montgomery
County, Indiana

James Busenbark

b: 28 Mar 1796 in Amwell Township, Hunterdon
County, New Jersey
d: 10 Feb 1874 in Montgomery County,
Crawfordsville, Indiana

Emmons Busenbark

b: 08 May 1829 in Union Township,
Montgomery County, Indiana
d: 08 Aug 1910 in Montgomery County, Indiana

Elizabeth Good

b: 30 Oct 1798 in Pennsylvania
d: 04 Oct 1842 in Montgomery County, Indiana

Elizabeth Jane Busenbark

b: 17 Oct 1859 in Hannibal, Missouri
d: 15 Apr 1922 in Montgomery County, Indiana

Samuel Gilliland

b: 02 May 1807 in Huntingdon County,
Pennsylvania
d: 19 May 1889 in Montgomery County, Indiana

Anna Laura Gilliland

b: 01 Jun 1838 in Montgomery County, Indiana
d: 18 Jan 1910 in Montgomery County, Indiana

Mary (Polly) Trousdell

b: 22 Jun 1813 in Butler County, Ohio
d: 04 Jun 1844 in Montgomery County, Indiana

Genealogical chart of Merle Fuson Coons (1887-1940)

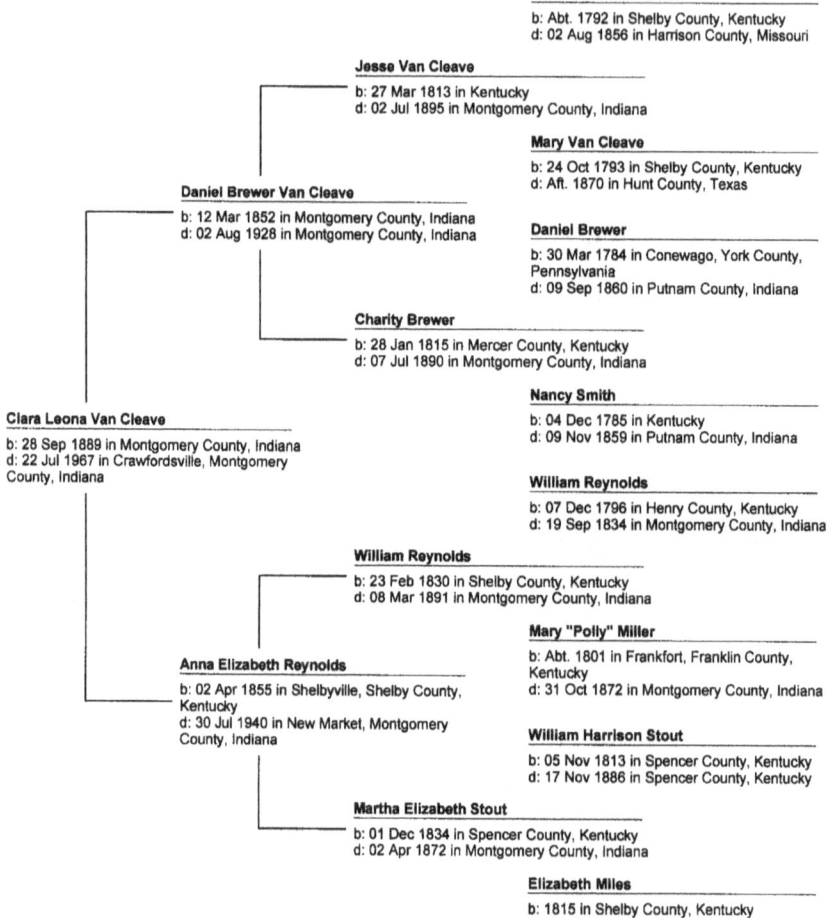

Thomas G Van Cleave

b: Abt. 1792 in Shelby County, Kentucky
d: 02 Aug 1856 in Harrison County, Missouri

Jesse Van Cleave

b: 27 Mar 1813 in Kentucky
d: 02 Jul 1895 in Montgomery County, Indiana

Mary Van Cleave

b: 24 Oct 1793 in Shelby County, Kentucky
d: Aft. 1870 in Hunt County, Texas

Daniel Brewer Van Cleave

b: 12 Mar 1852 in Montgomery County, Indiana
d: 02 Aug 1928 in Montgomery County, Indiana

Daniel Brewer

b: 30 Mar 1784 in Conewago, York County, Pennsylvania
d: 09 Sep 1860 in Putnam County, Indiana

Charity Brewer

b: 28 Jan 1815 in Mercer County, Kentucky
d: 07 Jul 1890 in Montgomery County, Indiana

Nancy Smith

b: 04 Dec 1785 in Kentucky
d: 09 Nov 1859 in Putnam County, Indiana

Clara Leona Van Cleave

b: 28 Sep 1889 in Montgomery County, Indiana
d: 22 Jul 1967 in Crawfordsville, Montgomery County, Indiana

William Reynolds

b: 07 Dec 1796 in Henry County, Kentucky
d: 19 Sep 1834 in Montgomery County, Indiana

William Reynolds

b: 23 Feb 1830 in Shelby County, Kentucky
d: 08 Mar 1891 in Montgomery County, Indiana

Mary "Polly" Miller

b: Abt. 1801 in Frankfort, Franklin County, Kentucky
d: 31 Oct 1872 in Montgomery County, Indiana

Anna Elizabeth Reynolds

b: 02 Apr 1855 in Shelbyville, Shelby County, Kentucky
d: 30 Jul 1940 in New Market, Montgomery County, Indiana

William Harrison Stout

b: 05 Nov 1813 in Spencer County, Kentucky
d: 17 Nov 1886 in Spencer County, Kentucky

Martha Elizabeth Stout

b: 01 Dec 1834 in Spencer County, Kentucky
d: 02 Apr 1872 in Montgomery County, Indiana

Elizabeth Miles

b: 1815 in Shelby County, Kentucky
d: Bef. 1836 in Spencer County, Kentucky

Genealogical chart of Clara Van Cleave Coons (1889-1967)

240

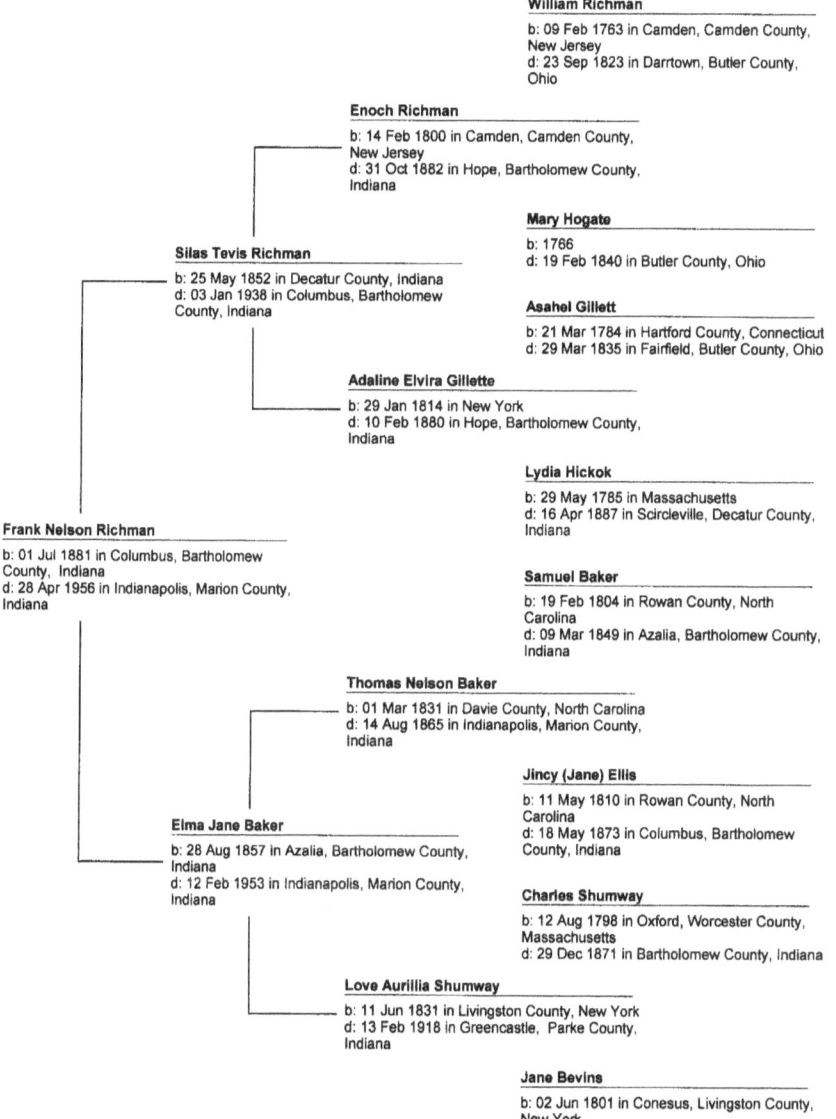

William Richman

b: 09 Feb 1763 in Camden, Camden County, New Jersey
d: 23 Sep 1823 in Darrtown, Butler County, Ohio

Enoch Richman

b: 14 Feb 1800 in Camden, Camden County, New Jersey
d: 31 Oct 1882 in Hope, Bartholomew County, Indiana

Mary Hogate

b: 1766
d: 19 Feb 1840 in Butler County, Ohio

Silas Tevis Richman

b: 25 May 1852 in Decatur County, Indiana
d: 03 Jan 1938 in Columbus, Bartholomew County, Indiana

Asahel Gillett

b: 21 Mar 1784 in Hartford County, Connecticut
d: 29 Mar 1835 in Fairfield, Butler County, Ohio

Adaline Elvira Gillette

b: 29 Jan 1814 in New York
d: 10 Feb 1880 in Hope, Bartholomew County, Indiana

Lydia Hickok

b: 29 May 1785 in Massachusetts
d: 16 Apr 1887 in Scircleville, Decatur County, Indiana

Frank Nelson Richman

b: 01 Jul 1881 in Columbus, Bartholomew County, Indiana
d: 28 Apr 1956 in Indianapolis, Marion County, Indiana

Samuel Baker

b: 19 Feb 1804 in Rowan County, North Carolina
d: 09 Mar 1849 in Azalia, Bartholomew County, Indiana

Thomas Nelson Baker

b: 01 Mar 1831 in Davie County, North Carolina
d: 14 Aug 1865 in Indianapolis, Marion County, Indiana

Jincy (Jane) Ellis

b: 11 May 1810 in Rowan County, North Carolina
d: 18 May 1873 in Columbus, Bartholomew County, Indiana

Elma Jane Baker

b: 28 Aug 1857 in Azalia, Bartholomew County, Indiana
d: 12 Feb 1953 in Indianapolis, Marion County, Indiana

Charles Shumway

b: 12 Aug 1798 in Oxford, Worcester County, Massachusetts
d: 29 Dec 1871 in Bartholomew County, Indiana

Love Aurillia Shumway

b: 11 Jun 1831 in Livingston County, New York
d: 13 Feb 1918 in Greencastle, Parke County, Indiana

Jane Bevins

b: 02 Jun 1801 in Conesus, Livingston County, New York
d: 27 Nov 1860 in Bartholomew County, Indiana

Genealogical chart of Frank Nelson Richman (1881-1956)

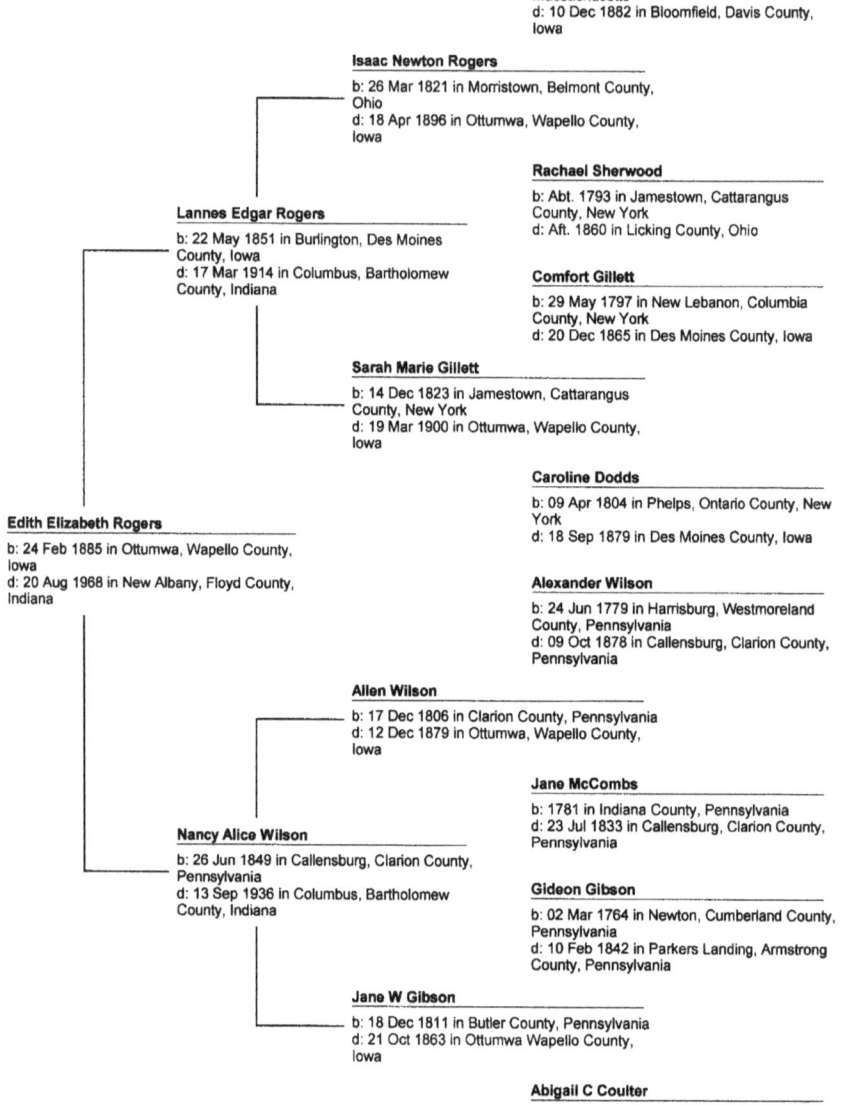

Michael Rogers

b: Oct 1796 in Newbury, Essex County,
Massachusetts
d: 10 Dec 1882 in Bloomfield, Davis County,
Iowa

Isaac Newton Rogers

b: 26 Mar 1821 in Morristown, Belmont County,
Ohio
d: 18 Apr 1896 in Ottumwa, Wapello County,
Iowa

Rachael Sherwood

b: Abt. 1793 in Jamestown, Cattarangus
County, New York
d: Aft. 1860 in Licking County, Ohio

Lannes Edgar Rogers

b: 22 May 1851 in Burlington, Des Moines
County, Iowa
d: 17 Mar 1914 in Columbus, Bartholomew
County, Indiana

Comfort Gillett

b: 29 May 1797 in New Lebanon, Columbia
County, New York
d: 20 Dec 1865 in Des Moines County, Iowa

Sarah Marie Gillett

b: 14 Dec 1823 in Jamestown, Cattarangus
County, New York
d: 19 Mar 1900 in Ottumwa, Wapello County,
Iowa

Caroline Dodds

b: 09 Apr 1804 in Phelps, Ontario County, New
York
d: 18 Sep 1879 in Des Moines County, Iowa

Edith Elizabeth Rogers

b: 24 Feb 1885 in Ottumwa, Wapello County,
Iowa
d: 20 Aug 1968 in New Albany, Floyd County,
Indiana

Alexander Wilson

b: 24 Jun 1779 in Harrisburg, Westmoreland
County, Pennsylvania
d: 09 Oct 1878 in Callensburg, Clarion County,
Pennsylvania

Allen Wilson

b: 17 Dec 1806 in Clarion County, Pennsylvania
d: 12 Dec 1879 in Ottumwa, Wapello County,
Iowa

Jane McCombs

b: 1781 in Indiana County, Pennsylvania
d: 23 Jul 1833 in Callensburg, Clarion County,
Pennsylvania

Nancy Alice Wilson

b: 26 Jun 1849 in Callensburg, Clarion County,
Pennsylvania
d: 13 Sep 1936 in Columbus, Bartholomew
County, Indiana

Gideon Gibson

b: 02 Mar 1764 in Newton, Cumberland County,
Pennsylvania
d: 10 Feb 1842 in Parkers Landing, Armstrong
County, Pennsylvania

Jane W Gibson

b: 18 Dec 1811 in Butler County, Pennsylvania
d: 21 Oct 1863 in Ottumwa Wapello County,
Iowa

Abigail C Coulter

b: 15 Jun 1782 in Sunbury, Northumberland
County, Pennsylvania
d: 02 Sep 1872 in Parkers Landing, Armstrong
County, Pennsylvania

Genealogical chart of Edith Rogers Richman (1885-1968)